PRINCIPLES OF M

PRINCIPLES OF MANAGEMENT

MG 1351

(Common to All Branches as per Anna University Syllabus)

By

K. ANBUVELAN
M.E., Ph.D.
P.G.D. C.C.S., M.I.S.T.E., M.I.E., M.I.C.I., M.I.C. F.R.C., C. Eng., (I)
Assistant Professor
Department of Civil Engineering
Bharath University, Chennai
Tamil Nadu

UNIVERSITY SCIENCE PRESS

(An Imprint of Laxmi Publications Pvt. Ltd.)

BANGALORE ● CHENNAI ● COCHIN ● GUWAHATI ● HYDERABAD
JALANDHAR ● KOLKATA ● LUCKNOW ● MUMBAI ● RANCHI
NEW DELHI ● BOSTON, USA

Published by :

UNIVERSITY SCIENCE PRESS

(An Imprint of Laxmi Publications Pvt. Ltd.)

113, Golden House, Daryaganj,
New Delhi-110002

Phone : 011-43 53 25 00
Fax : 011-43 53 25 28

www.laxmipublications.com
info@laxmipublications.com

Price : **Rs. 195.00** *Only.*

First Edition : 2007
Reprint : 2008

OFFICES

India

© **Bangalore**   080-26 61 15 61
© **Chennai**   044-24 34 47 26
© **Cochin**   0484-239 70 04
© **Guwahati**   0361-254 36 69, 251 38 81
© **Hyderabad**   040-24 65 23 33
© **Jalandhar**   0181-222 12 72
© **Kolkata**   033-22 27 43 84
© **Lucknow**   0522-220 95 78
© **Mumbai**   022-24 91 54 15, 24 92 78 69
© **Ranchi**   0651-221 47 64

USA

Boston

11, Leavitt Street, Hingham,
MA 02043, USA

UPM-9284-195-PRINCIPLES OF MANAGEMENT
Typeset at : Kalyani Computer Services, New Delhi.

C—16218/08/07
Printed at : Sheel Print-N-Pack, Delhi.

In loving remembrance,
I dedicate this book to
Mr. A. Kalaiselvan &
Er. M. Karunamoorthi
Family

CONTENTS

PREFACE

Due to the advances [продвинутой] in the field of Science and Technology especially Research & Development, the knowledge of Engineering and Management is essential for benefit and economic of the user to solve the day-to-day problems in practical applications.

A proper planning and organizing will reduce almost fifty percent of unwanted problems in the practical application which directly saves the time and cost. The knowledge of Indian and International aspects of management will help to increase the business promotion to global.

With this connection, the study of "Principles of Management" is essential for all kinds of student community to acquire the management concepts and practices for working in the present environment effectively and efficiently.

In such situation the author is really happy to present this textbook on this topic for the benefit of young student community as per Anna University Syllabus.

The book is written in a simple and easy-to-follow language, so that even an average student can grasp the subject by self-study. At the end of the book, Model question Papers & Glossary are given.

The complete details of the source material used for the preparation of the text matters are presented in the form of references at the end of the book.

Finally, the author is thankful to colleagues, students, friends and family members for their kind encouragement, cooperation and timely help extended during the preparation of the textbook.

Though every care has been taken in checking the manuscripts and proof reading, yet claiming perfection is very difficult. Suggestions for improvement are most welcome and would be incorporated in the next edition with a view to make the book more useful.

—AUTHOR

MANAGEMENT CONCEPTS

1.1 MANAGEMENT - INTRODUCTION ВВЕДЕНИЕ

➢ Management is that function of an industrial undertaking which organises, directs and controls various activities of the enterprise directed towards specific ends (objectives).

➢ The objectives of the enterprise are accomplished through the use of resource like men, money, material and machines.

➢ The management function of a concern is a major segment of co-ordination. Management entails the coordination of human effort and material resource toward the achievement of organisational objectives.

➢ **Harbison** and **Myers** observe Management as

(a) An economic source, [источник] because the management resources of a firm determine to a large extent its productivity and profitability. [продуктивность и рентабельность]

(b) A system of authority, because historically, first of all management developed Authoritarian Philosophy, and

(c) A class and status system, because entrance into the class of managers is based upon higher education and brain.

➢ Management embraces [обнимает"] all duties and functions that pertain [относиться к] to the initiation of an enterprise, its financing, the establishment of all major policies, the provision of all necessary equipment, the outlining of the general form of organisation under which the enterprise is to operate and selection of the principal officers.

➢ **Management** may be called an **Art** as well as **Science.**

(a) Management has **Scientific** basis because management techniques are susceptible to measurement and factual determination. [определение]

(b) Management is an **Art** because management means co-coordinating and getting things done through others.

➢ Management is actually an executive function which actively directs human efforts towards common goals.

интегрировать

➢ The main characteristics of the management is to <u>integrate</u> and apply the knowledge and analytical approaches developed by numerous other disciplines.

1.2 PRINCIPLES OF MANAGEMENT

➢ 'Principles of Management' implies a list of current management practices.

➢ Though **F.W.Taylor** developed principles of management, credits to **Henry Fayol**, a french management theorist for advocating and publicizing certain principles (or laws) for the soundness and good working of the management.

➢ Henry Fayol warned that the principles of management should be,

независимо от

➢ Flexible and not absolute - must be usable <u>regardless</u> of changing condition.

➢ Used with intelligence and with a sense of proportion, etc.,

➢ Henri Fayol listed 14 Principles that grew out of his experience; they are briefed under.

Разделение работы

1. **Division of work (or Labour)**

➢ Division of work means dividing the work on the principle that different workers (and different places) are best fitted for different jobs (or things) depending upon influences arising from geography, natural conditions, personal <u>aptitude</u> and skills.

➢ Division of work leads to <u>specialization.</u>

труд,

➢ Concept of division of <u>labour</u> can be applied to all kinds of work, managerial as well as technical.

Преимущество

Advantage of Division of Labour, since the same worker does the same work repeatedly,

(i) he gains proficiency and skill on the jobs,

(ii) rate of production increases,

iii) product quality improves,

iv) he is in a position to suggest changes in product, processing or methods of doing that work.

Disadvantage of Division of Labour

) Division of labour gives rise to loss of craftsmanship; workers become machine-minders and no more.

i) With the passage of time, the same job becomes dull and monotonous.

ii) Workers do not remain all round and one cannot work in place of another if he is absent. отсутствовать

Authority and Responsibility   Полномочия и ответственность

➢ Authority and responsibility should go together, hand-in-hand and must be related. связан

    исполнительный правосудие

➢ An executive can do justice with his responsibility only when he has the proper authority.

➢ Responsibility without authority or **Vice Versa** is meaningless.

Discipline   Дисциплина

       эффективность   предприятиях

➢ Discipline is absolutely necessary for efficient functioning of all enterprises.

➢ Discipline may be described as respect for agreements that are directed at achieving obedience, application and the outward marks of respect.

    послушание

Unity of Command   Единоначалие

➢ Unity of command means, employees and should receive order and instructions from one boss (or supervisor) only. In other words a worker should not be under the control of more than one supervisors.

➢ Unity of command avoids confusion, mistakes and delays in getting the work done.

Unity of Direction   Единство направления

    более широкий

➢ It is a broader concept than the unity of command.

➤ Unlike unity of command which concerns itself with the personnel, unity of directions deals with the functioning of the body corporate.

➤ Unity of direction implies that there should be one plan and one head for each group of activities having the same objective.

In other words, there should be one common plan for an enterprise as a whole.

6. Subordination of Individuals to General interest

➤ The interests of an individual person should be permitted to supersede or prevail upon the general interest of the enterprise.

➤ This is necessary to maintain unity and to avoid friction among the employees.

7. Remuneration

➤ Remuneration is the price to the employees for the services rendered by them for the enterprise.

➤ Remuneration should

➤ be fair, and

➤ bring maximum satisfaction to both employees and the employers.

8. Centralisation of Authority

➤ Centralization of authority means that the authority is in the hands of centre, i.e. the authority is not dispersed among different sections.

➤ In a business organisation, authority should be centralized only to that degree o extent which is essential for the best overall performance.

➤ The degree of centralization is decided by keeping in view the nature, size an complexity of the (business) enterprise.

9. Scalar Chain

➤ Managers may be regarded as a **Chain of superiors.** There should be a unbroken like of authority and command through all levels from the highest (i.e general managers) to the lowest ranks (employee).

> The chain of superiors should be short - circuited, when following it strictly will be detrimental to performance.

10. Order Заказ

> This promotes the idea that everything (e.g., materials) and everyone (human being) has his place in the organisation.

> Materials and human beings should be arranged such that right materials (things)/person is in the right place.

11. Equity of Treatment Равенство обращения

> Manager should have equality of treatment for all his subordinates.

> Manager should deal with his subordinates with kindness and justice.

> This will make employees more loyal and devoted towards the management/ enterprise.

12. Stability Стабильность

> Stable and secure work force is an asset to the enterprise, because unnecessary labour turnover is costly.

> An average employee who stays with the concern is much better than outstanding employees who merely come and go.

> Instability is the result of bad management.

13. Initiative Инициатива

> Initiative is one of the keenest satisfaction for an intelligent employee to experience.

> Managers should sacrifice their personal vanity in order to permit their subordinates to exercise their own initiative.

> A manager should encourage his subordinates to take initiative.

14. **Esprit de crops**   *культура*

погрёживать

> This principles of management emphasizes the need for team work (harmon
> and proper understanding) among the employees and shows the importance o
> communication is <u>obtaining</u> such team work.
> *получение*

1.3 FUNCTIONS OF MANAGEMENT

1.3.1 History

Landmarks of the conception and progress of western Scientific Management ca
be traced to the last 100 years or so. There are three well defined channels in whicl
these management thought and principles can be grouped. The x-theory, the y-theory
and the latest z-theory. Infact, our ancient scriptures like manushastra, Upanishad
describe vividly organisational behaviour individual and group behaviour etc. The
various doctrines and postulations to guide the rulers and the administrators of variou
countries of the world like India, Babylon, China, Greece may well form the
fundamental principles of managing human element, financial and trading aspects. Wel
recorded Kautilya's Arthashastra (400 B.C) is one such doctrine.

X-theory : This theory assumes that man is naturally lazy and dislikes work. He ha
little ambition and does not want to shoulder any responsibility but desires total security
Thus by <u>coercion</u>, control and directive or by suitable reward or bribe, he can be made
to work.

Y-theory : This theory assumes that work is a natural activity and that everybody
derives satisfaction in doing some work. It also base that everybody wish to develop
himself and thereby satisfying important human need for self-realization. This prompt.
him to take initiative and shoulder responsibility. Hence rules and regulations are
secondary and organisation objectives are only primary.

Z-theory (contingency theory) : This theory has been based on careful survey o
several organisations and postulates that an organisation should be tailored to suit the
requirements of tasks and people. For best results flexibility of the organisation is
must and the tasks, people and the organisation structure must fit together well.

1.4 SCIENTIFIC THEORIES

1. **FREDERICK WINSLOW TAYLOR, M.E., D.Sc., (1911), (Mechanica
Engineer) :** In consonance of U.S. President Roosevelt's remarks - "the
conservation of our national resources is only preliminary to the larger question o
national efficiency" and based on his observations and experiments, carried out on
the shop floor level, proposed certain principles like. Work-study, time-motion

study, task planning etc. to improve workshop efficiency. He founded the systems Engineering principles.

2. **MARY PARKER FOLLETT** (1863 - 1933) : In the 1920's Mary Parker Follett's comments and writing on leadership, power, law of situation, conflict integration and circular behaviour, empowerment, teams and networked organisations, importance of relationships within and among organisations, authority, control etc., were way ahead of her time. She examined the creative group process, crowd psychology, neighborhood and work, governance, the self-in relation to the whole and ideals of integration, synthesis and unifying differences. She was truly a prophet of management. Mary Follet proposed certain principles to motivate the human resources, based on behavioral science for securing high level of sustained efficiency.

    POWER :

    Control is coming more and more to mean fact-control rather than man-control. Central control is coming more and more to mean the correlation of many controls rather than a superimposed control. Circular behaviour is the basis for integration. If your business is so organised that you can influence a co-manager while he is influencing you, so organised that a workman has an opportunity of influencing you as you have of influencing him; if there is an interactive influence going on all through the time between you, power may be built up.

3. **FRENCHMAN HENRY FAYOL** (1841-1925) : He projected the subject as a general theme and proposed principles of universal applicability in any industry, office and administration. He belongs to the classical school of management theory and was writing and exploring administration and work about same time as F.W.Taylor in USA. While both have a task focus, their approaches are quite different. Fayol was particularly interested in authority and its implementation while Taylor concentrated on work organisation (e.g efficiency). Fayol's five functions still form the basis of much of modern management thought and action.

    a. Plan and look ahead
    b. Organize
    c. Command
    d. Co-ordinate
    e. Control (feedback and inspect)

    He also indent field 14 principles that he saw as common to all organisations.
    a. Specialization / division of labour
    b. Authority with responsibility
    c. Discipline

       d. Unity of direction
       e. Unity of command
       f. Remuneration
       g. Centralization
       h. Sub-ordination of individual interests
       i. Chain/line of authority
       j. Order
       k. Equity
       l. Lifetime jobs (for good workers)
       m. Initiative, and
       n. Esprit decorps.

4. **KORT LEWIN** (1890-1947) : "A Dynamic Theory of Personality" published in 1935 outlines Group Dynamics. He explored the following queries :

       a. Group productivity : Why was it that groups are so ineffective in getting things done?
       b. Communication : How influence is spread throughout a group.
       c. Social perception : How a person's group affected the way they perceived social events.
       d. Inter group relations.
       e. Group membership : How individual adjust to these conditions.
       f. Training leaders : Improving the functioning of groups (T-groups)

5. **CHARLES HANDY** : An organisational thinker, popularized a typology of cultures. Power culture, role culture, task culture and person culture.

6. **GEERT HOFSTEDE** (1991) : Researched into organisation cultures identified six independent dimensions of practices :

       a. Process - oriented versus results - oriented.
       b. Job - oriented versus employee orientated.
       c. Professional versus parochial.
       d. Open systems versus closed systems.
       e. Tightly versus loosely controlled, and
       f. Pragmatic versus normative.

7. Similar researchers like, organisational psychologist, Chris Argyris (1976) - Double loop learning, WARREN BENNIS - Leadership theories, PETER CHECKLAND - SOFT SYSTEMS APPROACHES, MUMFORD - PARTICIPATIVE SYSTEMS DESIGN and theories like. Complexity theory and chaos theory, paved ways for developing principles of scientific management.

Most theories were concentrating on the central theme of organisation and the work force. Mathematical and operation research techniques were applied only very recently as tools of management.

1.5 OBJECTIVES OF MANAGEMENT

The main objective of any management guideline is,

1. To have co-ordination between various agencies.
2. To effect economy and efficiency in execution.
3. To exercise control over the quality and workmanship.
4. To check and control the material quality.
5. To reduce the time period of execution of activities, and
6. To achieve optimum utilization of various resources.

1.6 PRINCIPLES OF SCIENTIFIC MANAGEMENT

There are three questions upper most in the minds when someone becomes interested in scientific management principles. First : wherein do the principles of scientific management differ essentially from those of ordinary management? Second : How and why are better results attained under scientific management than under the other types? Third : Is not the most important problem that of getting the right man at the head of the company? And if we have the right man, can we not leave the choice of the type of management safely to him?

In the case of scientific management the management assume, for instance, the burden of gathering together all of the traditional knowledge which in the past has been possessed by the workmen and then of classifying, tabulating and reducing this knowledge to rules, laws and formulae which are immensely helpful to the workmen in doing their daily work.

First : They develop a science for each element of a man's work, which replaces the old rule-of-thumb method.

Second : They scientifically select and then train, teach and develop the workman, whereas in the past he choose his own work and trained himself as best he could.

Third : They heartily co-operate with the men so as to insure all of the work being done in accordance with the principles of the science which has been developed.

Fourth : There is an almost equal division of the work and the responsibility between the management and the workmen. The management take over all work for which they are better fitted than the workmen, while in the past almost all of the work and the greater part of the responsibility where thrown upon the men.

Under scientific management, various parameters are studied by undertaking,

a. Work study
b. Task planning
c. Selection and training
d. Tools and materials
e. Worker management interrelationships etc., thereby the management and the execution team are prepared and wasteful areas are identified and improvements envisaged.

In today's environment of survival of the fittest, no individual methodology can be called as THE METHOD or an individual can be termed as the RIGHT MAN. Frequent reviews, analysis and recommendations of corrective steps, by a team of dedicated professionals, basing on the various observed data, obtaining by scientific methods from on the spot study or from similar situations, is the order of the day.

1.7 FUNCTIONS OF MANAGEMENT

Broadly the management function can be grouped as under, but it varies depending on the industry to a large extent.

1.   Administrative, financial and technical control.
2.   Planning strategy, recruitment and training of workers and staff.
3.   Procurement of plant, machinery, tools and tackles, raw material, spares etc.,
4.   Identification, outsourcing, sales and advertisement, packaging and delivery.
5.   Co-coordinating.

Administrative control is limit the expenditure and quantities of various items of work within the estimate. Financial control is to sanction the budget allotment and to monitor the income - expense table. Technical control is exercised on the execution of the works as per approved specification and any variation is promptly reported for necessary action. Rest of the points is self explanatory.

1.8 FUNCTIONS OF MANAGER

The managerial function differs from one type of industry to another and thus the role of the managerial team differs. Nevertheless, qualities of Manager: Intelligence, Motivation, Knowledge and opportunistic. Characteristics desirable are,

1.   Perseverance, hard work and ability to take risk.
2.   Independent, Imaginative, Innovative, Initiative, Creative and Dynamic.
3.   Responsible, Adaptable, self confident, will power and willingness to learn.
4.   Good salesmanship, organising skill, sociability and flexibility.

5.   Determination to succeed, ability to win friends, crisis management skills.
6.   High integrity, pleasing personality and manners, tactful and composed.

The above manager in perspective, the functions of THE MANAGERIAL TEAM are,

1.   Decision making.
2.   Organizing men and material for execution/production.
3.   Supervision.
4.   Controls and Rewards, Incentives.
5.   Income and expenditure division/costing.
6.   Marketing and Advertisement.
7.   Implementation of innovative ideas from subordinates or of own.
8.   Risk bearing and uncertainty bearing.
9.   Contingency planning.

Most of the above functions form a regular and routine of the managers. The items 7,8 and 9 involves strategically planning, involving more number of heads from various disciplines of management of the organisation or require the consultancy from outside.

Risk Bearing : This is the ability to withstand the effects of calculated planning turning otherwise and made to incur loss(es).

Uncertainty Bearing : The ability to face and act in situations. The worth of natural calamities. Fire, Theft, Unforeseen competition, steep raw material price increase and non-availability or shortage, political turmoil, depression, whims and fancies of clients etc., forming uncertainties in business.

Thus, a Manager or the Managerial function calls for continuous improvement in the execution of activities, newer ways to be innovated, tested and adopted after suitable modifications, realization of cost component of utilization of various resources, means and methods to reduce frivolous and wasteful resource consumption, time conscious, watch dog of improvements in other similar establishments etc.

1.9 REVIEW QUESTIONS

1.   Discuss the important functions of management.
2.   Describe whether management is a science or an art.
3.   What are the functions of a Manager.
4.   Explain Scientific Theories in Management.

MANAGEMENT THOUGHTS

2.1 Administration and Management

Management is a specialized activity required for the running of those social institutions which are composed of a group of human beings. The same management functions are to be found everywhere and as such, the management skill is transferable from one kind of social institution to another. Usually, this specialized ability is called "management" in business institutions and "administration" in others. The attempt to draw a distinction between "business administration" and 'business management' is thoroughly misleading and all recent studies have tried to avoid it as far as practicable. That there is no distinction even between management and public administration was pointed out by Fayol in his address to the Second International Congress of Administrative Science "All undertakings require planning, organization, command, co-ordination and control and in order to function properly, all must observe the same general principles. We are no longer confronted with several administrative sciences, but with one which can be applied equally well to public and private affairs". Persons who discharge management functions are universally called 'executives' but in business they are further known as 'managers'.

2.2 Levels of Management

In the past, the two broad levels of management used to be denoted by administrative management and operating management. The upper level of management was usually called "administrative management" and the lower level was known as "operating management". The use of these terms implies a division of the management functions into two separate groups, viz., thinking functions and doing functions. As pointed out earlier, fundamental management functions are undertaken by all managers, irrespective of their leels or ranks. Accordingly, it does not fit into the facts of the real life to draw any line of separation between thinking functions and doing functions. Furthermore, the use of these terms stems from the acceptance of two different social sciences management and administration which are not existing in fact.

The current practice is to denote the upper level of management by the term "top management". The lower level or echelon of management goes by the name of "middle management". The adoption of the term middle management undoubtedly suggests that there is a further level below it. Actually, the lowest level is composed of foremen and supervisors who also perform precisely the same management functions of planning, organizing, directing and controlling in differing degrees. To be sure, whoever performs the basic functions of management are to be called 'managers' in the technical sense of the term since their functions can be sharply distinguished from those of non-managers.

Levels of management become prominent in large-sized public limited companies. Three distinct levels of management along with their respective functions are stated below:

2.2.1 Top Management

Top management of a company is constituted by its broad of directors and the chief executive. Functions of top management include (1) to make an outline of planning through the formulaton of basic objectives and policies of the company, (2) to determine the basic pattern of the company's organization structure, (3) to arrange for effective co-ordination of all activities, (4) to make staffing of departmental and other important executives, (5) to prepare overall budgets and programmes for short-range and long-range operations, (6) to exercise overall control in respect of all operations, (7) to ensure continuity of the company through modernization and innovation of material resources and the executive development of human resources and (8) to maintain public relations with all outside parties for improving the company's image and protecting its interests.

2.2.2 Middle Management

Between top management and supervisory management, there is found to exist another level of management known as middle management. In large enterprises, middle management is bifurcated into two parts upper middle or intermediate management and lower middle management. Middle management is constituted by divisional, departmental and sectional managers and its functions include (1) to develop derivative objectives and policies and to prescribe procedures and methods in different areas, (2) to prepare departmental budgets and programmes in the context of overall planning, (3) to execute plans through orders, instructions and advice, (4) to exercise control in different areas through the application of quality standards and cost standards and (5) to effect co-ordination between top management and supervisory management.

2.2.3 Supervisory Management

Supervisory management is the lowest level of management and it is constituted by superintendents, foremen and inspectors. There are six important functions of supervisory management : (1) to supervise the actual operations through guidance, checking and overseeing, (2) to translate the plan into actions through the provision of facilities and resources and the creation of a favourable work environment, (3) to exercise control over the work-in-progress through applying quantity standards and time standards, (4) to send information and progress reports to higher management, (5) to motivate the personnel for improving productivity of the company and (6) to put all the managerial orders, instructions, policies and programmes into action and to make higher managerial accomplishments.

2.3   DEVELOPMENT OF MANAGEMENT THOUGHT

Management has become today a theory jungle by the contributions of scholars and writers from several disciplines like sociology, psychology, social psychology, cultural anthropology, political science, engineering, economics, mathematics, statistics and others. Having different backgrounds and adopting divergent approaches, these contributions have created a diversity in management thought. To understand the present state of management, it becomes necessary to trace the history of management thought. Management has been progressively developed through the following seven schools of thought.

1. Scientific Management.   F.W. Taylor is the founder of scientific management at the turn of this century. Taylor's ideas on scientific management took a tangible shape through the publication of his famous work, the Principles of Scientific Management in 1911. Apart from Taylor, other contributors to scientific management include Frank B. Gilbreth, Morris L. Cooke, Henry L. Gantt and Harrington Emerson. Gilbreth contributed to scientific management through motion study as Taylor did through time study. Morris Cooke wrote about the applicability of the principles and techniques of scientific management to non-business institutions like municipalities and universities.

2. Management Theory : Henri Fayol of France was the first of management theorists who were concerned with the principles of organization and the functions of management. Through his well known work General and Industrial Management, published in French in 1916, Fayol laid the foundation of management as a separate body of knowledge and viewed that management had universal application to all forms of group activity. Other important contributors to this school of management thought are Max Weber, Oliver Sheldon, James D. Mooney, Lyndall Urwick, Chester I. Barnard and Herbert A. Simon.

3. Human Relations. After the pioneering work of Mary Parker Follett on group behaviour and group dynamics, the conclusions of Hawthorne study were published by Elton Mayo and his associates in the latter 1930s and throughout the 1940s. Mayo's conclusions were that human behaviour is moulded by feelings or sentiments, that the group exercises a strong influence on individual behaviour and output, and that the financial incentive is less powerful than group standards and sentiments in determining output. Briefly, the Hawthorne study established that human beings are the most important and influential input for securing a greater output in any concern. Other contributors to this school of thought include Kurt Lewin, F.J. Roethlisberger and T.N. Whitehead.

4. Decision Science : In the 1950s, the contributions of economists, mathematicians and statisticians, or econometrists as they are jointly called, led to the development of another school of management thought which is known as decisionscience school. It is concerned with rational decision making by way of defining the problem, developing alternatives, evaluating such alternatives, and choosing the best possible solution thereof. According to this school, as decision making is the sole way in which managers can discharge their responsibility of managing, decision making should be taken as the central focus of the management study. Various mathematical models and analyses like linear programming, critical-path scheduling, inventory models, information models, simulation, etc. have been developed for quantitative measurement of decision results with the help of computers. Important contributors to this field include Herbert A. Simon, Russel Ackoff, Joy Forrester, Martin Starr and Kenneth Boulding.

5. Behavioural Sciences : Along with the growth of decision science school, there arose the behavioural sciences school after the World War II. Ideas of Mary Parker Follett, Chester I. Barnard and Elton Mayo were greatly extended by behavioural scientists. Reversing the findings of the human relations school which viewed that happy workers were productive workers, the behavioural sciences school puts emphasis on human behaviour as it relates to the goal achievement and efficiency improvement. With this end in view, behavioural scientists are mostly concerned with organizational change, motivation and leadership. This school contributes to our knowledge of organizational behaviour by showing the way of integrating individual goals with the organizational goals and of managing interpersonal conflicts. Important contributors to this school of thought include Herbert A. Simon, James G. March, Douglas McGregor, Chris Argyris, George C. Homans, Rensis Likert, Abraham Maslow, Frederick Herzberg, Joe Kelly and others.

6. Systems Theory. To reconcile the divergent views and approaches adopted in different schools of thought, the systems theory has been developed from the 1960s for integrating the past and present contributions by way of a systems aproach and for explaining the complexity and dynamicity of present-day organizations. The systems concept enables us to see the critical variables and constraints and their interactions with one another. Herbert A. Simon is the spiritual father of this school. Other major contributors to this school of thought are Daniel Katz, Robert L. Kahn and Richard A. Johnson.

SYSTEMS APPROACH. A system is defined as a set of regularly interacting or inter-dependent components that go to constitute a united whole. A series of flows connects the components and provides the means by which the components interact with one another. The systems approach to management has the same characteristics as are found in physical and biological systems. The systems have five essential characteristics. First, systems must have some specific components, parts, units or subunits which are called sub-systems of the system. The marketing unit, for example, is a subsystem of the enterprise system. Secondly, every system is encompassed, affected or influenced by a larger system which is called the suprasystem. The enterprise system, for example, is encompassed by the industrial suprasystem. Thirdly, all systems along with their subsystms must have some common objectives for unifying the components through their interrelationships. Fourthly, systems are of such a complex character that a change in one subsystem affects the other subsystems. Finally, all systems must receive inputs to survive and these inputs must be processed into outputs at such a rate that they maintain the viability of the system.

7. Contingency Theory. Allied to the systems theory, the contingency theory calls for a further refinement, extension and synthesis of past and present contributions in the sphere of management. The contingency view requires a consistency between the organization and its environment and among the various subsystems. Current management thinking is greatly influenced by both the systems approach and the contingency approach. These two approaches are recognized as the key to effective management in the 1980s. Both these approaches accept the dynamics and complexities of the organization structures and of the behaviour of their members. Important contributors to the contingency theory include Tom Burns, G.M. STalker, Joan Woodward, Paul R. Lawrence, L.W. Lorsch, Victor H. Vroom and Robert J. House.

CONTINGENCY APPROACH. The most recent development in the theory of management is what is known as the contingency theory or the situational approach. In all its operations, an organization affects and is affected. In all its operations, an organization affects and is affected in turn by its environment. The environment is composed of persons, physical resources, ecnomic and market conditions, climate, culture, attitude and laws. The environment exercises a potent influence on the enterprise and sets opportunities and limitations for the organization. Any successful organization recognizes the important environmental factors and tries to mould other factors. As a result, effective managerial principles and practices vary with the environment in which the organization operates, and any generalizations of principles are not practicable. In the sphere of organization design, leadership and motivation, the contingency approach to organizations has modified the traditional thinking on such matters. According to this approach, the organization structure, leadership styles and motivation patterns are contingent on the task, technology and environment of the organization.

Contributors from the UK. As regards the important contributors from the U.K. Boulton and Watt introduced in 1796 Production Management by way of work study, production planning, payment by results and cost-accounting procedure. Robert

Owen adopted a pioneering step in 1810 in the field of Personnel Management. Charles Babbage busied himself with an improved use of machines and the organization of human beings and published a work on the Economy of Machinery and Manufacturers in 1832. During the present century, a comprehensive work on management is The Philosophy of Management written by Oliver Sheldon in 1923. Besides, several publications of Lyndall Urwick and E.F.L. Brech have enriched our management knowledge.

Contributors from the U.S.A. In the U.S.A., Taylor's ideas on scientific management were greatly extended by his three important disciples, viz., Henry L. Gantt, Frank Gilbreth and Harrington Emerson. Contributions from businessmen include Lectures on Organization by Russel Robb in 1910; a publication entitled Organization Engineering by Henri Dennison in 1931; a comprehensive theory of organization under the title of Onward Industry by Mooney and Reiley in 1931; and Chester I. Barnard's book, The Functions of the Executive published in 1938. Barnard's book is recognized as a landmark in management thinking for introducing social aspects in the management process. The results of Hawthorne Research have been published by three important researchers, viz., Elton Mayo, F.J. Roethlisberger and T.N. Whitehead. Herbert A. Simon is the most important and versatile contributor to management thought over a period of three decades. He contributed to management from mathematics, cybernetics and computers approaches as well as from psychological, sociological and economic viewpoints. His book, Administrative Behaviour, is a modern classic on decision making. His another book, Organizations, equally proved his genius for integrating behavioural sciences into management thinking. He is the only Nobel prize winner in the management area. Peter F. Drucker is the most objective and prolific management analyst of the present time. Drucker is currently exercising a major influence on management thinking and practice by his several publications and many of his ideas have become the basic tenets of management at present. Last but not the least, the influence of the American Management Association and the Society for the Advancement of Management is tremendous on the growth of the management theory. Moreover, a galaxy of political scientists, sociologists, psychologists and anthropologists have made some significant contributions in recent years. Of all the social scientists, the name of Mary Parker Follett deserves special mention.

Mary Parker Follett (1868-1933). Follett has made valuable contributions through books and papers on group dynamics, human relations and authority exercise, some of which bear a stiking similarity with Hawthorne Experiments published in a subsequent period. She pointed out that any human group has a life of its own which is something more than the sum of the individual lives composing it and that the individual's thoughts and actions are always moulded by the group influence. In all co-operative endeavours, the group adds a plus value when properly directed. Conflicts between persons or between groups stem from differences which can be used as an avenue towards, and a vehicle of progress when such differences are integrated rathern than compromised or suppressed under domination. Exercise of authority is involved in leadership, control as well as in the execution of decisions and orders. In all such situations, the employee acceptance of authority would be satisfactory provided "Law of the Situation" is explained through the systematic presentation of facts. Briefly, instead of imposing power over people, the use of authority and the task of order giving should be depersonalised.

Taylor F.W. (1856-1915). Taylor is well known for his famous work, The Principles of Scientific Management, published in 1911. Although the work was professed to provide general principles of management, it was in reality found to contain certain principles of factory management or production management. To improve the productive efficiency of industrial concerns, he was preoccupied with machines and their operators. With this end in view, he developed time and motion study which was regarded as the "cornerstone of scientific management." The central theme in Taylor's work was the advocacy for separation of planning functions from doing functions, management taking more and more thinking functions from workers so as to make their work purely mechanical through the formulation of rules, laws and formulas. His insistence on the application of scientific methods or "one best way of doing jobs" are the principal contribution to management theory. His ideas on selection, training, compensation and discipline of workers have some rudiments of validity. He placed several new duties on management in the form of principles : (a) replacement of the old rule-of-thumb method by scientific one through the exact determination of each man's work on the basis of elementary motions or operations ; (b) scientific selection, placement and training of workers; (c) absolute co-operation between labour and management in the performance of work ; and (d) equitable division of work and responsibility between management and labour.

Taylor's scientific management inundated the whole industrial world in a sudden flood which, however, receded back in course of time. Taylorism has become a dead cult now for two misconceptions. Subsequent studies have revealed that complete separation of planning from doing under his functional foremanship is out and out an unrealistic principle. Secondly, the assignment of mechanical job to workers by breaking a task into elementary components is thoroughly unproductive, since it denies job-satisfaction to workers and makes them inanimate cogs in the industrial machinery. Organized labour misunderstood it as a device for speeding-up and rate cutting. Moreover, the claim of Taylor and his disciples that theirs was an "exact science" has be littled the importance of it. Rather than providing fundamental principles of general management, Taylorism is now held to be responsible for delaying the propagation of a true management science developed by Henri Fayol in 1916. That the Americans even now use the term scientific management can be explained historically. Taylorism is nothing but shadow of the present-day concept of scientific management even in the U.S.A.

Fayol, Henri (1841-1925). Henri Fayol, the French industrialist, is regarded in responsible quarters as the real father of management science. After graduating himself as a mining engineer in 1860, he immediately joined a coal mining company as its engineer and was promoted to the position of its Managing Director in 1888 for his conspicuous ability. When he became the chief executive of the company, it was on the verge of collapse. Under his leadership over a period of 30 years, the company came out as one of the largest coal and iron combines in the country with an exceptionally strong financial position. As a successful industrialist, Fayol had the opportunity to search for sound management principles and was able to analyse the management process correctly in course of his two lectures delivered in 1900 and 1908. Subsequently he tried to reduce his ideas into a coherent philosophy by the development of principles through his famous work, General and Industrial Management, published in French in 1916. From the date of his retirement in 1918 till 1925, he devoted himself to the task of popularising his theory of management in France.

The relative contributions of these two pioneers have been reviewed by Urwick in his foreword to the English translation of *General and Industrial Management* in the following words : "The work of Taylor and Fayol was of course, essentially complementary. They both realized that the problem of personnel and its management at all levels is the 'key' to industrial success. Both applied scientific method to this problem. That Taylor worked primarily on the operative level, from the bottom of the industrial hierarchy upwards, while Fayol concentrated on the Managing Director and worked downwards, was merely a reflection of their very different careers. But Fayol's capacity to see and to acknowledge this publicly was an example of his intellectual integrity and generosity of spirit. They gave France a unified management body more than twenty years before the same ideal began to be realized in Great Britain." Although Taylorism has undergone a profound change under the impact of new developments, Fayol's principles have stood the test of time and have been accepted as the core of management theory even upto the present time.

2.4   REVIEW QUESTIONS

1. Define Administration and Management.
2. Explain the different levels of management.
3. Differentiate Administration with management.
4. Explain the various schools of management thoughts ?

PLANNING

3.1 DEFINITION

Planning is the process of determining the objectives of the administrative effort and of devising means calculated to achieve them. In other words, planning is the preparation for action. It is an endeavor to apply foresight to human activity, and is based on knowledge and research.

Terry has defined planning in terms of future course of action. He says that, "Planning is the selection and relating to facts and making using of assumptions regarding the future in the visualization and formalization of proposed activities believed necessary to achieve desired result.

Mcfarland has defined as a concept of executive action that embodies the skills of anticipating, influencing and controlling the nature and direction of change.

According to Koontz and O'donnell, "Planning involves selecting enterprise objectives, departmental goals and programmes, and determining the ways of reaching them". Planning, thus, provides a rational approach to pre-selected objectives.

According to Philip Kotler, "Planning is deciding in the present what to do in future. It is the process whereby companies reconcile their resources with their objectives and opportunities.

3.2 TYPES OF PLANS

Planning may be of different types. We can classify some of the important types of plans according to the nature of planning below:

a.   **Financial or Non-Financial Plans**

➤ Most plans cannot be translated into action if there is no finance.

➤ Planning loses all its significance if sufficient financial resources are not mobilized.

➤ Plans that require financial resources are considered financial plans.

➤ Plans relating to the physical resources of an organization may be called non-financial plans.

b.   **Formal and Informal Plans**

➤ More thinking by managers refers to informal plans.

➤ When an informal plan is finalized and prepared for implementation, it is considered to be a formal plan.

c.   **Specific and Routine Plans**

➤ Any plan made with a particular object is known as.a specific plan.

➤ Day-to-day normal activities require some type of regular plan known as a routine plan.

d.   **Strategic and Functional Plans**

➤ Strategic planning is the overall planning of the enterprises objectives determined by the top management.

➤ A plan made in a functional area like production, purchase, marketing is referred to as a functional plan.

e.   **Long-range and Short-range Plan**

➤ It depends upon the organizational structure, nature of business, the kind of industry, etc.

➤ In general, a short-term plan refers to a period covering six to twelve months.

> A long-range plan usually involves a time interval of between three and five years.

> The modern concern is to plan for a decade or two.

f.   Administrative and Operational Plans

> Administrative plan provides the base for operative plans.

> Administrative planning is done by the top and middle - level management.

> Operational planning by the lower-level management.

3.3   STRATEGIES, POLICIES & PLANNING PREMISES

Strategies

> The term strategy has originally come from Greece around 400 BC and it refers to the technique of directing a military force in the light of the enemy force's action.

> In management, it has the same competitive implications. It is also regarded as interpretative planning.

> Strategy is related to the environment and its impact on the organization.

Policies

Policies are guidelines to action.

> They are the basic statements serving as guides to the thinking and action of subordinates in repetitive situations. They provide broad guidelines.

> According to Alford and Betty, "the mode of thought and the principles underlying the activities of an organization or an institution". It is a regular decision which is applicable to repetitive situations.

> Policy statement must be definite, clear and easily understandable.

➤ Policies made by the management should be reasonable and stable, flexible, based on proper and correct information and sound judgment, and, to accomplish their purpose, be communicated. Policies should be in writing.

Planning Premises

➤ A plan is based on certain assumptions called premises.

➤ The assumptions or premises are for a future setting or happenings.

➤ Premises are made about market conditions, price trends, tax policy, government policy, business cycles, etc.

➤ Premises represent the plan environment.

➤ Planning premises, their choice, evaluation and usefulness depends upon the abilities of the planner.

➤ Planning premises are,

     a.   External and Internal
     b.   Tangible and intangible
     c.   Controllable, semi-controllable, and Uncontrollable

3.4   IMPORTANCE OF PLANNING

The following points are the importance of planning.

a.   Selection of Optimum Goals

➤ Planning involves rational thinking and decision-making concerning a proposed course of action. It also implies selection of one course of action and rejection of outer possible courses of action.

➤ The selected course of action is naturally the one that promotes the overall organizational goals within the frame work of the resource availability and economic, social and political factors.

➤ For optimization of overall organizational operations, it may sometimes be necessary to sub-optimize i.e., to reduce the efficiency of some departments.

b.   Tackling increasing complexities

➤ An organization is a heterogeneous group of human beings who differs from one another in many respects.

➤ It is unlikely that they will work effectively and harmoniously in the interest of the organization.

➤ Unless they have a plan in the making of which they have had a share and, which they regard as common property.

➤ So, planning is essential to any goal-directed activity.

c.   Meeting environmental changes

➤ Business environmental changes move rapidly and sweepingly than can be imaged.

➤ Change in social values, increase in competition, new product discoveries, change in consumer tastes and preferences, have each the potential to upset any organization.

➤ Management should discern and exploit the emerging situation by adjusting and adapting the inputs and transformation process to suit the environmental changes.

➤ Only proper and effective planning can help the management to do so.

d.   Safeguard against Business failures

➤ Business failures are blamed on cut-throat competition, unpredictability of consumer tastes and preferences, rapid technological changes and abrupt economic and political development.

➤ In general, failure of business is caused due to rash and unscientific decision - making, which is a direct result of lack of proper planning.

e.   Unity of Action

  ➤ Planning enables the people within an organization to work effectively and harmoniously for accomplishment of common goals.

  ➤ It provides them a stake in their own future and thus induces them to do their utmost to meet the challenge.

f.   Effective Co-ordination and Control

  ➤ Planning makes it easy to exercise effective control and co-ordination.

  ➤ The work to be done, the persons and the departments which have to do it, time-limit within which it is to be completed and the costs to be incurred, are all determined in advance.

  ➤ This facilitates proper and timely measurement of actual performance and its comparison with the planned performance.

  ➤ In case, actual performance is not as per the plans, factors responsible for the same can be ascertained.

  ➤ In he absence of planning, there will be no scientific standards to measure and evaluate performance.

3.5   PRINCIPLES OF PLANNING

        The following are the principles of planning.

1.   Principle of the Contribution to Objectives

        Every plan and its components should help in the achievement of organizational objectives.

2.   Principle of the Primacy of Planning

        Planning is considered as the first and the foremost function to be performed in the process of management. It is followed by other managerial functions like organizing, staffing, directing and controlling.

3.   Principle of the Pervasiveness of Planning

Planning is all-pervasive and it percolates to all the levels of management from top to bottom.

4.   Principle of the Flexibility of Planning

Every plan should be made in such a way that it adjusts an adapts itself to charged circumstances. There must be a high degree of flexibility in every good plan.

5.   Principle of Periodicity

Long-term plans, medium-term plans and short-term plans are to be integrated and interrelated in such a way as to achieve the organizational objectives effectively and economically.

6.   Principle of Planning Premises

To develop consistent and co-ordinated plans, it is essential that planning be based upon carefully considered assumptions and predictions, known as planning premises.

7.   Principle of Efficiency of Operations

Every plan should be designed with its components like objectives, strategies, policies, procedures, schedules, budgets, etc. to accomplish efficient realization of the plans.

8.   Principle of Limiting Factors

There are various limiting factors like money, manpower, machinery, materials and management, which are to be taken into consideration while drafting a plan or taking a policy decision or devising a strategy.

9.   Principle of Revision

Every plan has to be executed, and in the execution, managers should check periodically the events and decisions, and if there is any necessity, to redraw and readjust their plan to achieve the organizational objectives. They should make provision for such change.

3.6   STEPS IN PLANNING

There are various steps involved in planning. There are as follows :

1.   Defining the Problem

The manager has to identify and define the problems which may appear at a future date and which may require proper planning.

2.   Establishing Objectives

Every Manager should clearly establish the objectives to be achieved by the enterprise. Objectives must be specific, informative and functional.

3.   Establishing the Planning Premises

Every plan has to be based on certain carefully considered assumptions and predictions, which are known as planning premises.

4.   Determining Alternative Courses of Action

The next step is to search for and examine alternative courses of action.

5.   Evaluation of Alternative Courses of Action

Every alternative course of action has to be evaluated, and the relative importance of each one of them should be ascertained.

6.   Selecting the Course of Action

After analyzing and evaluating the available alternatives, the manager has to select the best course of action.

7.   Formulating Derivative Plans

Every major plan has to be supported and developed by the preparation of other derivative plans. With in the framework of the basic plan, derivative plans are developed in each area of the business.

8.   Timing and Sequence of Operations

For every work, the manager has to prescribe the time frame, and within that, the work has to be started and completed. For smooth flow of work, it is better to maintain a sequence of operations.

9.   Participation and Follow-up

Each and every plan has to be communicated and explained in great detail to subordinates so that they are kept fully informed. It also helps in securing the co-operation and complete participation of the workers in executing the plans. Every plan and programme requires good follow-up. It helps in making some adjustments and modifications in the plan if necessary. Continuous follow-up can result in the effective execution of the proposed course of action.

3.7   LIMITATIONS OF PLANNING

Planning is, and should be, the primary function of management. It sets the frame of organization, direction, control and co-ordination of activities in any enterprise.

a.   Uncertainty

> Planning concerns the future, and nothing about the future is certain, except that it must be different from the present.

> Assessment of future can only be in terms of guesswork, probabilities, speculations, assumptions and conjectures.

> Uncertainty preferring the certainty of the present and past.

b.   Action - Packed Routine

> Managers are ever pre-occupied of rapping with day-to-day problems.

➢ This leaves them little time to think and plan about the problems of tomorrow.

➢ It is common to be over-concerned with the issues at hand which, if left unattended, might cause an immediate loss.

➢ Planning for the future does not appear to have the same urgency and can be conveniently postponed without fear of any loss for the present.

c.   Abstraction

➢ The planning process involves thinking about vague alternatives and concern with 'what if' question.

➢ Almost every conceivable thing is included in the realm of possibility.

➢ There seems to be nothing hard and fast, just assumptions, estimates, speculation and guess work, which can be tested only when the thing to which they relate actually take place.

➢ This often brings in distortion in planning.

d.   Rigidity

➢ Planning involves setting of objectives, and determination of the ideal course of action for their implementation.

➢ It implies that there will be no deviation from the chosen path.

➢ However, pursuit of vague, though predetermined, goals is against the very concept of business.

e.   Costly

➢ Planning is an expensive exercise both in terms of time and money.

➢ It necessitates the formulation of estimates, collection of necessary information and facts, and a careful analysis and evaluation of the various courses of action.

➢ To decide on the best and the most economical course of action for the enterprise, as also for each of its workers and departments.

3.8   REVIEW QUESTIONS

1.   What is planning? What are the steps involved in it?
2.   What are the planning premises?
3.   Discuss the importance of planning. What should be done to overcome its limitations?
4.   Why are strategies important?
5.   What do you understand by the term policy?
6.   Distinguish between a policy and a strategy.
7.   Explain the principles of planning?

OBJECTIVES

4.1 DEFINING OBJECTIVES

The terms `objective' and `goal' indicate an end result to be sought and accomplished. Goals and objectives both have value orientations and indicate desired conditions considered necessary to improve the overall performance of the organization. Three widely quoted definitions on objectives are given below.

➤ Objectives are goals established to guide the efforts of the company and each of its components.

➤ An organization goal is a desired state of affairs which the organization attempts to realize.

➤ Objectives indicate the `end point of a management programme'.

4.2 CHARACTERISTICS OF ORGANIZATIONAL OBJECTIVES

Just like any other management function, objectives have certain basic features. Generally speaking, enterprise objectives are visible and understood by all. They provide undeniable evidence of how well the man with the gun has performed. When objectives are defined and set, it is hard to plead ignorance, forgetfulness and misunderstanding. Apart from these simple descriptions, enterprise objectives have the following features:

1. Objectives Form a Hierarchy

In many organizations objectives are structured in a hierarchy of importance. There are objectives within objectives. They all require painstaking definition and close analysis if they are to be useful separately and profitable as a whole. The hierarchy of objectives is a graded series in which organization's goals are supported by each succeeding managerial level down to the level of the individual. The objectives of each unit contribute to the objectives of the next higher unit. Each operation has a simple objective which must fit in and add to the final objective. Hence no work should be undertaken unless it contributes to the overall goal. Usually the hierarchy or objectives in an organization is described through means-ends chain. Understanding the means ends chain helps us to see how broad goals are translated into operational objectives. In the organization the relationship between means and ends in hierarchical goals established at one level require certain means for their accomplishment. These means then become the sub-goals for the next level, and more specific operational objectives are developed as we move down the hierarchy.

2.   Objectives Form a Network

Objectives interlock in a network fashion. They are inter-related and inter-dependent. The concept of network of objectives implies that once objectives are established for every department and every individual in an organization; these subsidiary objectives should contribute to meet the basic objectives of the total organization. If the various objectives in an organization do not support one another, people may pursue goals that may be good for their own function but may be detrimental to the company as a whole. Managers have to trade off among the conflicting objectives and see that the components of the network fit one another. Because, as rightly pointed out by Koontz et al., "It is bad enough when goals do not support and interlock with one another. It may be catastrophic when they interfere with one another."

3.   Multiplicity of Objectives

Organizations pursue multifarious objectives. At every level in the hierarchy, goals are likely to be multiple. For example, the marketing division may have the objective of sale and distribution of products. This objective can be broken down into a group of objectives for the product, advertising, research, promotion managers. The advertising manager's goals may include: designing product messages carefully, create a favorable image of the product in the market, etc. Similar goals can be set for other marketing managers. To describe the single, specific goal of an organization is to say very little about it. It turns out that there are several goals involved. This may be due to the fact that the enterprise has to meet internal as well as external challenges effectively. Internal problems may hover around profitability, survival, growth, and so on. External problems may be posed by government, society, stockholders, customers, etc. In order to meet the conflicting demands from various internal and external groups, organizations generally pursue multiple objectives. Moreover, no single objective would place the organization on a path of prosperity and progress in the long run. According to Drucker, "To emphasize profit, for instance, misdirects managers to the point where they may endanger the survival of the business. To obtain profit today they tend to undermine the future." Where several goals are involved, maximizing one goal would usually be at the cost of another. Managers have to see that various goals exist is harmony and for this purpose they must assign a definite priority of 1, 2 or 3 depending on the importance of each objective. Such assignment of priorities helps to keep a perspective, especially when there are many goals for one position.

4.   Long and Short-Range Objectives

Organizational objectives are usually related to time. Long-range objectives extending over five or more years are the ultimate or `dream' objectives for the organization. They are abstractions of the entire hierarchy of objectives of the organization. For example, planning in India has got objectives like eradication of poverty, checking population growth through birth control etc., which reflect certain `ideals' the government wishes to accomplish in the long run. Short-range objectives (one year goals) and medium-range objectives (two to four-year period goals), reflect immediate, attainable goals. The short-range and medium-range objectives are the means for achieving long term goals and the long term goals supply a frame work within which the lower level goals are designed. Thus, all these goals reinforce each other in such a way that the total result is greater than the sum of the effects taken individually. That is why goal setting is called a `synergistic process'. In order to remain viable, every organization needs to set goals in all three time periods.

4.3   IMPORTANCE OF OBJECTIVES

Objectives are essential to organizations. Organizations produce and market economic products and services, universities provide teaching and research, governments provide welfare and security and so on. Organizations are attainment instruments. Without some purpose, there is no need for the organization. All organizations are goal seeking, that is, they exist for the purpose of achieving some goals efficiently and effectively. Objectives affect the size, shape, and design of the organization, and they are important in motivating and directing personnel. Objectives serve the following functions:

1.   Legitimacy

Objectives describe the purpose of the organization so that people know what a stand is for and will accept its existence and continuance. Thus, Ford `sells American Transportation', Chrysler `sells know-how' and Godrej `sells quality products'. Objectives help to legitimize the presence of organization in its environment. Now the organization can emphasize its uniqueness and identity.

2.   Direction

Objectives provide guidelines for organizational efforts. They keep attention focused on common purposes. Once objectives are formulated, they become the polar star by which the voyage is navigated. Every activity is directed toward the objectives, every individual contributes to meet the goals. `Without seeing the target, a manager would be like a blindfolded archer - expending useless effort and creating havoc.'

3.   Co-ordination

Objectives keep activities on the right track. They make behavior in organizations more rational, more coordinated and thus more effective', because everyone knows the accepted goals to work toward. In setting effective goals managers help members at all levels of the organization to understand how they can `best achieve their own goals by directing their behavior toward the goals of the organization.'

4.   Benchmarks for Success

Objectives serve as performance standards against which actual performance may be checked. They provide a benchmark for assessment. They help in the control of human effort of human effort in an organization.

5.   Motivation

Goals are motivators. The setting of a goal that is both specific and challenging leads to an increase in performance because it makes it clear to the individual what he is supposed to do. He can compare how well he is doing now versus how well he has done in the past and in some instances how well he is performing in comparison to others. According to Latham and Yuki goal specificity enables the workers to determine how to translate effort into successful performance by choosing an appropriate action plan. Suppose a publisher sets a goal of securing orders worth Rs. 5,000 in 6 months for a sales man and announces bonus for meeting this specification. This half yearly goal is a motivational tool that influences the salesman's behavior. Having a definite figure to shoot for is much more likely to stimulate his effort than instructions to `sell as much as you can'.

Psychologists preach the significance of setting goals in our private lives as well. You set the goal of cleaning your scooter on a Sunday morning. Despite the drudgery, you feel a sense of accomplishment a fulfilling your objective.

4.4   AREAS NEEDING OBJECTIVES

Peter Drucker, while working as a consultant for General Electric, identified eight key areas in which organizations would establish objectives. The areas were: (1) market standing, (2) productivity, (3) physical and financial resources, (4) profitability, (5) innovation, (6) manager performance and development, (7) worker performance and attitudes, and (8) public and social responsibility.

1.   Market Standing

Market standing and innovation are the foundation areas in management. Essentially an organization exists to obtain results in these areas only. Market standing is a question deciding on the optimum (not the maximum) of market share the firm is trying to capture ultimately. This requires a careful analysis of (i) customers and products or services; (ii) market segments (what groups are buying the product or service); and (iii) distribution channels (who is getting the product to the customers).

2.   Innovation

In every business there are three kinds of innovations: innovation in product or service; innovation in market place and consumer behavior and values; and innovation in the various skills and activities needed to make the products and services and to bring them to the market. The chief problem in setting innovation objectives is the difficulty of measuring the importance of various innovations. Management must, first of all, anticipate the innovation goals needed to reach marketing goals. It must also find out the technological developments in all areas of the business. For example, the survival of an insurance company depends on: the development of new forms of insurance, the modification of existing policies, finding out cheaper ways of selling policies and settling claims etc. Operating in a competitive world forces business firms to place emphasis on innovation goals.

3.   Productivity

Productivity is the ratio of an organization's inputs to its outputs. All business has the same resources to work with; it is the quality of management that differentiates one business from another. It must decide as to what inputs of labor, equipment and finances are necessary to produce the firm's outputs?

4.   Physical and Financial Resources

Every business must be able to attract resources - physical, financial and human - and put them to productive use to be able to perform well. Resource mobilization is a two-step process: anticipating the needs of the business and planning for obtaining the resources in an economical fashion. After mobilizing resources one also has to say "This is what is available; what do we have to be, how we have to behave, to get the fullest benefit?"

5.   Manager Performance and Development

In order to `stay in' and remain profitable every business needs strong, innovative managers. So it is highly important, especially in the case of large organizations, to set objectives relating to the quality of management performance, the development of managers at various levels in the organization.

6.   Worker Performance and Attitudes

Organizations must provide tangible benefits to the individuals working for its continued growth. Thus, workers want wages, managers want salaries, and owners want profits. These are the inducements that an organization must provide in order to obtain performance (contributions) from various groups. Most of the routine or normal work is performed by operative level employees in every organization. Unless goals are established in terms of output per employee, quality of product etc. the organizational activities may be disrupted by labor strife, union problems etc.

7.   Profitability

(i)   Profit objectives are important for accomplishing other objectives like covering risks in the business; (ii) ensuring supply of future capital for modernization and expansion; and (iii) satisfying customer needs. "A fundamental objective of the business firm is to produce and distribute products and services that the customer is willing to buy. Its reason for being is to create value. Utility must be created or consumers will spend their money elsewhere. Profits are essential to the survival and growth of the firm." They are the rewards for the effective utilization of resources in creating values for consumers. Instead of trying to maximize profits, the firm must try to create utilities for consumers.

8.   Public and Social Responsibility

To achieve the economic objective, a firm must produce the goods the consumer wants. If a firm is not able to create economic value for society, it may not stay in business along enough to make a profit. In recent years social responsibility of business has become a matter of concern for many business undertakings. Here 'responsibility' implies a sense of obligation on the part of the business toward the general public.

4.5   CRITERIA OF A GOOD OBJECTIVE

A good objective must be specific. Specificity is a highly desirable quality. Specificity provides direction towards which efforts could be channelised. A company's objective which reads "to achieve a common condition of employment for all employees, to at least present staff conditions, by 31st December, 1995," is clearly undesirable as it lacks specificity.

Secondly, an objective must be time-bound. "To reduce the selling expenses by 5% in the domestic market by 30th November, 1995", is clearly specific and time-bound objective. But to formulate an objective such as "to apply work study techniques to methods of working so that 70% of direct employees are achieving 100% performance" is of little use as it does not specify the time limit.

Thirdly, an objective should be as measurable and quantifiable as possible. This may not always be possible, but an attempt should be made to formulate the objective in measurable terms. Clearly, an objective like "to improve return on investment on new product lines" cannot be said to be a good objective.

The other criteria of a good objective are feasibility, rationality and consistency.

4.6   MANAGEMENT BY OBJECTIVES (MBO)

MBO is difficult to define, for organizations use it in different ways and for different reasons. In broad terms, it may be stated that MBO is an overall philosophy of management that concentrates on measurable goals and end results. It provides a systematic and rational approach to management and helps prevent management by crisis. MBO is based on the assumptions that people perform better when they know what is expected of them and can relate their personal goals to organizational objectives. It also assumes that people are interested in the goal-setting process and in evaluating their performances against the target. In the words of Odirone, MBO is a `process' whereby the superior and subordinate managers of an organization jointly identify its common goals, define each individual's major areas of responsibility in terms of results expected of him, and use these measures as guides for operating the unit and assessing the contribution of each of its members.'

4.6.1   MBO Process

The exact meaning of MBO (and its application) varies from organization to organization. In some, MBO is nothing more than a catchy slogan from the latest management jargon. MBOis dismissed as a joke, a gimmick for justifying the existence of personnel departments, a fad that will go away and a paper-shuffling hassle that won't stop. In other organizations, MBO represents an overall philosophy of management, a way of thinking that concentrates on achieving results. It is treated as a multifaceted tool for improving managerial as well as organizational performance. In order to understand the reasons for this diversity, it is necessary to look into the process of MBO.

1.   Goal Setting

Any MBO programme must start with the absolute and enthusiastic support of top management. It must be consistent with the philosophy of management. The long term goals of the organization must be outlined initially, like: What is the basic purpose of the organization? What business are we in and why? What are the long term prospects in other areas? After these long term goals are established, management must be concerned with determining specific objectives to be achieved within a given time capsule.

2.   Action Plan

The action plan is the means by which an objective is achieved. The action plan gives direction and ensures unity of purpose to organizational activities. It will wet out in detail exactly what is to be done, how the subordinate will proceed, what step will be taken and what activities will be engaged in as the subordinate progresses. It provides a specific answer to the question: `What is to be done?' Questions like who is responsible for each activity, what resources are needed, what the time requirements are - are also answered.

3.   Appraising Performance (Final Review)

This is that last phase of the MBO programme. In this step the actual results are measured against predetermined standards. Mutually agreed on objectives provide a basis for reviewing the progress. While appraising the performance of subordinates, the manager should sit with the subordinates and find out the problems encountered while accomplishing the goals . The subordinate, as in the periodic sessions, should not be criticized for failure to make sufficient progress; the atmosphere should not be hostile or threatening. A give-and-take atmosphere should prevail and the appraisal should be based on mutual trust and confidence between managers and subordinates. In actual practice this type of give-and-take session is extremely difficult to achieve and rarely reaches its potential value, unless managers are gifted with necessary interpersonal skills. Often, appraisal takes place for the purpose of determining rewards and punishments;' judging the personal worth of subordinates and not the job performance. As a result, appraisal sessions become awkward and uncomfortable to the participants and intensify the pressure on subordinates while giving them a limited choice of objectives. Insecure subordinates may come to `dread' the sessions and they may not feel free to communicate honestly and openly without fear of retaliation.

4.6.2   Benefits

Management by objectives moulds the planning, organizing directing and controlling activities in a number of ways.

1.   As objectives provide the basic foundation of planning, the programme of action is thoroughly tuned to the set of objectives. Instead of going through planning as a work or as a mental exercise in thinking, planning for performance can be made to prevail through a system of management by objectives.

2.   Delegation and decentralization in the sphere of organizing become effective and fruitful only when the subordinates are trained and allowed to work under a system of management by objectives.

3.   By clarifying the sense of direction and allowing subordinates to operate under greater freedom, management by objectives results in motivating managers to do the best possible work rather than enough to get by with the situation.

4.   Management by objectives leads to the adoption of managerial self-control. Managerial self-control has been found from experience to be associated with higher performance goals and broader vision.

5.   Management by objective has ushered an era of improved managing in the business world. It provides a practical means of allowing wider participation in goal setting and of accomplishing goals of the enterprise in a better way.

4.6.3   MBO - Problems

Each organization is likely to encounter specific problems in MBO practice but some of the common problems are given here.

1.   **Time and cost**. MBO is not as simple as it looks to be. It is a process which requires large amount of the scarcest resource in the organization time of the senior managers. This is particularly so at the initial stages, when MBO is seen as something over and above the normal work. Sometimes managers get frustrated and feel overburdened. Further, MBO generates paper work because large numbers of forms are to be designed and put into practice. Therefore, there is a problem of communication overload. However, such problems are transitory and emerge only at the initial stages. Once MBO becomes a part of the organizational life, these problems disappear.

2.   **Failure to Teach MBO Philosophy**. MBO is a philosophy of managing an organization in a new way. However, managers fail to understand and appreciate this new approach. They have a number of doubts about MBO like what purpose is served by MBO, how the performance is to be appraised, and how organization will benefit. MBO demands rigorous analysis as an integral element of the management process but the organization may not be used to rigour. Frequently both the base data and the expertise for analysis are not available. If corrective action is not taken early, the objectives become imprecise, control information may not be available and one would not know if something was achieved. This is done on a systematic basis and managers seldom appreciate this. They take MBO as another tool for control. Moreover, their old way of thinking puts difficulty in introducing MBO because they may not appreciate the full view of MBO.

3.   **Problems in Objective Setting**. MBO requires verifiable objectives against which performance can be measured. However, setting of such objectives is difficult at least in some areas. Objectives are more in the form of statement rather than in quantitative form. Of course, some objectives can be quantified and can be broken in

terms of time period but others lack this characteristic, for example, objectives of staff activities. In such cases, there is absence of basis for further course of action.

4.   **Emphasis on Short-term Objectives.** Sometimes, in order to be more precise, there is a tendency to emphasize on short-term objectives usually for a year or even less. No doubt, this may help in performance appraisal but there is always a danger in emphasizing short-term objectives at the cost of long-term objectives.

Sometimes, an organization's short-term and long-term objectives may be incompatible because of certain specific problems.

5.   **Inflexibility.** MBO represents the danger of inflexibility in the organisation, particularly when the objectives need to be changed. In a dynamic environment, a particular objective may not be valid for ever. In the context of revised objectives, change premises, or modified policies, it is useless to follow the old objectives. However, many managers often hesitate to change objectives during a period of time. Thus inflexibility created by applying MBO may cause harm than what it may contribute.

6.   **Frustration.** Sometimes MBO creates frustration among managers. This frustration may be because to two reasons. First, as experience shows, many organisations could not implement MBO properly, resulting into utter chaos. In this case, the organization is not able even to work with its old system. Second, introduction to MBO tends to arouse high expectations for rapid change, particularly among the young and junior managers. They begin to see the vision of a new world for their organization in terms of growth, profitability, and for themselves in terms of career advancement. If the rate of change is slower than expected due to any reason, managers begin to feel frustration and even disenchantment with MBO.

In spite of these obstacles and problems in MBO, it continues to be a way of managing the organization. In fact many of the problems and weaknesses of MBO can be overcome by implementing it properly.

4.6.4   MBO - Limitations & Specifications

Limitations. But management by objectives is fraught with certain difficulties in actual practice.

First, subordinate managers are to be trained and coached for working under a philosophy of management by objectives.

Secondly, managers are to be provided with proper guidelines for goal-setting on their part by way of disseminating the planning premises and of imparting a knowledge of the network of company objectives and policies.

Thirdly, the possibility of setting easy goals by managers in quantitative terms only without caring for their qualitative aspects is to be guarded against.

Fourthly, the tendency to overlook long-run objectives and to put emphasis on short-run objectives is to be checked on the part of managers.

Fifthly, as changes in top-level objectives call for a corresponding change in lower-level objectives, inflexibility in objectives may be introduced by the failure to revise lower-lever objectives, an inflexibility in objectives.

Finally, unless the entire pattern and style of managing are suitably adjusted to it, the system may degenerate into a management gimmick. As a matter of fact, the success of MBO programmes in industrial enterprises is as low as 20 to 40 per cent.

Specifications for Objectives

A number of considerations are involved in setting objectives which are supposed to play a dominant role in management.

First, after defining the purpose and mission of business as to what the nature of business is, what is should be and what it will be, the objectives are formulated for any purposeful action. Otherwise, the objectives become good intentions or pious desires. In the context of the clear definition of the business, objectives become the strategies for committing resources and initiating actions. Developed in this way, objectives give direction to the business and provide standards for measuring performance.

Secondly, the translation of major objectives into derivative objectives should always be effected in intelligible, tangible and meaningful terms. Unless individual objectives are specified in definite terms of expected results and they are well understood by lower-level executives and operators, no successful accomplishment is practicable. Furthermore, in the hierarchy of objectives, the individual objectives must fit into the mould of overall objectives for the company to ensure effective management.

Thirdly, objectives should be set in realistic terms rather than in idealistic terms. Objectives which are not attainable and which signify the merge hope of top executives demoralize employees and retard their performance. But realistic objectives based on measured expectations provide incentives and job satisfaction for high performance.

Fourthly, short-range objectives should be recognized as distinct steps in the realization of long-range objectives. Otherwise, the achievement of long-range objectives becomes difficult, if not impossible. Long-range objectives involving plans for the distant future fail to make the individual objectives tangible and meaningful and to provide sensible standards for control. Such objectives may also appear as idealistic to the employees. All these difficulties can be removed by setting short-range objectives as different steps in long-range objectives.

Fifthly, as company objectives are of multiple characters, there arises the necessity of balancing various objectives through a greater concentration of resources and efforts on one or two objectives at a time. Rather than spreading resources over all objectives and stressing everything, the objectives are to be selective. Main and dominant objectives are given more care than others through the constant adjustment of short-run emphasis on such objectives.

Finally, the dynamic business environment makes the company objectives dynamic in nature, and such objectives call for changes along with changing time and situations. Although objectives are more stable than other plans, the periodic adjustment of objectives becomes necessary to keep pace with the progress of time and to cope with the expanding size of the business. Once a change is introduced in overall major objectives, the derivative objectives must also reflect the same degree of change to fit into the hierarchy of objectives.

4.6.5 Prerequisites for Installing MBO Programme

MBO is a philosophy, rather than a mere technique. As such, its installation requires a basic change in the organizational culture and environment. Many of the organizations could not use MBO successfully because of the lack of appreciation of this fact. Many of the organizations are designed so as to undermine the MBO Philosophy. This is because they could not create the proper environment required for the adoption of MBO. Below are stated some of the prerequisites and problems contained therein for installing the MBO programme:

1.   Purpose of MBO: MBO is a means rather than an end. It has to achieve certain things in the organization; it has to solve some problems. Thus, the organization should be very clear about the purpose for which it is being implemented. As already discussed, Howell has suggested a three stage evaluation of MBO : management appraisal and development, improvement of the productivity and profitability, and long-range planning. Thus, an organization facing serious competition in both, in its product and factor markets and in the grip of secular decline, will tend to use MBO primarily for immediate improvements in productivity and profitability. On the other hand, an economically affluent organization might contemplate using MBO to change its management style so that it conforms to a more advanced and germane model of man-in-the-organization. In both these cause, the details and emphases of the system will vary. Thus, if the purpose of MBO is not precisely defined and particular techniques in MBO suitable to the purpose are not emphasized, there is every possibility that MBO does not produce the results as anticipated.

2.   Top Management Support. The presence or absence of top management support is a critical factor in determining the degree to which an MBO programme will be successful. Many studies on MBO suggest that out of the several factors determining the success or failure of MBO, no single factor had greater correlation than the subordinate's perception of superior's attitude towards MBO. Thus subordinates who can see their superiors as having a positive approach towards MBO are themselves also like to show a positive attitude. MBO is a way of managing on a day-to-day basis rather than an exercise of writing objectives once a year. The manager has   a   responsibility   of (i) personally discussing with each subordinate the objectives that were set; (ii) evaluating progress made in achieving these objectives; and (iii) assisting and supporting the subordinate by removing obstacles that hinder his work accomplishment. Mere verbal or printed commitment is not enough. Vigorous involvement amongst the top management is essential and this must be seen and perceived as such throughout the organization. In short, an MBO programme is not an end in itself, rather a means to an end. Management support for using objectives to plan and to control, working on a continuous basis, increases the probability of success of a programme.

3.   Training for MBO: Another critical factor in implementing MBO is the existence of some type of training programme for people who will be operating under it. Systematic training is required in the organization for disseminating the concepts and philosophy underlying MBO. The training should start with the concepts, philosophy, and need for MBO. If people in the organization are not clear about the reasons for which MBO is being undertaken, they will fear and may show their resistance because people tend to show fear to what they do not understand. This fear can lead to suspicion and mistrust which, in turn, undermines people's enthusiasm which is very important during the initial stages of MBO. One consultant on MBO has remarked that 'the importance of orientation and training should not be overlooked. I think it is important when you move into a programme like this, if you are starting from scratch, that people understand why and how your are developing the programme. Sometimes there is a certain amount of fear involved when a programme of this kind is involved.'

4.   **Participation:** Success with MBO required a commitment on the part of each individual involved in this type of system. Their commitment, in turn, is a function of their identification with and participation in the system. The subordinate should not perceive that MBO is another technique being used by his superior to control his performance. Such undesirable perception may be avoided by encouraging the subordinate to play an active role in the preliminary phases leading to the actual writing of the objectives. Subordinate's role should include (i) the identification of important areas of accountability of his job; (ii) the determination of mutually agreeable performance measures; and (iii) the identification of this present performance level. However, the areas and scope for participation may vary in their relative emphasis according to the functional areas or hierarchical level to which an individual belongs. There cannot be a standard set of participation and each organization may make its own diagnosis about the extent and type of participation it desires under given conditions. In this context, Newport observes : 'A change to participative management involves the establishment of a situation in which people are active rather than passive, responsible rather than irresponsible, and basically more independent than dependent. Yet our heritage is one for the most part of a belief in the necessity for highly structured organizational arrangements. To change such management ideologies adopted from generation to generation is a time consuming process.

In evaluating whether participation will work or not, following questions should be asked:

(i)   Has the type of participation required been carefully thought out?
(ii)   Does higher management really mean to share certain managerial prerogatives that supposedly go with their rank?
(iii)   Is participation perceived as a trap by subordinates?
(iv)   Have subordinates the right skills and knowledge in order to shed their defences, and participate meaningfully?

5.   Feedback for Self direction and Self control: One of the strong points in MBO system is that within this system a man can direct and control his own performance. For such a purpose, a man, who has performance objectives and knows how well he is achieving them, should know `where he stands' and `where he is going' so that he can make necessary adjustments to achieve the desired results on his own. As such feedback is necessary. Feedback is an essential ingredient in sustained learning and improvement in situations. By feedback, here, is not meant merely the regular supply of control information to each manager. The interpersonal aspect of feedback is equally important. Feedback under MBO should take two forms. First, the individual should get periodic reports on where he stands on an overall performance basis. This is required specially when the subordinate requires help from the superior. Second, feedback is necessary in the form of periodic counseling and appraisal interview. The superior helps to evaluate progress, to identify problems, and to offer planning suggestions.

6.   Other Factors. Besides the above major considerations, there are several other factors that influence the success of MBO. To the extent those responsible for implementation are aware of the various problems, they can make provisions in advance to overcome these. These are as follows :

(i)   Implementing MBO at Lower Levels. If the full benefits of MBO are to be realized, it must be carried all the way down to the first line of the organization. There is a tendency for active participation in objective setting itself and for periodic feedback and review to diminish, the further down the management leader the programme gets. It such a tendency prevails, to that extent, the utility of MBO will be effective.

(ii)   MBO and Salary Decision. One of the most elusive aspects of MBO is to tie the organization's compensation system with the MBO programme. Though this problem does not arise at initial level, later on, this becomes a crucial issue. This is because rewards and penalties are among the accepted ways of exercising organizational authority over its members. There are various problems to the organizational remuneration with MBO. First, there is the problem of equating the degree of difficulty to the achievement of various objectives in various functional areas. Second if, the monetary differences between the superior and the average performer is not perceived being significant, the superior performer will lose enthusiasm to continue his outstanding performance. At the same time, minimum increases for average performers can also be discouraging. They may be doing their best work, and getting only a minimum increase may be perceived as punishment. However, such an opportunity may not exist in the organization. Third, some argue that to link MBO with reward - penalty systems would amount to bringing in the piece rate system from the shop floor to the manager's office. Thus, linking MBO with reward and penalty is really a difficult problem. One way to overcome this problem is that rewards and penalties may be thought of in qualitative terms also, instead of the usual monetary alternatives.

(iii) **Conflicting Objectives**. One of the outcomes of MBO programme is that to a degree it builds a competitive climate. This is because MBO generates commitments. But it is often found in practice that over-commitment leads to competitive rivalry with respect to claims on the scarce resources of the organization. This may be dangerous if it exceeds the limits. The accomplishment of result in organizations largely requires interdepartmental cooperation and integration of efforts. The persons responsible for introducing MBO must be certain that competing objectives are not set. Some educational effort is needed to enable managers to adopt an overall approach to performance objectives. At the same time, MBO programme itself should not encourage sub-optimizing efforts in the short run. Intergroup and intragroup performance reviews at regular intervals should reveal the human dynamics of such sub-optimal behavior.

4.6.6 MBO in Indian Organizations

In India, there is very limited experience of MBO. In fact very few organizations have applied MBO and very few of them have shared their experience with others. MBO came to India initially through the multinational companies operating in India. At the initial stage, overseas corporate offices of multinationals provided expertise to the Indian associate companies. It was in 1969 that MBO made a systematic entry through a management institution : Administrative Staff College of India, Hyderabad, organized top management seminar on MBO in which heads of many organizations participated. Many of them appreciated the role of MBO as a system of management and applied it in their organizations.

4.7 REVIEW QUESTIONS

1. What do you mean by Management By Objectives (MBO).
2. What is the importance of setting organizational objectives in a modern complex organization.
3. Discuss the benefits and difficulties for MBO.

Objectives

systems would amount to bringing in the shop-floor rats, so to say, from the shop floor to the manager's office. Thus, making MBO awkward and grossly unwieldy, a difficult problem. One way to overcome this problem is list reviews, and possibly may become thought of and qualitative traits also, instead in the usual monetary measures.

(iii) **Conflicting Objectives.** One of the outcomes of MBO generally, it may, to a degree it hampers a cooperative climate. This is because MBO encourages comparisons that may often lead in practice that over-component leads to competitive rivalry, with respect to claims of the scarce resources of the organization. This may be dangerous if it exceeds the limits. The accomplishment of MBO in organizations largely requires interdepartmental coordination and integration of actions. The persons responsible for introducing MBO might be comparing competing objectives are not set. Some educational effort is needed to push managers to adopt an overall approach to performance objectives. At the same time, MBO programme itself should not encourage sub-optimizing efforts in the short run. Intergroup and intragroup performance reviews at regular intervals should reveal the human dynamics of such an optimal behavior.

4.6.6. MBO in Indian Organizations.

In India there is very limited experience of MBO. In fact, very few organizations have applied MBO, and very few of them have shared their experience with others. MBO came to India initially through the multinational companies operating in India. At the initial stage, overseas corporate offices of multinationals provided expertise to the Indian associate companies. It was in 1967 that MBO made a systematic entry through a management institution. Administrative Staff College of India, Hyderabad, organized top management seminar on MBO in which heads of many organizations participated. Many of them appreciated the role of MBO as a system of management and applied it in their organizations.

4.7. REVIEW QUESTIONS

1. What do you mean by Management By Objectives (MBO).
2. What is the importance of setting organizational objectives in a modern complex organization.
3. Discuss the benefits and difficulties for MBO.

FORECASTING

5.1   INTRODUCTION

Planning is "a systematic economic and rational way of making decisions today that will affect tomorrow", then forecasting becomes an integral part of the planning process, specially, strategic planning which is long-range in nature.

Lyndall Unrwick defined forecasting as, "it is involved to some extent in every conceivable business decision. The man who starts a business is making an assessment of a future demand of its products. The man who determines a production programme for the next six months or twelve months is usually also basing it on some calculation of future demand. The man, who engages staff, and particularly Young staff, usually has an eye to future organizational requirements.

Business forecasting refers to a systematic analysis of past and present conditions with the aim of drawing inferences about the future course of events. Louis Allen defines forecasting, as "a systematic attempt to probe the future by inference from known facts."

Neter and Wasserman have defined forecasting as :

"Business forecasting refers to the statistical analysis of the past and current movement in the given time series so as to obtain clues about the future pattern of those movements."

5.2   FEATURES OF FORECASTING

Based on the above definitions the following features are explained below:

1.   **Involvement of future events:** Forecasting relates to future events. Forecasting is the essence of planning because planning also aims at deciding what is to be done in the future.

2.   **Depends upon past and present event:** Actually, forecasting is made by analyzing the past and present relevant data. It takes all the factors into account, which affect the functioning of the enterprise.

3.   **Happening of future events:** Forecasting defines the probability of happening of future events. Therefore, happening of future events can be precise only to a certain extent.

4.   **Makes use of forecasting techniques:** As can be gathered from what has gone before that forecasting is a systematic attempt to probe the future with a view to drawing certain useful infer ness. Such a probing obviously demands a proper and full analysis of known facts with the help of various qualitative and quantitative forecasting techniques.

5.3   ELEMENTS OF THE FORECASTING PROCESS

J.W. Redfield describes the following elements of forecasting process:

1.   Prepare the groundwork.
2.   Establishing future business.
3.   Comparing actual with estimated results.
4.   Refining the forecasts.

5.3.1   Prepare the Groundwork

The group work preparation requires a thorough study, investigation, and analysis of the company, its products, its market share, its organizational structure and the industry. The investigation will involve the past performance of all these factors, their growth over a period of time and the extent of their inter-relationships and interdependence. The aim is to build a foundation on which future estimates can be based.

5.3.2   Establishing Future Business

The future expectancy of the business can be reasonably computed from the past data as well as the input from the key executives of the organization, sales personnel and other specialists. This forecast is developed with the participation of the key personnel and is officially communicated to all. Thus all these people assume responsibility for meeting these forecasts and accountability for any deviations from this forecast.

5.3.3 Comparing Actual with Estimated Results

The forecast estimates over the future years provide benchmarks against which the actual growth and results can be measured and compared. If there are significant variations between the two, one way or another, the reasons for such deviations can be investigated and analyzed.

5.3.4 Refining the Forecasts

In the light of any deviations found, the forecast can be refined to be more realistic. If some conditions have changed during the periodic evaluation, then the new values of the variables can be incorporated in the estimates. Thus, these constant revisions and refinements and improvements would add to the experience and skill in forecasting, since proficiency in forecasting can only be gained through practice and experience.

The above elements indicate a systematic approach to the problem of forecasting. As a materiality, these elements are found in any research procedure.

5.4 PLANNING AND FORECASTING

Even though both planning and forecasting are known as equals, there basic difference. Planning is more comprehensive which includes many sub process and elements in order to arrive at decisions. These decisions may be in terms of what is to be done, and when to be done. Conversely, forecasting involves the estimate of future events and provides parameters to the planning. It may also involve many sub process and elements but these are used to project what will happen in future.

Forecasting may not require any commitment of action but may help in planning the future course of action, whereas commitment of actions is the basic ingredient of planning.

The major decisions in planning are made at the top level. But forecasting is normally taken at middle level or lower level.

5.5   ADVANTAGES OF FORECASTING

Forecasting plays a vital role in the process of modern management. It is an important and necessary aid to planning and planning is backbone of effective operations. Thus the importance or advantages of forecasting are stated below :

1.   It enables a company to commit its resources with greatest assurance to profit over the long term.

2.   It facilities development of new products, by helping to identify future demand patterns.

3.   Forecasting by promoting participation of the entire organization in this process provides opportunities for team work and brings about unity and co-ordination.

4.   The making of forecasts and their review by managers, compel thinking ahead, looking to the future and providing for it.

5.   Forecasting is an essential ingredient of planning and supplies vital facts and crucial information.

6.   Forecasting provides the way for effective coordination and control. Forecasting requires information about various external and internal factors. The information is collected from various internal sources. Thus, almost all units of the organization are involved in this process, which provides interactive opportunities for better unity and coordination in the planning process. Similarly, forecasting can provide relevant information for exercising control. The managers can know their weakness in forecasting process and they can take suitable action to overcome these.

7.   A systematic attempt to probe the future by inference from known facts helps integrate all management planning so that unified overall plans can be developed into which divisions and departmental plans can be meshed.

8.   The uncertainty of future events can be identified and overcomes by an effective forecasting. Therefore, it will lead to success in organization.

5.6   LIMITATIONS OF FORECASTING

The following limitations of forecasting are listed below:

1.   **Basis of Forecasting:** The most serious limitations of forecasting arises out of the basis used for making forecasts. Top executives should always bear in mind that that bases of forecasting are assumptions, approximations, and average conditions. Management may become so concerned with the mechanism of the forecasting system that it fails to question its logic. This critical examination is not to discourage attempts at forecasting, but to sound caution about the practice of forecasting and its inherent limitations.

2.   **Reliability of Past Data:** The forecasting is made on the basis of past data and the current events. Although past events / data are analyzed as a guide to the future, a question is raised as to the accuracy as well as the usefulness of these recorded events.

3.   **Time and Cost Factor:** Time and cost factor is also an important aspect of forecasting. They suggest the degree to which an organization will go for formal forecasting. The information and data required for forecast may be in highly disorganized form; some may be in qualitative form. The collection of information and conversion of qualitative data into quantitative ones involves lot of time and money. Therefore, managers have to trade off between the cost involved in forecasting and resultant benefits. So forecasting should be made by eliminating above limitations.

5.7   TYPES OF FORECAST

There are three types of forecasts, which many business organizations rely on are:

(i)   Demand (Sales) forecast.
(ii)   Economic forecast and
(iii)   Technological forecast.

Demand or sales forecasts are fundamental to a company's planning and control decisions. They give the expected level of demand for the company's products or services through some future periods.

Economic forecasts involve such matters as future state of the economy; inflation rates etc, and have a profound influence on the success of future business activities.

Technological forecasts usually focus on the rate of technological progress or the nature of technological developments in areas related to the business and technology.

5.8   FORECASTING TECHNIQUES

Forecasting technique can be classified into two major categories.

(i)   Qualitative forecasting technique.
(ii)   Quantitative forecasting technique.

5.8.1 Qualitative Techniques

1.   Jury or Executive opinion (Dolphi Technique)
2.   Sales force estimates.
3.   Customer expectations.

Jury or Executive Opinion

The jury of expert opinion sometimes referred to as the Dolphi technique; involves soliciting opinions or estimates from a panel of "experts" who are knowledgeable about the variable being forecasted. In addition to being useful in the creation of a sales or demand forecast this approach is used to predict future technological developments. This method is fast less expensive and does not depend upon any elaborate statistics and brings in specialized viewpoints.

Sales Force Estimates

This approach involves the opinion of the sales force and these opinions are primarily taken into consideration for forecasting future sales. The sales people, being closer to consumers, can estimate future sales in their own territories more accurately. Based on these and the opinions of sales managers, a reasonable trend of the future sales can be calculated. These forecasts are good for short range planning since sales people are not sufficiently sophisticated to predict long-term trends. This method known as the "grass roots" approach ends itself to easy breakdowns of products, territory, customer etc, which makes forecasting more elaborate and comprehensive.

Customer Expectations

This type of forecasting technique is to go outside the company and seek subjective opinions from customers about their future purchasing plans. Sales representatives may poll their customers or potential customers about the future needs for the goods and services the company supplies. Direct mail questionnaires or telephone surveys may be used to obtain the opinions of existing or potential customers. This is also known as the "survey method" or the "marketing research method" where information is obtained concerning Customer buying preferences, advertising effectiveness and is especially useful where the target market is small such as buyers of industrial products, and where the customers are co-operative.

5.8.2   Quantitative Techniques

Quantitative techniques are based on the analysis of past data and its trends. These techniques use statistical analysis and other mathematical models to predict future events. Some of these techniques are:

1.   Time series analysis.
2.   Economic models.
3.   Regression analysis.

Time Series Analysis

Time series analysis involves decomposition of historical series into its various components, viz., trend, seasonal variations, cyclical variations and random variations. Time series analysis uses index numbers but it is different from barometric technique. In barometric technique, the future is predicted from the indicating series, which serve barometers of economic change. In time series analysis, the future is taken as some sort of an extension of the past. When the various components of a time series are separated, the variations of a particular phenomenon, the subject under study stay say price, can be known over the period of time and projection can be made about future. A trend can be known over the period of time, which may be true for future also. However, time series analysis should be used as a basis for forecasting when data are available for a long period of time and tendencies disclosed by the trend and seasonal factors are fairly clear and stable.

Economic Models

Utilize a system of interdependent regression equations that relate certain economic indicators of the firm's sales, profits etc. Data center or external economic factors and internal business factors interpreted with statistical methods. Often companies use the results of national or regional econometric models as a major portion of a corporate econometric model. While such models are useful in forecasting, their major use tends to be in answering "what if"? Questions. These models allow management to investigate and in major segments of the company's business on the performance and sales of the company.

Regression Analysis

Regression Analysis are statistical equations designed to estimate some variables such as sales volume, on the basis of one or more 'independent' variables believed to have some association with it.

5.9   REVIEW QUESTIONS

1.   What is forecasting and explain its features?
2.   What are the elements of forecasting process?
3.   What are the advantages of forecasting?
4.   Write down the limitations of forecasting?
5.   What are the types of forecasting?
6.   Explain briefly forecasting techniques.
7.   Explain quantitative forecasting techniques.
8.   Describe Regression analysis.
9.   "Forecasting is a systematic analysis of past and present conditions." Explain.
10.   Explain the importance of forecasting.

6

DECISION MAKING

6.1   INTRODUCTION & DEFINITIONS

Decision-making is an integral part of every manager's job. Decision-making has a wide-range, covering matters from selection of the venue for holding a meeting, to significant issues such as, assignment of resources, hiring and firing of personnel, rate of dividend, merger, etc. In the words of John MacDonald, "The business executive is by profession a decision-maker. Uncertainty is his opponent, overcoming it is his mission. Whether the outcome is a consequence of luck of wisdom, the moment of decision-making is without doubt the most creative event in the life of the executive."

Decision-making is not the monopoly of top management alone, though it is true that decisions made at this level are of far-reaching importance for the organization as a whole. In fact, managers at all levels are engaged in decision-making of one kind or another, the significance of their decisions differing in proportion to the duties assigned and authority delegated to them.

Definitions

George R. Terry : "Decision-making is the selecting of an alternative, from two or more alternatives, to determine an opinion or a course of action."

Andrew Szilagyi : "Decision-making is a process involving information, choice of alternative actions, implementation, and evaluation that is directed to the achievement of certain stated goals."

Henry Sisk and Cliffton Williams : "A decision is the selection of a course of action from two or more alternatives; the decision-making process is a sequence of steps leading to that selection."

6.2   IMPORTANCE OF DECISION-MAKING

Decision-making is an indispensable component of the management process. It permeates all management and covers every part of an enterprise. In fact whatever a manager does, he does through decision-making only; the end products of manager's work are decisions and actions. For example, a manager has to decide (i) what are the long term objectives of the organization, how to achieve these objectives, what strategies, policies, procedures to be adopted (planning); (ii) how the jobs should be structured, what type of structure, how to match jobs with individuals (organizing); (iii) how to motivate people to peak performance, which leadership style should be used, how to integrate effort and resolve conflicts (leading); (iv) what activities should be controlled, how to control them, (controlling). Thus, decision-making is a central, important part of the process of managing. The importance of decision-making in management is such that H.A. Simon called management as decision-making. It is small wonder that Simon viewed decision-making as if it were synonymous with the term 'managing'. Managers are essentially decision makers only. Almost everything managers do involves decision-making. Decision-making is the substance of a manager's job. In fact, decision-making is a universal requirement for all human beings. Each of us makes decisions every day in our lives. What college to attend, which job to choose, whom to marry, where to invest and so on. Surgeons, for example, make life-and-death decisions, engineers make decisions on constructing projects, gamblers are concerned with taking risky decisions, and computer technologists may be concerned with highly complex decisions involving crores of rupees. Thus whether right or wrong, individuals as members in different organizations take decisions. Collectively the decisions of these members give 'form and direction to the work an organization does'. Some writers equate decision-making with planning. In fact, Koontz and O'Donnell viewed 'decision-making as the core of planning', implying that is not at the core of organizing or controlling. However, instead of taking extreme positions it would be better to view decision-making as a pervasive function of managers aimed at achieving goals. According to Glueck there are two important reasons for learning about decision-making: (i) Managers spend a great deal of time making decisions. In order to improve managerial skills it is necessary to know how to make effective decisions. (ii) Managers are evaluated on the basis of the number and importance of the decisions made. To be effective, managers should learn the art of making better decisions.

6.3   FACTORS INVOLVED IN DECISION-MAKING

There are two kinds of factors to be considered in decision-making in favor of any alternative. These may be classified as (a) tangible and (b) intangible factors.

Tangible factors

Among the tangible factors relevant to decision-making the important ones are (a) sales; (b) cost; (c) purchases; (d) production; (e) inventory; (f) financial; (g) personnel and (h) logistics.

The effect of any decision on one or more of the tangible factors can be measured and therefore it is easy to consider the pros and cons of every decision. Decisions based on these factors are likely to be more rational and free from bias and feelings of the decision-maker.

Intangible factors

Among the intangible factors which may influence decision-making in favor of any alternative, the important ones are the effects of any particular decision (a) prestige of the enterprise; (b) consumer behavior, (c) employee morale; and so on.

Accurate information and data about these factors is not easy to obtain. Therefore, intuition and value-judgment of the decision-maker will assume a significant role in the choice of a particular alternative.

6.4   TYPES OF DECISIONS

Though managers are constantly called upon to make decisions and all managerial decisions are important in their own ways, some decisions have a limited scope while others involve the entire organization in a significant manner. For better understanding of the managerial decisions, we may classify them as follows:

1.   **Personal and organizational decisions**. This classification was first mooted by Chester Barnard. Accordingly, personal decisions are concerned with the managers as individuals rather than the organizations. As against this, organizational decisions are made by the managers in their official capacities and within the constraints set by their formal authority. Since personal decisions are based on subjective evaluation of the managers, these can neither be delegated nor there any interference or influencing

from the top. But organizational decisions may be, and often are delegated to subordinates.

In order to avoid bias in decision-making, which may be harmful both to the organization and the decision-maker, a clear distinction between personal and organizational decisions has constantly to be maintained, though it is often a difficult task.

2.   Strategic and operational decisions. Strategic decisions, which are often table for their novelty and complexity and involve uncontrollable factors such as actions of competitors or the state of the economy, are invariably made by the top management. Increasing the rate of dividend, expansion of business, etc., are the examples of strategic decisions.

Operational decisions are concerned with day-to-day operations of the enterprise. They do not involve much discretion or independent judgment on the part of managers, as the parameters within which the decisions have to be made, are often clearly defined.

3.   Structured and unstructured decisions. Structured decisions are those which are made within the limits set by the policies, procedures, tradition or custom. They do not require creativity or independent judgment on the part of the manager. As against this, unstructured decisions have neither any existing policies or procedures, nor any tradition or custom as their basis. For this reason, they call for a great deal of imagination and independent judgment, and hence are often within the purview of the top management only.

4.   Crisis and research decisions. Crisis decisions are those which are made to meet unanticipated situations which do not allow much scope for extensive investigation and analysis of the factors relevant to them. They have to be made instantaneously under pressure of circumstances.

As against this, research decisions are those which are made after a thorough analysis of pros and cons without any pressure.

5.   Initiative or forced decisions. Initiative decisions are the hall-mark of aggressive managers who search for or create situations calling for decision-making by them. Most of such decisions may not be needed in many cases. As against this, forced decisions are those where the managers have no alternative but to make decisions, either under orders from their superiors or due to pressured persuasion by subordinates.

6. **Problem and opportunity decisions.** Problem decisions are concerned with resolving problem situations which have arisen as anticipated, or otherwise. On the other hand, opportunity decisions pertain to taking advantage of an opportunity for increased profits, growth, etc. The frequency of opportunity decisions will depend on how far the manager is prepared to take risks and his skill for recognition of an opportunity.

6.5 COMMON DIFFICULTIES IN DECISION-MAKING

Some common difficulties faced in making decisions and implementing them are as follows.

Incomplete information

This is a major problem for every manger. Lack of information leaves a manager adrift in a sea of uncertainty. Not only this, most decisions involve too many complex variables for one person to be able to examine all of them fully.

Un-supporting Environment

The environment - physical and organizational - that prevails in an enterprise affects both the nature of decisions and their implementation. If there is all round goodwill and trust and if the employees are properly motivated, the manager is encouraged to take decisions with confidence. On the other hand, under the opposite circumstances he avoids decision-making.

Non-Acceptance by Subordinates

If subordinates have a stake in the decision or are likely to be strongly affected by it, acceptance will probably be necessary for effective implementation. On the other hand, subordinates may not really care what decision is reached. In such situations, acceptance is not an issue. Democratic leadership style which encourages subordinates to suggest, criticise, make recommendations or decide upon policies or projects is an effective device for gaining their acceptance and commitment.

Ineffective Communication

Another important problem in decision-making is the ineffective communication of a decision. This makes implementation difficult. The manager should, therefore, take care to communicate all decisions to the employees in clear, precise and simple language.

Incorrect Timing

In decision-making, the problem is not merely of taking a correct decision. It is also of selecting an appropriate time for taking the decision. If the decision is correct but the time is inopportune, it will not serve any purpose. For example, if the manager wants to decide about introducing a new product in the market, he should take the decision at a correct time. Otherwise, he may lose the market to his competitors.

6.6   GUIDELINES FOR EFFECTIVE DECISION MAKING

Decision making is an arduous task. A successful and correct decision is gratifying to the decision maker but he also experiences frustration when he faces ill-structured and uncertain situations and when his decision fails to achieve the decision objectives. Yet, managers must make decisions as it is their most important responsibility to their organization. They cannot afford to display an attitude of "sailing around the world without landing", and "talking about a subject without getting it". The success of an executive depends on his ability to make the right decision at the right time and to pursue its effective implementation. The following guidelines are offered as an aid to effective decision making.

1.   Define the Goals

The decision maker should define the goals that he seeks to achieve by making a decision. The goal of a decision is derived from his objectives which in turn are a part of the total organizational objectives. Thus, the goal of a decision should be compatible with and contribute to larger goals.

2.   Ensure that the Decision Contributes to the Goal

Once the goal has been determined, it becomes the criterion for making the decisions, as well as for evaluating its results. Often, an executive seeks to achieve not one but more than one goals through a decision. For example, the goal of a marketing decision may be not only to increase the sales volume but also increase the profit margin. These goals may not always be compatible. It requires the decision maker to balance the conflicting goals in such a manner that he can achieve all the goals simultaneously.

3.   Adopt a Diagnostic Approach

A decision maker has to be a diagnostician in many ways. He has to identify and define the problem. Further, he has to diagnose what and how much information is relevant to the problem being attacked, and where he will get it. Development and evaluation of alternative also require diagnostic abilities. He also has to diagnose the surrounding situation comprising the internal and external environmental forces. Thus, effectiveness in decision making significantly depends on an executive's diagnostic abilities.

4.   Involve Subordinates in Decision Making Process

Involvement of subordinates in decision making process serves many purposes. It improves the quality of the decision, particularly if the decision maker does not possess all the special abilities required for making a particular decision. It is more likely to happen than not, as every decision has several aspects such as administrators, technical, human relations and financial aspects. The most important stage at which subordinates' participation can enhance the decision quality is the stage of development and evaluation of alternative solutions to problems. Their participation can bring not only new insights to the problem. but also elicit their commitment to implement the decision. Those who participate in making a decision tend to become ego involved in it, and thereby committed to its successful implementation.

5.   Ensure successful implementation of the Decision

Event he best decision will not yield satisfactory results unless it is implemented effectively. Successful implementation of a decision significantly depends on the extent of understanding of the decision and its implications, and motivation of the subordinates who have to carry it. An executive can enhance his effectiveness in both these directions by promoting upward communication. He should also be able to know when and what kind of guidance is needed by them, and be willing to extend it to those who need it. He can be more effective if he successfully welds his subordinates into a team with himself as the team leader.

6.   Evaluate the Results

The purpose of a decision is to accomplish some goal which will not be attained without it. The results of the decision should, therefore, be evaluated in terms of its predetermined goals.

7.   Be Flexible

The decision maker should adopt a flexible approach not only in making the decision but also after the decision has been put into implementation. If it is not yielding the desired results, he should modify, discard, or replace it with another decision which may produce better results.

6.7   DECISION-MAKING - THE QUANTITATIVE WAY

Introduction

The administration of a modern business enterprise has become an enormously complex exercise. There has been an increasing tendency to turn to quantitative techniques and models as a potential means for solving many of the problems that arise in such an enterprise. Management in action is decision-making. We consider decision-making in business to be a process whereby management, when confronted by a problem, selects a specific course of action or solution from a set of possible courses of actions. Since there is generally some uncertainty about the future, we cannot be sure of the consequences of a decision made. The process of making decisions in a business has the same essential characteristics as problem-solving behaviour in general.

Business Decisions

The business manager wants to choose the course of action that is most effective in attaining the goals of the organisation. In judging the effectiveness of different possible decisions, we must use some measuring unit. The most commonly used measure in making decisions is the amount of profit in monetary terms but for our purpose here, we will take only a few of these.

1.   Decisions under certainty or uncertainty.
2.   Decisions made for one time-period only or a sequence of inter-related decisions over several time-periods.

3.   Decisions where the opponent is nature (a family planning, a picnic) or a thinking opponent (setting the price of a product after considering the actions of the competitors).

The following general process of solution is adopted for all types of decision situations:

1.   Establish the criteria that will be utilized. One of the criteria may be maximization of profit. In a capital budgeting decision, we choose the project with the highest pay off.

2.   Select a set of alternatives for consideration.

3.   Determine the model which will be used and the values of the parameter of the process, e.g., we may decide that the algebraic expression of the model of total expenses is:

Total Expenses = a+ b units sold.

The parameters are "a" and "b" and their values would have to be determined in order to use the model.

4.   Determine that alternative which optimizes or falls in line with the criterion that has been chosen in item 1 above.

Abstraction

Real life problems are very complicated in nature. In empirical situation, there is a large number of inherent "facts," Moreover, every potential course of action triggers off a chain reactions - of course an effect and interaction - and there is no end to this process. Consider the problem of erection of a factory building. Much time is spent on gathering factual information about the project, e.g., the exact location, the physical features of the building ; a minute study of the climatic conditions of the potential sites and their bearing on most of the construction; the raising of finance and the cost of finance raised. By far the most important decision is in respect of the alternative uses to which these funds can be put in the present and future periods. If the manager as a decision-maker prefers to collect all the facts before he acts, it follows that he will never act. It is to be appreciated that it is beyond the comprehension of human mind to consider every aspect and dimension of an empirical problem. Some characteristics of the problem must be ignored if at all a decision is to be made. In other words, it is for the decision-maker to abstract from the empirical situation those factors which he considers to be the most relevant to the problem he faces. In this way, abstraction initiates the solution of many a human problem.

Model Building

Once the selection of the critical factors or variables has been made by the decision-maker, the next step is to have their combination in a logical manner so as to form a counter-path or model of the empirical situation; ideally, it strips a natural phenomenon of its complexity. It, therefore, duplicates the essential behavior of the natural phenomenon with a few variables, simply related. The more the simplicity of the model, the better it is for the decision-maker, provided the model serves as a reasonably reliable counter-path of the empirical order.

The advantages of a simple model are :

1.   It economizes on time as well as on thought.
2.   It is within the reach of comprehension and ability of the decision-maker.
3.   If occasion arises, the model can be modified quickly and effectively.

The aim of the decision-maker in constructing a model is to approximate reality as far as possible. In other words, a model is a de facto approximation of reality. Replication of reality seems to be a lofty aim and meeting it would consume an infinite length of time. Besides, such an elaborate model would be beyond the reach of human comprehension. Therefore, the manager as a decision-maker wants the simplest possible model that predicts outcomes reasonably well and consistent with effective action on his part.

Solutions

Having constructed the model, it is possible to draw certain conclusions about its behavior by means of a logical analysis. The decision-maker bases his action or solution on these conclusions. The effectiveness of a model depends upon the logical analysis used in drawing conclusions and the abstraction of critical variables from our example. The decision-maker may decide that an interest rate of 12% matches the annual opportunity cost of money for his firm. He can make his decisions on the construction of the factory premises by calculating the present value of the cash flows and would not have to consider the alternative uses of which his funds can be put to in detail.

Errors

Generally, there are two possible types of errors in decision-making to start with. He can err in applying logic to the process of reasoning from premises to conclusions to solutions. The concern may be able to obtain funds at the cost of 12% but management may have decided not to raise any new capital. The premise that one can use the interest rate to represent an opportunity cost is valid, but the conclusion that the use of interest rate applies to all investments is erroneous.

Secondly, there may be a mistake in selecting the variables or the variables selected are not adequate for the construction of the model in our example. The decision-maker has taken into account the time value of money but has ignored the risk element that is associated with the use of money. It is not possible to eliminate errors of this type altogether because it would amount to a consideration of all conceivable pertinent variables and would preclude decisive action. Abstraction does violate reality to some extent but it is a necessary condition for problem-solving. This is one reason why decision-making carries with it the possibility of errors.

Model-Building Techniques

There are several ways of representing the models. Common place repetitive problems as those of eating, walking and opening doors are a matter of thinking in the mind of the decision-maker in an informal and intuitive manner. Such problems are resolved without the aid of a formal model. If the problem is somewhat more complex or unusual, we spend more time on it. It is possible to express to the extent of selecting the important elements of the problem and proceeding to examine and experiment with them. The nature of variables determines the technique of describing and relating selected variables. If the variables are amenable to a quantitative representation, then there are strong reasons for selecting a mathematical representation of the model. Mathematics has a theoretical rigour of its own, and so it ensures a certain orderly procedure on the part of the investigator. It demands specificity in respect of the variables that have been abstracted and the relationships assume to be existing amongst them. For example, it is more difficult to make implicit assumptions in a mathematical model than in a literary model. Secondly, mathematics is a potent tool for relating variables and for deriving logical conclusions from the given premises. Mathematics facilitates the solution of problems of bewildering complexities and also facilitates the decision-making process where quantitative analysis is applicable.

In the recent past, especially since World War II, a host of business problems have been quantified with some degree of success, leading to a general approach which has been designated as operations research. Undoubtedly, the quantitative representation of business problems is much older than operations research, considering the practice of accountancy. However, recently, the use of quantitative techniques has covered all the areas of modern business.

A word of caution is necessary for those businessmen who are found to employ quantitative techniques for business decisions. The conclusion derived from a mathematical model contains some degree of error because of the abstraction process. It is a matter of judgment as to when to modify the conclusion in view of the magnitude of error. Operations research supplements business judgment; it does not supplant it. Moreover, there are many business problems which cannot be given a quantitative representation and so they require the use of qualitative models and solutions. Within the constraints mentioned here, quantitative analysis can become an extremely productive technique for managerial decision-making. Problems which would perplex the initiation of the most experienced executives may, on some occasions, be resolved with relative ease.

6.8   REVIEW QUESTIONS

1.   Define 'decision-making'.
2.   What is the importance of decision-making?
3.   Discuss tangible and intangible factors relevant to decision making?

7

ORGANIZATION

7.1   INTRODUCTION

Organization is the task of mobilizing resources. It is a structure involving a large number of people engaging themselves in a multiplicity of tasks, a systematic and rational relationship with authority and responsibility between individuals and groups. It involves dividing the entire work into manageable units, departmentation, decentralization, delegation and span of control.

7.2   DEFINITIONS

LOUIS A. ALLEN : Organization is a mechanism or structure that enables living things to work effectively together. The evolution of all forms of life and of human society demonstrates the need for organization.

OLIVER SHELDON : Organization is the process of combining the work which individuals or groups have to perform with facilities necessary for its execution that the duties so performed provide the best channels for efficient, systematic, positive and coordinated application of available effort.

BARNARD : Organization is a system of consciously coordinated activities or forces of two or more persons.

MOONEY and RAILEY : Organization is the form of every human association for the attainment of a common purpose.

JOSEPH L. MASSIE : Organization is the structure and process by which a cooperative group of human beings allocates its tasks among its members, identifies relationships and integrates its activities towards common objectives.

KOONTZ and O'DONNELL : Organization is the establishment of authority and relationships with provision for coordination between them, both vertically and horizontally in the enterprise structure.

ALVIN BROWN: The part which each member of an enterprise is expected to perform and the relations between such members, to the end that their consistent endeavor shall be most effective for the purpose of the enterprise.

A study of the above definitions makes it clear that organization involves identification and grouping of work, defining responsibility; delegation of authority establishment of structural relationships; and coordination of interrelated activities. Organization is concerned with (a) the attainment of objectives by grouping the activities, (b) dividing these activities into different departments, divisions, sections and between individuals, (c) providing authority, delegation, coordination and communication, (d) providing physical facilities like buildings, equipment, etc. for the smooth and successful performance of the tasks; and (e) establishing clear structural relationships among individuals and groups.

7.3   PRINCIPLES OF ORGANIZATION

1.   **Unity of objectives:** The entire organization and every part of it should be function effectively to accomplish the basic objectives of the enterprise.

2.   **Efficiency:** All the accomplishments of the organization should be at the lowest possible cost. There should not be any waste of human resources.

3.   **Span of control or span or management:** Urwick states that a manager can directly supervise a limited number of people. No superior at a higher level should have more than six immediate subordinates.

4.   **Division of work:** Specialization and division of work should result in separate departments "established to reflect the most efficient breakdown of enterprise activities". Each area of specialization must be interrelated.

5.   **Functional definition:** The duties and responsibilities must be properly defined. There should not be duplication or overlapping of activities.

6.   **Coordination:** The efforts of everyone in the organization must be coordinated to achieve common goals. Coordination is the orderly arrangements of collective efforts to accomplish a common organizational goal.

7. **Scalar principle (Chain or command):** The line of authority flows, from the topmost to the lowest managerial level, and this continuation chain of command should not be broken.

8. **Unity of direction:** There must be only one plan for a group of activities directed towards the same goal. "One person one plan" is the best way of achieving unity of direction.

9. **Unity of command:** Each subordinate should have one superior only. Dual command is always dangerous and confusing.

10. **Delegation:** Delegation should be made up to the lowest competent level. Delegation of authority increases efficiency and smooth operation.

11. **Responsibility:** The superior is responsible for the activities of the subordinates, and the subordinates are responsible to their superiors for their performance. Authority should be consistent with responsibility.

12. **Balance:** There should be a reasonable balance between centralization and decentralization, different sizes of various departments, limited span and longer lines of management.

13. **Communication:** A good organization must have an effective channel of communication for smooth flow of information.

14. **Personal ability:** Ultimately, an organization means people. Proper selection, placement and training of people will go a long way in developing a favourable organizational climate.

15. **Flexibility:** The organization should adopt built-in devices for any change, expansion, etc. with least disturbance. The organizational structure should not be rigid. It should be able to adapt itself to all future changes.

16. **Continuity:** There must be a provision for continuity of management and enterprise. Management development programmes should be encouraged.

17. **Exception principle:** All routine, normal and programmed matters should be handled at the lower level itself. Only exceptionally vital decisions of unusual nature should be handled by superiors, as they have limited time.

7.4   FORMAL AND INFORMAL ORGANIZATIONS

An organization may be formal or informal. In most organizations, formal groups will function as it is essential to execute specific tasks of the concerned formal organization. Chester Barnard states that an organization will be a formal one when the activities of two or more persons are consciously cordial to a given objective. It refers to the structure of positions with clearly defined functions and relationships as determined by the top management. A formal organization is mainly guided by its rules, systems and procedures. In a formal organization, authority, and responsibility and relationships must be clear, fixed and definite. A formal organization is generally based on delegation of authority and it is a legally constituted one. In fact, a formal organization is created and propagated through organization charts, rule books, manuals, procedures, models, etc. Chester Barnard states that a formal organization comes into existence when persons are (a) willing to communicate with one another, and (b) willing to act and share a common purpose. William Brown states that "I personally believe that the more formalization that exists, the more clearly we will know the bounds of discretion which we are authorized to use and will be held responsible for; and prescribed policies make clear to people the area in which they have freedom to act."

A formal organization according to Keith Davis "is a pinnacle of man's achievement in a disorganized society. It is man's orderly, conscious, intelligent creation for human benefit. A formal organization is a system of well-defined authority positions and responsibility centres".

Informal organization can be beneficial to management. Keith Davis states that work groups are important as they provide various benefits. Some of them are as follows.

> ➢ Informal work groups blend with the formal organization to make a workable system for getting work done.

> ➢ Informal work groups lighten the work load for the formal manager and fill in some of the gaps in the manager's abilities.

> ➢ Informal work groups provide satisfaction and stability to the organization.

> ➢ They provide a very effective channel of communication within the organization.

> ➢ Managers will be more careful and effective with the informal work groups.

Management can neither establish nor abolish an informal organization. But any sensible management will try to live with an informal organization and can effectively develop its influence on such an organization for its advantage. It should see than an informal organization remains secondary to the formal organization.

7.5   STEPS IN ORGANIZATION

Once the necessary plans and objectives are formulated, the organizational process can be started. Every type of activity has to be grouped into workable units of similar activities. All the work has to be classified, employees identified and an arrangement made for the assignment of work to the employees. Terry states that organization is the establishment of effective behavioral relationships among selected work places so that their groups can work together efficiently.

The logical steps in the process of organization are as follows:

➢ Determine and formulate objectives, strategies, plans and policies.
➢ Determine the activities involved to accomplish the objectives.
➢ Grouping of similar activities into tasks, sections and departments.
➢ Define responsibility and accountability for every person.
➢ Delegate the required authority to perform the task.
➢ Integration of activities through authority relationships and communication networks.
➢ Provide adequate physical facilities to perform the tasks effectively.

7.6   IMPORTANCE

Organization is the backbone of the management; it helps the enterprise in its progress and prosperity. Today, organization has become more important than ever before because of the many advantages it offers to the modern-day complex society.

1.   Encourages specialization. Specialization is the direct result of organization, which helps in increasing the productivity and efficiency.

2.   Eliminates the problem of duplicating and overlapping. Proper and clear division and delegation of authority and responsibility avoid duplication and overlapping.

3.   Brings order and cohesiveness. Determining a clear line of authority will bring in order in the concern. Everything in its place and a place for everything can be introduced by organizing the concern.

4.   Improves administration. Administrative policies and day-to-day operation of the enterprise will become effective and functional with proper organization.

5.   Stimulates creative thinking. A good organization provides maximum opportunity for creative people to develop their ideas for the benefit of the concern. It also provides the ways and means of doing things in a better way.

6.   Facilitates effective communication. With the clear definition of authority, an organization can develop the most efficient channels of communication.

7.   Helps in providing a balanced emphasis on various activities. Organization, by clearly defining the importance of activities through divisions, departmentation, etc. gives more priority for urgent and important problems. Routine problems can be decided at the lower or middle level. Managing change, managing crisis, managing credibility become easy through proper organization.

8.   Helps to build up and expand the enterprise. An organized enterprise can build up a team of executives and workers who can develop much faster. Organized team effort helps in expanding the firm. Today, every organization is expanding the firm. Today, every organization is expanding smoothly into unimaginably large-sized units because of organized effort.

9.   Helps in the smooth delegation of authority. When executives delegate authority downwards, that can get the things done smoothly. It also helps in fixing responsibility for task. A good organization clearly defines the authority, responsibility and relationship.

7.7   SOME CLASSICAL PRINCIPLES OF GOOD MANAGEMENT

Before we would close this chapter, we would record some classical principles of organization designing and operations which bear repetition even in today's context.

Ten Commandments of Good Organization - American Management Association (AMA)

The Ten Commandments were formulated by the AMA as sound principles of a good organization. These are summarized (and adapted) below:

(1) Well-defined responsibilities for each management level.
(2) Matching responsibility with authority.
(3) No change in the assignment of a level (authority and responsibility) without prior consultation.
(4) Each one should take orders from only one (unity of command).
(5) No by-passing of levels in issuing executive orders.
(6) Chasten subordinates privately; not in the presence of his colleagues or juniors.
(7) Attend to all conflicts among levels concerning authority and responsibility.
(8) Orders concerning advancement, wages and discipline to be approved by the executive immediately superior to the one directly responsible.
(9) No executive or employee should be a critic of his own boss.
(10) An executive whose work is subject to inspection should be helped to enable him to appraise independently the quality of his own work.

Uuwicks' Ten Principles of Organization

Ten principles of organization were propounded by the noted management scientist, Lyndall F. Urwick. These are adapted and reproduced here:

(1) Principle of the Objective: Every organization and every part of it must be an expression of the purpose of the undertaking concerned or it is meaningless and therefore redundant.

(2) Principle of Specialization: The activities of every member of any organized group should be confined, as far as possible, to the performance of a single function.

(3) Principle of Coordination: The purpose of organizing per se, as distinguished from the purpose of the undertaking, is to facilitate coordination, unity of effort.

(4) Principle of Authority: In every organized group, the supreme authority must rest somewhere. There should be a clear line of authority from the supreme authority to every individual in the group.

(5)   Principle of Responsibility: The responsibility of the superior for the acts of his subordinate is absolute.

(6)   Principle of Definition: The content of each position - the duties involved, the authority and responsibility contemplated, and the relationships with other positions should be clearly defined in writing and published to all concerned.

(7)   Principle of Correspondence: In every position, the responsibility and the authority should correspond.

(8)   The Span of Control: No person should supervise more than five, or at the most six, direct subordinates whose work interlocks.

(9)   Principle of Balance: It is essential that the various units of an organization should be kept in balance.

(10)   Principle of Continuity: Reorganization is a continuous process; in every undertaking specific provision should be made for it.

7.8   REVIEW QUESTIONS

1)   Define organization?
2)   What are the principles of organization?
3)   Describe formal and informal organizations.
4)   Write down the steps in organization.
5)   Explain the principles of organization.

DEPARTMENTATION

8.1   INTRODUCTION

Departmentation is a means of dividing the large and complex organization into smaller, flexible administrative units. It is the organization-wide division of work into various manageable units or departments. It refers to horizontal differentiation in an organization. It is the grouping of activities and employees into departments. It is a method of arranging activities to facilitate the accomplishment of organizational objectives.

Departmentation is defined as the establishment of a distinct area, unit or subsystem of an organization over which a manager has authority for performance of specified activities and results. In simple words, the organizational process of determining how activities are to be grouped is called departmentation.

8.2   THE NEED FOR DEPARTMENTATION

Departmentation is necessary because it involves grouping of people or activities into a single department or unit to achieve organizational goals. Departmentation is essential because of the following reasons:

➢ Departmentation permits an organization to take advantage of specialization.
➢ Departmentation enables each person to know the particular part he is expected to play in the total activities of the company.
➢ Departmentation facilitates communication, coordination and control and contributes to the organizational success.
➢ Departmentation provides an adequate platform around which the loyalties of organizational members may be built.
➢ It enables a manager to locate the sources of information, skills and competence to take certain vital managerial decisions.

8.3   IMPORTANCE'S OF DEPARTMENTATION

The major importance of the departmentation is along following lines.

1.   **Advantages of Specialisation.** Probably the most important single principle in an analysis of the classical approach to organisational design is specialisation of work. This principle affects everyone every day. The basic advantage of the specialisation lies in terms of efficiency with which the work is performed because a person focuses his attention on a narrow aspect of the work and he gets mastery over that aspect. Naturally this results into performing the work more efficiency. Thus if the managerial function is conceived as a set of activities facilitating the work of the organisation, these activities can be carried out more efficiently and effectively through the division of work leading to a specialisation of managerial function.

2.   **Fixation of responsibility.** Departmentation helps in fixing the responsibility and consequently accountability for the results. Responsibility can be discharged properly when it is clear, precise, and definite. Through departmentation, the work is divided into small units where it can be defined precisely and responsibility can be fixed accurately. The manager concerned to whom responsibility is given can be delegated corresponding authority. When both responsibility and authority are clearly specified, a manager knows what exactly he has to do in the organisation. This helps the manager to become more effective.

3.   **Development of Managers.** Departmentation helps in the development of managers. Development is possible because of two factors. First, the managers focus their attention on some specific problems which provides them effective on-the-job training. Second, managerial need for further training can be identified easily because the managers' role is prescribed and training can provide them opportunity to work better in their area of specialisation. Thus need for training and its methods can be easily identified.

4.   **Facility in Appraisal.** Managerial performance can be measured when the area of activities can be specified and standards in respect of these can be fixed. Departmentation provides helps in both these areas. When a broader function is divided into small segments and a particular segment is assigned to each manager, the area to be appraised is clearly known; the factors affecting the performance can be pointed out more easily. Similarly, standards for performance can be fixed easily because factors

affecting the work performance can be known clearly. Thus performance appraisal will be more objective when departments have been created.

5.   Feeling of Autonomy. Departmentation provides motivation by developing feeling of autonomy to the extent possible. Normally departments are created in the organisation with certain degree of autonomy and freedom. The manager in charge of a department can take independent decisions within the overall framework of the organisation. Thus he enjoys satisfaction of being important to the organisation. This feeling itself is a source of better performance among managers.

8.4   ADVANTAGES OF DEPARTMENTATION

Following are the advantages of departmentation:

(i)   Advantage of managerial specialisation

Departmentation enables enterprises to avail of the advantages of managerial specialisation. Infact, in whatever way are departments created; it is sure that each departmental head is a specialist in matters pertaining to his department. This specialisation means increased efficiency of operations, leading to more profits for the enterprise.

(ii)   Expansion and growth of enterprise facilitated

The device of departmentation facilitates growth and expansion of the enterprise. Depending on growth requirements of business, more departments may be created in the enterprise; or within the same department, more sub-departments may be created - to handle additional work load.

(iii)   Decentralization facilitated

Departmentation facilitates the implementation of the policy of decentralization of authority. In fact, many departmental heads may be granted full powers to run their departments efficiently - through systematic decentralization. Decentralization is likely to motivate departmental heads and boost their morale-all leading to higher efficiency and increased profits for the whole organisation.

(iv)   Fixation of responsibility facilitated

Departmentation facilitates fixation of responsibility on departmental heads, as their roles and functions are clearly specified. Management, accordingly, can also install a system of 'Responsibility Accounting'; and ensure its advantages to the organisation.

(v)   Performance appraisal and managerial development

On the basis at the functioning of departments, it is easier for management to undertake performance appraisal of departmental heads and their subordinates. Performance appraisal findings may provide useful clues to initiating schemes of managerial development.

(vi)   Facilitates intra-departmental co-ordination

Since people in a department perform interrelated jobs and tasks pertaining to the subject matter of that department; therefore, it could be said that departmentation facilitates intra-departmental co-ordination. Moreover, people in the department develop better social informal relations because of frequent interactions.

(vii)   Administrative control facilitated

Departmentation facilitates administrative control on the part of top management. In view of the nature and functioning of departments; top management can devise and implement broad but suitable controls over departmental heads.

8.5   BASIS OF DEPARTMENTATION

The activities of an organization can be grouped into departments on any of the following bases:

1.   **Function:** Departments can be created on the basis of functions like production, sales, personnel, finance, etc. This is the most popular basis of departmentation.

2.   **Product or service:** Large companies with different product lines can set up separate departments for each product or service that it produces or provides. Specialized product knowledge and fixing of specific responsibilities are the merits of this division. This is also called divisionalization.

3.   Customers: Departmentation may be done on the basis of the customers of the concern. A marketing company may have separate departments to cater to the wholesalers, retailers, mail-order customers, etc.

4.   Location: This is also called territorial division or departmentation. A company may have separate departments to serve the southern region, northern region etc. It has the advantage of the intimate knowledge of local conditions.

5.   Time: When a working unit called a department works in different shifts, for each shift the working unit or department may be separate.

6.   Process: Different departments can be created on the basis of functional processes, e.g., bleaching department, drying department, printing department, etc.

7.   Combination: One or more bases can be adopted to constitute a department according to the necessity of the organization.

The following factors are to be considered in forming departments in an organization.

1.   Cost factor: The cost of creating a new department should be considered. It should be economical.

2.   Functional specialization: A new department should be based on this important factor of functional specialization. For every separate function like marketing, personnel or purchase, a separate department has to be created to secure the economies and benefits of functional specialization.

3.   Control centre: One should see whether creation of a department can serve as an effective control centre for that particular group of activities.

4.   Integration of different activities: Various connected activities can be brought together into one department. Sometimes even different activities which are not closely related can be brought together.

5.   Personnel factors: While creating a department, one has to see whether there is a proper personnel manager to manage the department effectively.

8.6   IDEAL PRINCIPLES OF DEPARTMENTATION

Some of the ideal principles of departmentation are suggested below:

(i)   Principle of attainment of enterprise objectives

According to this principle, the basis of departmentation must be such that there is greatest facility, in the most effective and efficient attainment of enterprise objectives.

(ii)   Principle of comprehensive departmentation

By the principle of comprehensive departmentation, we mean that the entire organisational functioning is covered by the chosen basis of departmentation i.e. no aspect of organisational functioning is overlooked, in creating departments, in the organisation.

(iii)   Principle of inter-departmental co-operation

Departmentation must be so done in an organisation, that there is maximum inter-departmental co-operation; and that the possibilities of interdepartmental conflicts are minimized.

(iv)   Principle of promotion of specialisation

The process of department creation must promote both managerial and operational specialisation so that maximum organisational efficiency is achieved; as a result of such specialisation.

(v)   Principle of cost-benefit analysis

The notion of 'cost-benefit analysis' must be kept in mind, by management; while creating departments, in the organisation. According to this principle, the benefits obtained from creation of departments must exceed their operational costs; otherwise organisational profitability will be reduced.

(vi)   Principle of top-management control

According to this principle, the basis of departmentation must facilitate top-management's overall control over all departments.

A derivative principle here is that departmentation basis must ensure exact fixation of responsibility on departmental heads vis-à-vis the performance of their departments. Then only, is it possible for top-management to exercise control over departmental performances.

(vii)   Principle of special attention to Key-Result Areas (KRA)

Departments must be created on such a basis, in an organisation; that special attention is paid to key-result areas (KRA), during departmental performance.

KRA are those which vitally affect the long-term survival and growth of an enterprise. KRA may include profitability, market standing, public relations etc. as determined by the top management.

(viii)   Principle of best utilization of resources

According to this principle, departmentation must be so done in an organisation; that there is ensured a best utilization of precious organisational resources like raw materials, manpower, machinery, technology and other inputs. There must not be any duplication of efforts or wastage of resources, by the departments created in the organisation.

(ix)   Principle of autonomous feeling to departmental heads

According to this principle, the basis of departmentation must be such that departmental heads have the feeling of maximum autonomy in their operational life; so that they function with creativity and innovative considerations in mind. Such autonomy will motivate them to work according to the best of their abilities and competence.

(x)   Principle of flexibility

The basis of departmentation must lead to the emergence of a flexible departmental set-up; so that in view of volatile and turbulent external environmental influences, more departments (or sub-departments) may be added to the existing set-up or some departments (or sub-departments) deleted from the existing set-up.

(xi)   Principle of human consideration

The ideal basis of departmentation must not only rest on technical or financial considerations; it must give due weightage to human considerations i.e., needs, values, attitudes, expectations, feelings etc. of people working in the organisation. Then only will departments created in the organisation lead to maximum organizational efficiency and maximum human satisfaction.

8.7   REVIEW QUESTIONS

1)   What is departmentation? State its need and significance.

2)   What are different bases of departmentation?

3)   State and explain the ideal principles of departmentation.

4)   Why is there a need for departmentation?

5)   Point out the advantages of departmentation.

THE CONCEPT OF AUTHORITY

9.1 MEANING OF AUTHORITY

According to Barnard, "Authority is the character of a communication (order) in a formal organisation by virtue of which it is accepted by a contributor to, or member of, the organisation as governing the action he contributes that is, as governing or determining what he does or is not to do, so far as the organisation is concerned."

In the words of Simon, authority may be defined as "the power to make decisions which guide the actions of another. It is relationship between two individuals - one superior, the other subordinate. The superior frames and transmits decisions, with the expectation that they will be accepted by the subordinate. The subordinate expects such decisions, and his conduct is determined by them."

9.2 CHARACTERISTICS OF AUTHORITY

The following characteristics of authority deserved special notice:

1. Basis of getting things done. Authority provides the basis of getting things done in the organisation. It refers to the right to affect the behavior of others in the organisation with a view to performing certain activities to accomplish the defined objectives.

2. Legitimacy. Authority is accepted as it has certain legitimacy about it, that is to say, it implies a right to secure performance from others. Such right may be legal or format, or it may be supported by tradition, customer accepted standards of authenticity. The right of a manager to affect the behavior of his subordinates is given to him by virtue of his position or office of the said organisation.

3. Decision-making. It is a pre-requisite of authority. The manager can command his subordinates to act of abstain from acting in a particular manner only when he has made decisions as regards the course of activities to be performed by him.

4.   Subjectivity in implementation. Though authority has an element of objectivity about it, its exercise is significantly influenced by subjective factors, such as the personality of the manager who is empowered to use it, as also of the subordinate or group of subordinates with reference to whom it is to be exercised.

9.3   DISTINCTION BETWEEN AUTHORITY AND POWER

Sometimes two terms 'authority and power' are used interchangeably because of their common objective of influencing the behavior of people on whom these are exercised. However, there is a difference between these two. While authority is the right to command, power is the capacity to command. The traditional concept of hierarchy finds its essential rationale that someone has the right to command someone else and that the subordinate person has the duty to obey the command. This is implied in the notion of official legitimacy, legal in nature rather than social and informal. However, the right to command does not necessarily connote the capacity to command. For example, a person in the society may have capacity to influence the behavior of others by his money power or muscle power but he may not have right to do so.

Sometimes, right and capacity are clearly separable and can be identified easily, but at other times, the two get intermingled. For example, commanding others on the basis of money or muscle power is clearly separable but in an organisation two managers of equal status and authority may have different type of command in actual practice. The difference arises because one manager may acquire more power due to his personal factors. Here authority and power go together and distinction is not easy. In fact, there is a continuum of authority-power relationship. At one end, right and capacity would be one, while at the other end, both would be completely separable. Between these two extremes, it is possible to find a number of variations. Thus the major difference between authority and power can be identified as follows:

1.   Authority is legitimized by certain rules, regulations, laws, and practices. In the case of power, there is no such legitimization.

2.   Authority is institutional and originates because of structural relationships. Power emerges because of personal factors and varies with the individuals. In the management of an organisation, authority is the central element of formal organisation and systematic communication. Power reflects the political realities within the organisation and relates to the subtler, more informal patterns of action and interaction that occur.

3.   Authority exists in the context of organizational relationship, mostly in superior-subordinate relationships either direct or otherwise. Power relationship many exist between any two persons and organizational relationships may not be necessary.

Although these differences have been suggested, it is important to recognize that much of the controversy surrounding right and capacity to control has involved ascertain degree of semantic confusion. Much heat has been generated as to whether authority, defined to include capacity, really flows down from the top in traditional fashion or whether it arises from the bottom as a kind of consent of the governed. For example, Barnard has supported the later view when he has emphasized the flow of authority upward due to the consent of governed. Notwithstanding this, the distinction between authority and power exists on the above lines at least on conceptual level.

9.4   SOURCES OF AUTHORITY

Some disagreement has developed in management literature about the sources of authority. The basic source of disagreement arises because of the question 'who legitimizes power and gives it the status of authority? 'Who designates the areas in which a manager may legitimately exercise power, that is, exert his authority?" One view is that authority derives from higher levels; that is normally referred to as the theory of formal authority. However, according to another approach, legitimization comes from below and flows upward. Accordingly, authority is conferred by those below a given manager. To the extent this legitimization upward fails to occur, real authority is lacking. This controversy here has much common with that between economic man and administrative man theory. The discussion here is concerned with the specific nature of formal and acceptance theories and with the conflict between them.

9.5   REVIEW QUESTIONS

1)   What is authority? Why do people accept authority?
2)   Distinguish between power and authority.

DELEGATION OF AUTHORITY

10.1 MEANING OF DELEGATION

To delegate means to entrust authority to a deputy so as to enable him to accomplish the task assigned to him.

In the words of Louis A.Allen, "Delegation is the dynamic of management; it is the process a manager follows in dividing the work assigned to him so that he performs that party which only he, because of his unique organizational placement, can perform effectively, and so that he can get others to help him with what remains".

According to E.F.L.Brech, "Delegation means the passing on to others of a share in the four elements of the management process; that is to say, in the command of the activities of other people and in the responsibility for the decision that will determine the planning, coordination and control of the activities of such other people".

In the words of Koontz and O'Donnel, "The entire process of delegation involves the determination of results expected, the assignment of tasks, the delegation of authority for accomplishment of these tasks, and the exaction of responsibility for their accomplishment."

10.2 THE PROCESS OF DELEGATION

The steps in the delegation process have been narrated above. We may have a brief look into their contents.

Business is run for results. The tasks set for the delegates himself and what he assigns (delegates) to the delegates, must accordingly be stated in terms of results.

No holder of a task can ever achieve the results that he is called upon to yield without the means to do so. This 'means' is the authority.

If the means is wider than the ends, part of it will go waste or be misused; if it is narrower, lacks adequacy, the ends will not be achieved. The means must therefore match the ends; authority and the task-results, accountability - must go together.

Finally, no manager (delegator) can or is allowed to abdicate responsibility even for the portion that he has delegated. His responsibility is total and continuous. He must therefore control - enforce accountability - which is another chapter of the art and practice of delegation.

10.3   TYPES OF DELEGATION

Formal, Informal and Specific Delegation.

It is customary in management literature to distinguish between: (a) formal and informal delegation; and (b) general and specific delegation.

As concepts the groupings have some merits; in practice, they overlap, as they are bound to do, the structural and human dynamics being what they are.

In a formal delegation, the delegated assignments and the accompanying authority for each delegate are spelt out, on a piece of paper. In the informal type, the delegation goes by a climate of understanding between the superior and the subordinate. As a crude analogy, in a household, the husband knows what is expected of him, so does, perhaps the housewife without so much as a charter of distribution of tasks and authority.

Whether a delegation is formal or informal, it ought to be clear. A lack of clarity as to who will do (and decide) what and who wields what authority - is a breeding ground of confusion. Confusion denudes management efficiency through consequential delays, inaction, wasteful file-shuttling and misunderstanding.

It is the merit of a formal delegation that it makes for clarity. It is all spelt out there, for all to see; it is circulated; everybody knows who is what, what he must do and achieve and what authority possesses. It clears operations of doubts and ambiguities.

A comment is often made that a formal delegation is rigid. It hamstrings initiative, curbs talents, stunts vitality, erodes adaptability to change. Even if these were true, and the alternative was uncertainty, confusion, they are better tolerated. But the fears of inflexibility in a formal delegation, and the consequences that are postulated, need not be true. The delegation charter is the body of outline in a field of sports which helps discipline and adherence to the rules of the game. Provided the supervisor-subordinate relations are warm and healthy, no manager need suffer inhibition in the full play of his talents and initiative merely because he is known to possess certain well-defined tasks and authority.

Delegation can also be general or specific. It is said to be general when the task is broadly set, leaving it to the delegate how he would work out the details. A sales manager, who is given charge of a sales territory with broad targets and authority, without being told in so many words as to how he should go about it, has a general delegation. A general delegation would perhaps remove some of the inflexibility claimed against a formal delegation but could add some of the uncertainties of an informal delegation in the field of operation of the delegated task. These contradictions have to be carefully balanced in framing a charter of general delegation.

10.4   PRINCIPLES OF DELEGATION

Delegation can be effective only if it conforms to certain well-established principles, which are as follows:

1.   Delegation to conform to desired objectives

The nature and extent of duties and authority to be delegated should be in tune with the objectives to be accomplished. Before assigning duties and delegating authority to his subordinate, the manager should be clear in his mind as to what he expects from them. This means that delegation should be only after he has determined his objectives, policies, plans, and also the specific jobs to be performed for the accomplishment of the objectives.

2.   Responsibility not delegatable

A manager can delegate only authority, not responsibility. Responsibility is never delegated. By assigning duties and delegating authority to his subordinates, a manager cannot turn a blind eye to how the assigned duties are performed, and how the delegated authority is exercised. The ultimate responsibility for the performance of duties and exercise of delegated authority remains with him.

3.   Authority to match duties

Delegation of authority can be meaningful only when it enables the subordinate to discharge his duties effectively. Just as an ill-equipped soldier cannot fight a battle successfully, similarly an inadequately - authorized subordinate cannot succeed in accomplishing the assigned task.

Assignment of a task without adequate authority will render a subordinate ineffective. Authority without matching responsibility will make him dictatorial. An ideal delegation is that where there is a proper balance between delegated authority and assigned duties.

4.   Unity of command

The principle of unity of command states that a subordinate should be commanded by one superior only. This means that a subordinate should be assigned duties and delegated authority by one superior only and he should be accountable for the performance of the assigned duties and exercise of the delegated authority to that same superior.

If there are many superiors to command a subordinate, it will create uncertainty and confusion, as the subordinate will find it difficult to determine which superior's order should be carried out first, and to whom he should approach for solution of his problems.

5.   Limits to authority to be well-defined

A manager cannot properly delegate authority unless he fully knows what his own authority is. To avoid confusion in this respect, there should be written manuals and orders to indicate the limits of authority and area of operations of each manager.

10.5   ADVANTAGES OF DELEGATION

Delegation offers several advantages. Important amount these are as follows:

1.   Basis of effective functioning

Delegation provides the basis for effective functioning of an organisation. It establishes relationships through the organisation and helps in achieving coordination of various activities in accomplishing enterprise objectives.

2.   Reduction in managerial load

Delegation relieves the manager of the need to attend to minor or routine types of duties. Thus, he is enabled to devote greater attention and effort toward broader and more important responsibilities.

3.   Benefit of specialized service

Delegation enables the manager to benefit from the specialised knowledge and expertise of persons at lower levels. Thus, purchasing may be delegated to the purchase manager, sales to the sales manager, advertising to the advertising manager, accounting to an accountant, legal matters to a lawyer, and personnel functions to a personnel manager.

4.   Efficient running of branches

In the modern world, where a business rarely confines its activities to a single place, only delegation can provide the key to smooth and efficient running of the various branches of the business at places far and near.

5.   Aid to employee development

Delegation enables the employees of business to develop their capabilities to undertake new and more challenging jobs. Also, it promotes job satisfaction and contributes to high employee morale.

6.   Aid to expansion and diversification of business

With its employees fully trained in decision - making in various fields, the business can confidently undertake expansion and diversification of its activities. Because, it will already have a competent team of contented workers to take on new responsibilities.

10.6   IMPORTANCE OF DELEGATION

Delegation has a distant origin. According to the Old Testament, when Moses was faced with a problem, which he and his followers found difficult to resolve, he was advised by his father-in-law, Jethro, as follows: "What you are doing is not good. You and the people with you will wear yourselves out, for the thing is too heavy for you: you are not able to perform it alone. Listen now to my voice. Choose able men from all the people, and let them judge the people at all times; every great matter they shall bring to you, but any small matter they shall decide themselves; so it will be easier for you and they will bear the burden with you".

Delegation is a universal process. Wherever human beings live or work in groups, one or the other form of delegation is practiced by them. The head of the family delegates some of his powers to other members of legislatures. Members of legislature delegate their authority to an elected leader who, in turn, delegates some of his authority to the cabinet members chosen by him.

In fact, the need for delegation arises because it is impossible for an individual, howsoever competent and capable he may be, to manage and control anything done even on a modest scale. Physical and mental limitations of an individual become all the more pronounced when it comes to management of a business enterprise. As E.F.L. Brech has put it, "The tasks involved in the management process of a particular enterprise are too large, either because the amount of responsibility, or mental energy and so on, called for are too big for one individual; or because the task entitled require rather more than one individual can make available single - handed."

Or, as Lounsbury Fish says, "An individual is only one manpower. Single-handed, he can accomplish only so much in a day. The only way he can achieve more is through delegation - through dividing his load and sharing his responsibilities with others".

Through delegation, an individual can multiply himself and perform several simple and complex tasks. Take the case of the principal of a college. His responsibility is to run the college properly and he has the necessary authority for this purpose. But cannot discharge his responsibility without delegation. He cannot simultaneously look after sports, games, and other extra curricular activities. He cannot also find time to attend to the office, incoming and outgoing letters and, above all, proper discipline in the college. For discharging his responsibility efficiently, the principal needs to delegate authority to a number of persons such as class teachers, games teachers, teachers in charge of extra-curricular activities, office superintendent, and so on.

Delegation enables a person not only to discharge his responsibility but also to discharge it efficiently and economically, because in that case he can secure the benefits of specialized knowledge and expertise of several persons. For a business with branches situated at different places, there is no alternative to delegation. Delegation ensures continuity in business, because managers at lower levels are enabled to acquire valuable experience in decision - making and they gain enough competence to fill higher positions in case of need.

10.7   EFFECTIVE DELEGATION

It takes two parties for delegation to be effective-a superior willing to delegate and give his subordinates real freedom to achieve delegated tasks and a subordinate willing to assume added responsibilities, develop solutions to problems independently and learn through the, painful though, process of trial and error. The barriers to delegation, as we have seen, are purely psychological and can be reduced through improved communication between managers and subordinates leading to better understanding. The following guidelines have been advanced by different writers to help managers delegate effectively.

The Subordinate

1.   Select subordinates in the light of the task to be performed. Provide guidance, help and information to them. Maintain open lines of communication.

2.   Do not be overawed by the errors committed by subordinates. Remove the elements of fear and frustration. Allow them to learn through mistakes. One does not learn to play tennis/cricket by reading a book. Require completed work.

3.   Allow the subordinates to see the big picture. The subordinate needs to know why his work is both necessary and important.

4.   Provide sufficient authority to subordinates for accomplishing goal assignments.

5.   Reward acceptance of responsibility. Perspiration does not go very far without a little inspiration.

The Organization Culture

1.   Create an atmosphere of trust and risk taking.
2.   Use constructive criticism to help the subordinate grow.
3.   All delegations should be in writing.

The Authority Structure

1.   Equate authority with responsibility; too much authority may be abused; too little authority may frustrate the subordinates.

2.   Restrain any inclination to override, interfere with or undermine the delegation.

The Control Systems

1.   Prevent illegitimate usurpation of authority by establishing broad controls.

2.   Provide standards so that the subordinate can measure and evaluate his performance against the standard.

It would seem easy and simple to delegate the task to subordinates observing the above guidelines. But as rightly pointed out by Robert Fulmer, delegation is almost never simple. It is in fact, a skill that separates men from the boys in management. Delegation demands a closer look at all the contingent factors like size, task complexity, costliness of the decision, organizational culture, qualities of subordinates etc. The subordinate must be willing to make a determined effort and the supervisor must be willing to extend freedom and cooperation, in turn. Koontz and O' Donnell have listed some personal qualities that can contribute to effective delegation. An effective delegator should:

➢   Give other peoples' ideas a chance.
➢   Allow subordinates to take decisions independently.
➢   Be a patient counselor and not a 'hovering hawk'.
➢   Repose confidence and trust in subordinates.
➢   Know how to use controls judiciously.

10.8   LIMITS OF DELEGATION

There are certain conditions in a business system, both internal and environmental, those evoke tendencies toward centralization and work against decentralization and delegation of authority and responsibility. Some of them reflect wider, uncontrollable forces; others are open, relatively, to manipulation. We shall take not here of these important influences:

i. Some decisions are irreversible, especially in the short run; others can be reversed or corrected but at a high cost in terms of money or embarrassment. This is so, regardless of the size of the commitment which may be large, medium or even small. An example is say, when a dealership has to be awarded to one among an excluded category.

ii. Some decisions involve large commitments in terms of money, time or direction, or a combination of them. Even an initial move (not so large in itself) can trigger off the wide commitment chain. It is unsafe to delegate such initial decisions to juniors.

iii. Certain decisions are apt to create an uncomfortable precedent - being off the track or running counter to recognized enterprise policy. Regardless of the individual content (importance) of such decisions, they are better retained at a high level.

iv. A certain decision, of not moment in so far as it goes, might create repercussions - a chain reaction elsewhere. An example is the waiver of the minimum educational qualification of a worker of a factory for his promotion. The repercussions may extend throughout the industrial relations climate of the enterprise: Such a decision should not be delegated.

v. Decisions where the personal (semi-judiciary) judgment of the senior is called into play. An example is passing of orders of major punishments on grounds of discipline - involving, say, dismissal or termination of service. The decision may be retained at a high level regardless of the level of employees concerned.

vi. The traditional make up of the enterprise influences the degree of decentralization and delegation. With a series of able and authoritarian administrators at the top dominating an enterprise, say, for a half a century, the tradition is likely to release tendencies against decentralization and delegation.

vii. In enterprises owned and managed by a dynasty or familial group decentralization tends to be confined to members of the family. The nodal points of decision and control remain in the hands of a few. Professionalization of management, in such a situation, has impact on the lower routine echelons of management and on the advisory specialist services.

viii.   Policy decisions are usually retrained at higher management levels. Besides the principles of size and commitment, this is also conditioned by the need to observe uniformity.

ix.   The growth, diversity and complexity of an enterprise evoke tendencies of decentralization and delegation on functional, territorial or product lines or a combination of the two or more criteria.

x.   Often adequacy of trained and competent managers imposes a constraint on decentralization and delegation. Key positions, in such a situation, tend to be held by a few senior and well-tried executives.

xi.   A situation of flux (may be, in a particular phase of an organization's life cycle) or a quick change is apt to put a brake on the progress of decentralization and the delegation scheme. A delegation system does not function well unless in a stable system and a comparative monotone of repetitive management.

xii.   The environment, the institutional framework and the laws of the land cast their strong influence on in-company delegation and decentralization. In a controlled system many facets of enterprise operations and decision are bound by regulatory measures and forms of a prescriptive nature.

While, in a situation as this, overall and absolute decentralization is constrained, there is nothing to prevent flow of delegation of authority at the top down the scalar chain.

10.9   REVIEW QUESTIONS

1.   What are the principles of delegation?
2.   Discuss the types of delegation.
3.   How delegation can be made more effective.
4.   What are the steps in delegation?
5.   Define delegation? Why is it essential for the smooth functioning of an enterprise?

11

CENTRALIZATION AND DECENTRALIZATION

11.1   CENTRALIZATION

According to Allen, centralization is the systematic and consistent reservation of authority at central points within the organization. In centralization little delegation of authority is the rule; power and discretion are concentrated at the top levels. Control and decision making reside at the top levels of the management. The more highly centralized the organization, the more control and decision making reside at the top. However absolute centralization is untenable because it would mean the subordinates have no duties, power or authority. Most organizations start out centralization of authority initially. Such an arrangement helps the manager to be in touch with all operations and facilitates quick decision - making. Centralization may be essential in case of small organizations to survive in a highly competitive world. But as the organizations to survive in a highly competitive world. But as the organization becomes more complex in terms of increasing size, interdependence of work-flow, complexity of tasks and spatial physical barriers within and among groups, a function requisite for efficiency is to move decision-making centres to the operating level. Thus, the larger the size of an organization, the more urgent is the need for decentralization. This does not mean that decentralization is good and centralization is bad. Centralization or decentralization may be, in part, merely the result of circumstances. There are certain special circumstances forcing managers to reserve authority and centralize decision-making power:

1.   **To facilitate personal leadership.** Centralization generally works well in the early stages of organizational growth. Working under a talented and dynamic leader, a small firm can derive advantages in the form of quick decisions, enterprising and imaginative action, and high flexibility. Centralization enables a small organization to capitalize on the loyalties, ability and experience of its most talented top management people. Under this arrangement the manager is in touch with all operations, makes all decisions, and gives all instructions. Thus, centralization can project the personality and skills of one outstanding leader more meaningfully.

2.   To provide for Integration. Under centralization, the organization moves like one unit. It keeps all parts of the organization moving together harmoniously toward a common goal. It assures uniformity of standards and policies among organizational units. The danger of actions drifting and getting off course is minimized. The manager acts like a unifying force and provides direction to enterprise activities. In the process duplication of effort and activity are also avoided. To see that all units do the same thing in the same way or at the same time without wasteful activity, centralization is essential.

3.   To handle emergencies. Centralization is highly suitable in times of emergency. The resources and information can be mobilized quickly and efficiently. Quite often emergency situations like declining sales, introduction of a highly sophisticated competitive product, government policy changes may force the organization to cut down costs, maintain inventories at an optimum level, utilize resources effectively and instantaneously. Centralization of decision-making ensures prompt action necessary to meet the emergencies.

11.2   DECENTRALIZATION

Decentralization is the systematic effort to delegate to the lowest levels all authority except that which can be exercised at central points. It is the pushing down of authority and power of decision-making to the lower levels of organization. The centres of decision-making are dispersed throughout the organization. However, the essence of decentralization is the transference of authority from a higher level to a lower level. Decentralization, in recent years, has come to be accepted as a golden calf of management philosophy. It has come to be associated as a fundamental principle of democratic management where each individual is respected for his inherent worth, and constitution. As pointed out earlier, absolute centralization (where there is no room for subordinates) or absolute decentralization (where there is no coordinated, organized activity) is fictitious in practice; it is a matter of degree along a continuum. Generally speaking, decentralization is said to be greater:

➤ When more decisions are made at lower levels.
➤ When more important decisions are made at lower levels.
➤ When more functions are affected by decisions made at lower levels.
➤ When the checking on the decisions made at lower levels is minimal.

11.3   TYPES OF DECENTRALIZATION

There are three approaches to assign authority and responsibility to lower level people in an organization. It is quite possible to provide for decentralization in varying degrees among various departments in the organization. For example, production and sales departments may be decentralized because of the urgency to take quick decisions; finance department may be centralized due to the need to obtain funds for the organization as a whole. Three types of decentralization are discussed below:

1.   Profit centers. Under profit centre decentralization the organization is first divisional zed on a product basis; each division is given the management and physical tools and facilities it needed to operate as an integrated and self-contained unit. Each division operates on a competitive basis; orders its own materials, schedules its operations and negotiates the sale of its finished products. It is accountable for the profit it earns or the loss it sustains. To use 'profit centres' authorities suggest that each one possess:

a.   Operational independence having control over most operational decisions affecting profits (volume, production methods etc.)

b.   Complete freedom to buy and sell in alternative markets both inside and outside the organization.

c.   Separate, identifiable income, expense and assets from the organization so that they can operate independently and calculate their own profit.

Thus, a profit centre is a relatively autonomous organizational unit 'that can be differentiated clearly enough from the rest of the organization so that costs it incurs or revenues it generates can be reasonably accounted for and associated with it.' However, it is not always easy to find organizational submits independent enough from each other so that they may be almost as different business. One important limitation identified in the profit-centre concept is cost. Creation of profit centres demands enormous doses of investment with no guarantee of adequate returns. On the positive side, profit centre decentralization provides a strong incentive to divisional management to improve the efficiency of its operations. It is remarked that 'The division head, instead of merely a production boss, is a manager in every sense of the word; actually, he operates in somewhat the same manner as the head of an independent business. This gives him the greatest possible encouragement to use every iota of management ability he can command'.

2.   Cost expense centres. Where it is difficult to find out revenue with a unit but is relatively easy to determine the costs of operation, cost centres are established. In the case of corporate legal staff or accounting staff it may be quite difficult to determine how much revenue is generated but it can be a cost centre since we can determine the costs necessary to run it. In a cost centre, a manager would be responsible for using resources within the overall cost or budgetary limitations. By keeping the costs under specified limitations he incurs an additional responsibility to provide required support to the rest of the organization.

3.   Investment centres. Investment centres are quite common in the case of multi product enterprises like General Motors, General Electric, Hindustan Lever Ltd. etc. In order to measure product performance, decentralization by investment centres is usually advocated and the managerial response - obligations would include responsibilities for the 'acquisition, use, and disposition of fixed-use resources'.

11.4   ADVANTAGES OF DECENTRALIZATION

The important advantages of decentralization are as follows:

1.   Relief to top executives. Decentralization enables the top executives to devote greater attention and effort to important issues. They may not be able to do this if they keep their hands full with problems of a routine nature.

2.   Motivation of subordinates. Systematic decentralization results in development of initiative, responsibility, and morale among employees. Because the authority to make decisions is placed in the hands of employees who have the responsibility to execute them, the employees are more sincere and hardworking in performing their jobs.

3.   Intimate relationships. In a decentralized unit, employees have greater opportunities to come in close contact with one another. This results in improved communication, so that employees can benefit from expertise and experience of one another.

4.   Sense of competition. In a decentralized enterprise, its departments and division are independent of one another. As a result, the management can experiment with new ideas and processes in any department without any risk of its adverse effect on the functioning of other departments.

5.   **Effective control.** Though each of the departments and divisions is granted freedom in running its affairs, the control function is not adversely affected. This is because for judging the performance of each unit, an important yardstick is its profitability and the rate of return on investment.

11.5.   DISADVANTAGES OF DECENTRALISATION

Decentralization has also certain limitations, important among which are as follows:

1.   **Lack of coordination.** Under decentralization, each division or department of the enterprise enjoys substantial freedom in the formulation of policies and action plans. This creates a difficult problem of coordination.

2.   **Costly.** Only a very large enterprise can afford the high operating costs of maintaining a decentralized set-up. This is because under decentralization, each division of the enterprise has to be self-sufficient in every respect, e.g., production, marketing, accounting, personnel, etc. This may not only result in duplication of functions, but may also lead to wastage of resources, because often one or the other facility remains under-utilized in each division.

3.   **Lack of able managers.** A decentralized enterprise has to depend on divisional managers. But it is difficult to find persons who are adequately equipped to run a division independently.

11.6   DISTINCTION BETWEEN DELEGATION AND DECENTRALISATION

Even though delegation and decentralization may be interchangeable terms, in reality there is considerable difference between then. The following are the main points of distinction:

Delegation	Decentralization
1. It is an act, or a process.	1. It is the end-result of delegation and dispersal of authority at various levels.
2. It refers to relationship between two individuals. ie., a superior and his immediate subordinate(s).	2. It refers to a relationship between the top management and various departments and divisions in the enterprise.

Delegation	Decentralization
3. It is vital to management process. Only through delegation of duties, subordinates can be involved in the activities aimed at the accomplishment of enterprise objectives.	3. It is optional in the sense that the top management may or may not favour a deliberate policy to work for a general dispersal of authority.
4. Control over a subordinate's performance is exercised by his superior who constitutes the source of delegation of authority.	4. Even the power to control may be delegated to the department concerned.

For example, suppose, the chief executive of a company authorizes the production manager to make appointments to all such positions under him in the case of which the maximum salary does not exceed Rs.1,000. This is a case of delegation of authority. But suppose the same authority is given to all departmental managers (marketing, finance etc.), it would be called decentralization of authority.

When departmental heads or those below them are granted authority in respect of the following it would be decentralization:

a.   Sanctioning increase in wages and salaries.
b.   Sanctioning disbursement of travel expenses.
c.   Sanctioning promotions.
d.   Sanctioning purchase of goods, machines, etc.

In a decentralized enterprise, there may even be separate balance sheet and profit and loss account for each division.

11.7   EFFECTIVE DECENTRALIZATION

Like delegation, decentralization has a technique by which it can be effectively achieved. When an organization decides in favor of votes for decentralization, it has to take some concrete steps to make it more effective. Effective decentralization requires a balance of the necessary centralization of planning, organization, motivation, coordination, and control.

1. Establish Appropriate Centralization

If decentralized management is to flourish, it is necessary to provide for a centralized authority which will act as a nerve centre of the enterprise. Here plans would be formulated, appropriate organization structure would be decided and coordination and control mechanisms would be provided. Within such a broad administrative framework individual operating components of the organization would be established as profit centres. The central authority ensures close coordination between various operating units and secures maximum total performance. Without the strong cement of centralized planning, organization, coordination and control the diversified company is in danger of coming apart at the seams'.

2. Development of Managers

Effective decentralization demands a large number of highly competent managers who are capable of exploiting their mental faculties fully and independently in the service of the organization. They must be able to look ahead, to plan for themselves and to run a business. In order to develop managers, the organization should take certain steps: (i) Managers do not develop overnight Instead; they develop through the painful process of trial and error. Every manager should be allowed to take decisions independently and commit mistakes initially. One must develop management ability by managing; one must learn to make decisions by making decisions only. (ii) Senior executives must enthusiastically accept the principle of delegation and know the technique of doing it.

3. Provide for Communication and Coordination

The inherent dangers in decentralized management must be recognized by all managers working in an independent fashion. Decentralization tends to create rivalry and conflict among operating divisions. Departmental managers constantly jockey for power and prestige, they compete for scarce resources and in order to show performance they may be working at breakneck speed at the cost of other departments. The remote control from headquarters may prove to be ineffective as the enterprise grows in size and complexity. To prevent the disintegrating tendencies arising from out of a tunnel vision on the part of each divisional manager, it is necessary to provide for communication and coordination among operating divisions at regular intervals. Coordinating executives and committees may be appointed to meet this end. The dangers of too much fragmentation can be avoided by laying special emphasis on interdepartmental coordination, mutual help and cooperation.

4.   Establish Adequate Controls

Profit centre decentralization demands an appropriate control system that will distribute the resources, assign costs fairly and indisputably to the operations unit that utilizes or incurs them. Budgets can be prepared and standards devised to see whether various units are going in the desired direction. To ensure accountability managers at all levels should be allowed to participate in budget formulation. This would not only make managers feel responsibility but also ensure an objective standard to measure performance and reward the same suitably.

Decentralization is not a panacea. It cannot be plugged into any situation and be expected to work well. It is quite possible that interdepartmental (or divisional) tensions and rivalries can trouble the top management with an unmanageable number of problems.

Decentralization, no doubt is highly beneficial but at the same time it is complex and challenging. Effective decentralization requires a contingency perspective which examines particular functions and departments, in a dispassionate manner. Much depends on how the philosophy of decentralization is being translated into practice. As a matter of fact, a programme of decentralization should not be initiated until the following points have been properly settled:

Top management is willing to share authority for decision-making with others.

Middle management is capable and is willing to accept new responsibility.

Policies are adequate to guide decision-making but not unduly restrictive.

Control system exists to evaluate effectiveness of middle management decisions.

Existing structure must lend itself to, or can be modified to, facilitate decentralized operations.

11.8   REVIEW QUESTIONS

1.   Define "Centralization". Distinguish between centralization and decentralization.
2.   Discuss various types of decentralization that is practiced in organizations.
3.   What are the primary advantages of a decentralized organization?

LINE & STAFF RELATIONSHIPS

12.1   CONCEPT OF LINE AND STAFF

Even in conceptual framework, line and staff are defined from two viewpoints. One of the viewpoints is that they denote different functions within the organization. The other viewpoint is that they refer to authority relationships in the organization. According to functional approach, line functions are those that are related directly with the attainment of the organizational objectives and staff functions are those that help line functions in attaining the objectives. In this form, Allen has defined line and staff as follows:

"Line functions are those which have direct responsibility for accomplishing the objectives of the enterprise and staff refers to those elements of the organization that help the line to work most effectively in accomplishing the primary objectives of the enterprise."

Thus the organizational objectives are the basic determinant of line and staff functions and with the change in the objectives, line and staff functions may change. Thus what may be line function in one organization may be staff function in another. For example, personnel function in an employment agency is line but it is staff in manufacturing organization. In a manufacturing - organization whose basic objective is to produce and sell goods, production and marketing are line functions and others such as finance, personnel, legal etc. are staff functions. Further, within a department, there may be line and staff functions, for example, in marketing selling may be line function but market research is staff function. A person performing staff function is called staff manager or simply staff.

Koontz and others have defined line and staff authority as follows:

"Line authority becomes apparent from the scalar principle as being that relationship in which a superior exercise directs supervision over a subordinate - an authority relationship in direct line or steps. The nature of staff relationship is advisory. The function of people in a pure staff capacity is to investigate, research, and give advice to line managers to whom they report."

12.2   DIFFERENTIATION BETWEEN LINE & STAFF

The differentiation between line and staff is necessary for the following reasons:

1.   To Provide Specialized Services: In managing the complex organization in dynamic environment, a manager' requirement of knowledge is varied and it is not possible for him to have all such knowledge. For this purpose, a manager needs the services of specialists. Such services are needed throughout the organization. However, both managers requiring and using such services and specialists providing the services must understand the nature of relationship existing them, otherwise they may lead to conflicts reducing organizational efficiency.

2.   To Maintain Adequate Checks and Balances. Sound management requires the system of countervailing forces in the organization so that authority delegated to individuals or groups is kept within prescribed bounds by counter-balancing authority. The system of checks and balances requires that 'each force or activity throughout the organization is opposed by a counterforce which operates as a check and thereby sets up a balance of force. Through the balance of forces, the energies of each activity are regulated. 'Effective control, in particular, requires appropriate checks and balances of this kind. The authority for planning and doing is separated to some extent under line and staff. Managers performing duties need assistance from persons who are not directly under their control.

3.   To Maintain Accountability. Organization being a co-operative endeavor requires the services of various persons. Each person has a definite role to play in the organization. This casts certain responsibilities on him. However, the responsibility should be clearly defined in the context of contributions. Thus persons should be identified who are accountable for end results. It ensures that persons would exercise authority for end results. The line and staff relationship makes this identification possible.

There are many reasons for misunderstanding and difficulty in identifying line and staff. Many managers fail to identify the clear distinction between line and staff which often leads to overstepping the use of authority leading to conflict between line and staff. Difficulty in identification of line and staff arises because of the confusion in the type of organization structure, failure to identify authority limitations, and classification of line and staff.

12.3   LINE RELATIONSHIP

A line manager has clearly defined role to play in the organization which requires understanding of the nature of line authority. Line authority exists between superior and his subordinate. In the organizing process, activities are assigned to the individuals making them responsible for the proper performance of these activities. Authority is delegated to these individuals to perform the activities. These individuals, in turn, assign some of the activities to persons working below them in the hierarchy and delegate them authority. This process goes on creating superior - subordinate relationships in the organization. The direct relationship between a superior and his subordinate is created through the enforcement of line relationship. Such a relationship works as follows:

1.   **as a Chain of Command.** A command relationship exists between each superior and subordinate. Line authority is the heart of this relationship because it entitles a superior to direct the work of his subordinate. In this relationship, a superior has uncontrolled authority, except those controls prescribed by the organization or regulated by the environmental factors, of giving orders to his subordinate and subordinate has no alternative except to obey those orders.

2.   **as a Channel of Communication.** Line authority can be treated as channel of communication between members of the organization. Communication, up and down in the organization, flows through the line relationship. Barnard has emphasized the role of line relationship as a channel of communication by suggesting that line of communication should be established and every member of the organization should be tied into the system of communication by having someone to report to and others to report him. Such a line can be maintained easily through line of command.

3.   **as a carrier of Responsibility.** The line relationship carries ultimate responsibility for the work assigned. Though the process of assigning activities goes on till the level where actual work is performed by operatives, each individual is accountable for the proper performance of the activities assigned to him.

12.4   STAFF RELATIONSHIP

The relationship between a staff man and the line manager with whom he works depends in part on the staff duties. A man who only gathers facts or only checks on performance will have relationships with line manager that are different from those of a man who has concurring authority. Therefore, there will be quite variations between line and staff relationships. Such relationships may run along a continuum with only advice at one extreme point and functional authority at other extreme point. In between, two more situations represent compulsory staff consultation and concurring authority.

12.5 TYPES OF STAFF

Staff support to line executives may be in any of the following ways:

a. **Personal staff:** Personal staff consists of a personal assistant or adviser attached to the line executive at any level. His main function is to aid and advise the line executives as also to perform any other work assigned to him.

b. **Specialized staff:** The staff in this case has expert knowledge in specific fields such as accounting, personnel management, public relations, chemical or industrial engineering, etc. For each of these functions, there may be an expert or group of experts placed under a separate department.

c. **General staff:** The staff in this case also consists of experts in different fields. But generally, this category of staff operates at higher levels and is meant to aid and advice the top management.

12.6 EVALUATION

Merits

1. **Expert advice:** Line executives, and through them the enterprises as a whole, benefit a great deal from the expert advice and guidance provided by the staff officers.

2. **Relief to line executives:** Staff executives carry on detailed analysis of each important managerial activity. As such, line executives do not have to undertake specialized investigation of each problem-situation, for which they may not always be competent.

3. **Training of young staff executives:** A line and staff organization offers an opportunity to young staff executives to acquire expertise in their respective fields of activity.

Demerits

1. **Confusion.** It may not always be possible to determine the pattern of authority relationships between line and staff executives, which might create confusion.

2. **Expertise not aided by authority.** Staff executives may be experts in their fields of activity but they only have an advisory role. They lack authority to implement their advice.

3. **Centralization.** In a line and staff organization, line executives alone have the power to make and execute decisions. Thus, it tends towards centralization of authority in a few hands.

12.7   LINE-STAFF CONFLICT

The conflict between line and staff may be attributed to: (a) personal backgrounds of the line and staff personnel, resulting in different attitudes to the organizational activities: and (b) tendency on the part of both line and staff to play disruptive political games because of consciousness as regards differences in their authority positions.

Generally, staff people are relatively young, better educated and more sophisticated in appearance and articulation of their viewpoints. They also suffer from a notion that their ideas if implemented will produce miraculous results. However, their problem is that they generally lack the command authority to translate their often grand ideas into action, and have therefore to pursue the exasperating course of persuasion and political game-playing.

As against this, line personnel view their staff counterparts as a source of irritation because the advice and recommendations emanating from the latter may involve change in the status quo, experimentation with altogether new ideas, and high expectations as regards what can be accomplished. Line personnel also regard the staff personnel as making unreasonable demands on their time, though without any useful results. In the process, while the line people accuse the staff people of being impractical and empty visionaries, the staff people return the compliment by saying that line people are unimaginative, obstinate and afraid to change the status - quo.

However, the line-staff conflict may be inevitable and even welcome in a limited way, because it forces the staff people to be more practical and result-oriented, and the line people to be less dogmatic and resistant to change. But through effective coordination and formalized standardization, much of the ill effects of such conflict may be avoided.

12.8   OVERCOMING LINE-STAFF CONFLICT

Line and staff, both are necessary for the successful functioning of an organization. Therefore, they should work together to enhance the smooth functioning of the organization. However, some conflict may arise between the two. Since the conflict arises either because of misunderstanding between the two or because of the organizational situations in which they are working, attempts should be made to overcome these problems and situations. In particular, attempts can be directed towards (1) understanding of authority relationships (2) proper use of staff (3) completed staff work, and (4) setting congenial organizational climate.

Understanding Authority Relationships

The first basic approach in overcoming the problem of line-staff conflict is the proper understanding of line-staff authority relationships. This can be done in better way by following guidelines.

1.   Line people have the ultimate responsibility for the successful operation of the organization. Therefore, they should have authority for making operating decisions.

2.   Staff people contribute to achieve organizational objectives by making recommendations and providing advice in their respective fields. In some situations, they may be granted functional authority through which they can ensure that their recommendations are put in operation.

3.   Since in most cases, solicitation of advice and acceptance of that is usually at the option of the line people, it becomes imperative for the staff to offer advice and services whenever these are not solicited but staff feels that these will be helpful in arriving at suitable decisions.

4.   Barring few exceptional situations where time factor is of utmost importance for decision making, line should be impressed upon for compulsory consultation and giving serious thinking to the advice rendered by staff.

5.   Staff people should sell their ideas to line people. They should rely more on the authority of knowledge and competence rather than authority of position.

Proper Use of Staff

Staff people are needed in the organization because line people are not able to solve the problems which require special knowledge and expertise. The effectiveness of line people depends to a large extent on how they make use of staff. For making proper use of staff, following points are important.

1.   There should be encouragement and education to line people as to how to make maximum use of staff effectively. Line people can not make use of staff unless they know what a specialist can do for them. Staff people also have responsibility to let line people know how they can contribute for the better performance of line activities.

2.   In order to make proper use of staff, they should not be kept busy in unimportant work because it does not serve any meaningful purpose. Instead, they should be assigned critical work in the area of their specialty.

3.   Staff people should be involved at the basic stage of planning of an activity, rather than when the problem becomes critical. When they are involved at the level of planning, many of the problems may not arise at all because care must have been taken against those problems.

4.   If line people have taken some actions directly affecting staff activities without consulting staff people, they should be informed immediately about these.

The information will help in removing misunderstanding, if any, created in the minds of staff people. At the same time, staff people will be informed about the actions going on in their area of activities and can pinpoint the drawback in action, if it exists.

Completed Staff Work

Generally ideas staff arrangement results in completed staff work. Completed staff work is the study of a problem, and presentation of a solution, by a staff man in such a manner that all that remains to be done on the part of the line manager is to indicate his approval or disapproval of the completed action. The concept of completed action is emphasized because the more difficult the problem is, more the tendency is to present the problem to the line manager in piecemeal fashion. The completed staff work requires more rigorous exercise on the part of staff people but it results into two things. First, the line superior is protected from half-baked ideas, voluminous paper work, and immature oral presentations. Second, staff people who can put forward their ideas in the form of completed staff work command more respect and value which help in getting their ideas accepted.

While making recommendations, staff people should study the problem carefully, listing all possible alternatives and effect of these alternatives of problem-solving and clear recommendations for action. They should also provide how recommendations can be put into practice, get clearance from persons likely to be affected by recommended action, and suggestions about avoiding any difficulties involved.

Setting Congenial Organizational Climate

Congenial organizational climate full of mutual trust and respect, self-restrain and control, coordinative approach, and mutual help is a vital factor for successful operation of any managerial process including line and staff relationship. However, two points that need special emphasis in this respect are: (1) recognition of line and staff as necessary element for organizational functioning, and (2) recognition of need for change.

The first aspect is related to the fact that line and staff authority relationship lays the foundation for an organizational way of life. Staff is necessary to take the advantage of specialization. Line managers should recognize the importance of staff people. They should develop a feeling that staff people help in attaining organizational objectives. On the other hand, staff people must convince the line people to sell their ideas, rather than enforcing their ideas through the use of authority. The second aspect is related to the recognition of need for change and overcoming resistance to change. Managers in the organization, particularly line managers, resist change especially when new way of working creates initial problem. A recommendation from staff people means a change in the operation in some way. Therefore, there is a need for analyzing important factors underlying resistance to change and relevant actions to be undertaken. Normally a change is better accepted when it fits in the overall goals and interests of people in the organization and they are informed and consulted before the introduction of change. Therefore, change process should be such that it creates less offence. Staff people have to share the responsibility of bringing change in their respective areas without creating undue friction in the organization.

12.9   REVIEW QUESTIONS

1.   Explain line and staff organization.
2.   Distinguish between line and staff organization.
3.   Explain the various types of staff.
4.   Discuss elaborately the nature of conflict between line and staff.

NATURE AND PURPOSE OF STAFFING

13.1 INTRODUCTION

Perhaps the most important resources of an organization are its human resources - the people who supply the organization with their work, talent, creativity and drive. Without the competent people, at the operational as well as managerial levels, organizations will either pursue inappropriate goals or find it extremely difficult to achieve appropriate goals once they have been set. People are, in fact, the vital resources for an effective organization.

People are the essential ingredient in all organizations, be the organizations business, governmental, religious, educational, and the way in which people are recruited, selected, and utilized by the leadership largely determines whether the organization will achieve its objectives successfully. It is then not too surprising that management is concerned constantly with the management of human resources - with the way in which these resources are developed and utilized, with the assumptions made about them, with the formulation of personal policy, with the methods and procedures used in dealing with the company work force. Staffing function of management deals with these aspects.

13.2 STAFFING

In simple words, staffing is the processing of obtaining and maintaining capable and competent people to fill all positions from top management to operative level. This includes securing, recruiting, selecting, training, appraising and maintaining the individuals in organizations. Let us pull the views of management scholars on the definition of staffing:

➢ Staffing is the function by which managers build an organization through the recruitment, selection, development of individuals as capable employees.
➢ Staffing is the executive function which involves the recruitment, selection, compensating, training, promotion and retirement of subordinate managers.

➤ Staffing is concerned with the placement, growth, development of all those members of the organization whose function is to get things done through the efforts of other individuals.

➤ Staffing is the whole personnel function of bringing in and training the staff and maintaining favorable conditions of work.

13.3   RESPONSIBILITY FOR STAFFING

As far as the responsibility for staffing is concerned, different scholars have different opinions. Some contend that the responsibility for staffing in an organization should rest upon the personnel department. That is why large organizations have their own personnel departments separately. But some scholars strongly feel that the responsibility for effective execution of staffing of personnel function rests upon all the members in the organization. As Koontz has pointed out, "neither the personnel department nor any other service group is the proper place for staffing function". Staffing is the unassigned, unspecified and implied duty of every manager. In small organizations, where staffing process is comparatively easier, the owner-managers or executives perform the entire staffing function on their own. On the other hand, large business firms tend to maintain separate personnel department to look after the staffing function. The personnel department assists guides and directs the line executives in performing the staffing activities effectively. A line manager cannot alone perform all the activities alone-such as selecting the large number of employees, recruiting them, providing those training, fixing their compensation, maintain their wage records etc. in a big firm. A manager may not have sufficient time at his disposal to perform these multifarious staffing functions. Lack of time apart, a manager may not possess specialized knowledge, skills in performing these activities. Organizations relieve the manager by creating a separate department known as personnel department by creating a separate department known as personnel department the primary responsibility of which is to recruit, select and supply the qualified and dedicated employees to various work units in an organization.

13.4   MANPOWER PLANNING (MPP)

Human resources have one unique feature; it is the only human resources which appreciate with time if sufficient care is taken to impart skill and knowledge. Human resources become an asset in the long run. Organizations which employ and utilize other resources can improve the efficiency of operations only when they have trained manpower. Manpower planning and development on a comprehensive basis assumes greater importance in organizations.

Manpower planning is basically a strategy for procurement, development, and allocation and utilization of an organization's human resources.

Manpower planning:

> is an on going process (it is not a static exercise)
> includes the planning and development of human resources.
> is not just forecasting demand and supply of human resources.
> is not simply a matter concerned with individual career planning and development.
> is not just a planning for changing organizational structure.

Though some firms drift along for several long years without paying adequate attention to human resource programmes, but long-term organizational success cannot be achieved without reasonable effort toward manpower planning. The importance of systematic and comprehensive manpower planning is recognized by organization due to the following reasons:

a.   It is vital for determining personnel needs of the organization in future.
b.   It enables the organization to cope with changes in competitive forces, markets, technology, products, etc.
c.   Manpower planning is an essential component of strategic planning.

In addition to the above, manpower planning focuses on the working conditions and relationships in which individuals function. Manpower planning ensures optimum use of available human resources. It also assesses the future skill requirements of personnel and determines the future levels of recruitment. It provides adequate control measures to ensure that necessary resources are available as and when conditions of business change. Manpower planning also anticipates redundancies and avoids unnecessary dismissals. On the whole, it provides a basis of management and organizational development programmes.

13.5   HUMAN RESOURCE PLANNING (HRP)

HRP basically involves applying the fundamental planning process to the human resource needs of an organization. To be effective, any human resource plan must be derived from the long-range plans of the organization. Unfortunately, HRP is quite often than not, isolated from organizational planning. A common error which human resource planners make is that they focus their attention on the short term replacement needs. They do not tie in with the long-range plans of the enterprise. Focusing on short-term replacement needs is a natural consequence of not integrating human resource planning with organizational planning. Human resource planning and organizational planning must be integrated logically and fruitfully. A non-integrated approach almost always leads to surprises which force the personnel / human resource planners to focus on short-term crisis.

13.6   AIMS AND OBJECTIVES OF HUMAN RESOURCE PLANNING (HRP)

The major aims of human resource planning are to ensure that the organization:

a.   obtains and retains the quality and quantity of manpower it needs;
b.   makes the best use of its manpower resources;
c.   is able-to anticipate the problems arising from potential surpluses or deficits of manpower.

13.7   STEPS IN HUMAN RESOURCE PLANNING

Sometime back there was a lot of ad holism in the matter of recruitment of personnel. This was happening because no prior estimates are made about the manpower needs in a continuous way in organizations. Organizational units never used to maintain an up-to-date record of employees - about their service, resignation, termination, recruitment, death, or disablement etc. Especially in small organizations employees do not get sufficient notice about their approaching retirement. Organizations too, are not prepared for their replacements. Organizations used to make ad hoc decisions in the crisis, in the form of granting extensions to the existing members, and causing frustration among those who are aspiring for higher jobs. Effective human resource planning does not create such embarrassing situations.

In every organization it is necessary to (a) analyze the current manpower supply; (b) tap various recruitment sources whenever and wherever necessary; (c) estimate various factors which generate manpower demands; (d) prepare a rational manpower recruitment plan; and (e) undertake educational, training and development schemes. All these are related to human resource planning.

HR provides, in general, the structure, impetus and assistance. HRP consists of four basic steps:

1.   Determining the organizational objectives.
2.   Determining the skills and expertise required to achieve the organizational and departmental objectives.

3.   Determining the additional human resource requirements in the light of the organization's current human resources.

4.   Developing action plans to meet anticipated human resource needs.

1.   Determining Organizational Objectives

First of all, human resource plans must be based on overall organizational objectives. That is to say, the objectives of human resource planning must be derived from organizational objectives.

The organizational objectives indirectly specify the human resource requirements in terms of number and characteristics of employees. Organizational objectives are basically designed to provide an organizational unit and its members a direction and purpose. The objectives are to be stated in terms of expected results. The organizational goal-setting process begins at the top of the organization with a statement of central purpose. Then, the long-range objectives and strategies are formulated based on the stated central purpose for which organization has come into existence. Based on the long term objectives, the short-term performance objectives are specified. The divisional, departmental objectives are then derived from company's short-term objectives. This process of goal setting is labeled as 'cascade approach' to objective-setting. The cascade approach should not be misunderstood as a form of 'top-down' planning whereby objectives are passed down to the lower levels of the organization. Actually, the basic idea is to involve all levels of management in the planning process. One advantage of involving all the levels of management in organizational planning is that it leads to an upward as well as downward flow of information during the planning stage. Again, this ensures that the objectives are communicated and coordinated throughout the organization. The cascade approach to goal setting thus involves both the operating and divisional managers in the overall company planning process. The human resource development identifies the particular shortcomings and strengths in the organizational personnel, and provides this information to the management. This information is significant in influencing the overall direction of the organization.

2.   Determining the Skills and Expertise Required

Once the organizational, divisional, departmental and individual unit objectives are established, it is the responsibility of the operating managers to determine the skills and expertise required to meet the respective objectives. The key point to note is that the managers should (in addition to the skills and abilities of the present employees) determine the skills and abilities required to meet the objectives. To take hypothetical example, suppose the objective of marketing department is to increase total sales by 20% (of a certain item). Once this objective has been established, the marketing manager must determine precisely how this objective can be translated into human resources. A logical starting point in this connection is to review the present/current job descriptions. Managers should, then, determine the skills necessary to meet the set objectives. Finally, the manager should translate the needed skills and abilities into types and number of employees.

3.   Determining the Net Additional Human Resource Requirements

Having determined the types and number of employees required to achieve the company objectives, the manager must analyze the requirements in the light of the current as well as anticipated human resources of the organization. This requires a thorough analysis of the presently employed personnel as well as forecasting the changes in employment.

Skills inventory. The skill inventory is also called personnel register. This is prepared to determine the net additional requirements of human resources. The Skills inventory provides consolidated information about the organization's human resources. It provides a running commentary on all employees in the organization. A skills inventory, in its simplest form, includes a list of names, characteristics and skills of the employees in an organization. A more comprehensive skills inventory contains the following information:

a.   *Personal data*. Age, sex, marital status of employee.
b.   *Skills*. Educational qualifications, skills, job experience, training etc.
c.   *Special qualifications*. Membership in professional groups, special achievements.
d.   *Salary and job history*. Past as well as present, salary date of increment, various positions held previously prior to the current employment.
e.   *Company data*. Benefit plan date, retirement information, seniority etc.
f.   *Capacity of the individual*. Test scores on psychological and other tests, information about health etc.
g.   *Special preferences of individuals*. Type of job, geographic location etc.

The advantages of preparing a skills inventory can be summarized thus:

a.   It provides a means of quickly and accurately evaluating the skills and abilities that are available in an organization.

b.   It helps in determining the net human resource requirements in the present as well as future.

c.   It helps in taking some crucial managerial decisions - such as accepting a new project, to bid on a new contract, or to introduce a new design or product.

d.   It also aids the management in planning the future employee training and management development programmes.

e.   It helps management in recruiting and selecting new employees.

4.   Developing Action Plans

Soon after determining the net human resource requirements, a manager must develop action plans to achieve the desired results. If the net requirements indicate a genuine need for additional employees, plans must be made to recruit, select, induct, and train new personnel. On the contrary, if a reduction in personnel is necessary (of course, it is a rare case) plans must be made to realize the necessary adjustments through attrition, layoffs or discharges. The action plans so developed should utilize the skills of the present as well as newly recruited personnel to the fullest extent possible.

13.8   REVIEW QUESTIONS

1.   Define staffing.
2.   What is the importance of staffing as function of management?
3.   Define Human Resource Planning (HRP). What are the main objectives of human resource planning?
4.   Write short notes on Manpower Planning (MPP).

STAFFING - SELECTION PROCESS & TECHNIQUES

14.1 SELECTION

Section is a deliberate effort of the organisation to select a fixed number of personnel from a large number of applications. Identifying sources of manpower recruitment and attracting the people to offer for employment, though not strictly the part of employee selection, may be considered as the base for selection. When an organisation gets applications from more candidates than the actual requirement, the organisation has to devise methods through which it can divide these applications into categories those who will be offered employment and those who will not be offered employment. Since more candidates will be rejected than those hired through this process, this is also called as the process of rejection instead of selection. For this reason, selection is frequently described as a negative process in contrast with the positive programme of recruitment.

14.2 SELECTION PROCESS

A selection process involves a number of steps. The basic idea is to solicit maximum possible information about the candidates to ascertain their suitability for employment. Since the type of information required for various positions may vary, it is possible that selection process may have different steps for various positions. For example, more information is required for the selection of managerial personnel as compared to workers. Similarly, various steps of selection process may be different for various organisations because their selection practices may differ. For example, some organisations conduct selection tests of various types while others may not use these. However, a standard selection process has the following steps; screening application forms, selection tests, interview, checking of references, physical examination, approval by appropriate authority and placement. Below is a discussion of the various steps.

1. **Screening of Applications.** Prospective employees have to fill up some sort of application forms. These forms have variety of information about the applicants like their personal bio-data, achievements, experience, etc. Such information is used to screen the applicants who are found to be qualified for the consideration of employment. The information may also be used to keep permanent records of those persons who are selected. Based on the screening of applications, only

those candidates are called for further process of selection who are found to be meeting the job standards of the organisation. When the number of applicants meeting the job standards far exceeds the actual requirements, the organisations decides a suitable number of candidates who will be called for further selection process.

2.   **Selection Tests.** Many organisation hold different kinds of selection tests to known more about the candidates or to reject the candidates who can not be called for interview etc. Selection tests normally supplement the information provided in the application forms. Such forms may contain factual information about candidates. Selection tests may give information about their aptitude, interest, personality, etc. which can not be known by application forms. Types of tests and principles of testing have been discussed in detail in this part of the chapter.

3.   **Interview.** Selection tests are normally followed by personal interview of the candidates. The basis ideal here is to find out overall suitability of candidates for the jobs. It also provides opportunity to give relevant information about the organisation to the candidates. In many cases, interview or preliminary nature can be conducted before the selection tests. For example, in the case of campus selection, preliminary interview is held for short listing the candidates for further process of selection.

4.   **Checking of References.** Many organisatios ask the candidates to provide the names or referees from whom more information about the candidates can be solicited. Such information may be related to character, working, etc. The usual referees may be previous employees, persons associated with the educational institutions from where the candidates have received education, or other persons of prominence who may be aware of the candidates' behaviour and ability. In our country, references are not given adequate importance because of their biasness but these can give very useful information which may not be available otherwise.

5.   **Physical Examination**: Physical examination is carried out to ascertain the physical standard and fitness of prospective employees. The practice of physical examination various a great deal both in terms of coverage and timing. While many organisations do not carry physical examinations at all, others carry on a very comprehensive basis. Some organisations only have general check up of applicants to find the major physical problems which may come in the way of effective discharge of duties. In the context of timing also, some organisations, locate the physical examination near the end of the selection process, other place it relatively early in the process. This letter course is generally followed when there is high demand for physical fitness.

6. **Approval by Appropriate Authority**: On the basis of the above steps, suitable candidates are recommended for selection by the selection committee or personnel department. Though such a committee or personnel department may have authority to select the candidates finally, often it has staff authority to recommend the candidates for selection to the appropriate authority. Organisations may designate the various authorities for approval of final selection candidates for different categories of candidates. Thus for top-level managers, board of directors may be approving authority. In university, it may be syndicate / executive committee. When the approval is received, the candidates are informed about their selection and asked to report for duty to specified persons.

7. **Placement.** After all the formalities are completed, the candidates are placed on their jobs initially on probation basis. The probation period may range from three months to two years. During this period, they are observed keenly, and when they complete this period successfully, they become the permanent employees of the organization.

14.3   SELECTION TESTS

In India, the use of psychological and other tests is gaining popularity. A test is an instrument designed to measure selected psychological factors. Monappa and Saiyadain define tests as follows: 'Psychological tests are essentially and objective and standardised measure of a sample of behaviour.

Three important concepts in this definition are objective, standardised, and sample of behaviour. Objective in this definition refers to the validity and reliability of measuring instruments. Validity of a test refers to the content of measurement, that is, it is measuring the relevant qualities of the candidates. Reliability refers to the consistency with which a test yields the same results throughout a series of measurement. Both these aspects are very important in a test. The second aspect of definition is standardised which refers to uniformity of procedure in administering and scoring the test, as well as of testing conditions which include the time limit, instructions, tester's state of mind and health, and other facilities while administering the test. The third aspect of definition is sample to behaviour which refers to the fact that a total replication of reality in the testing situation is not possible. Test items are representative of eventual behaviour, and need not closely resemble the behaviour the test is to predict.

14.4   TYPES OF TESTS

The use of tests in selection is so widespread that these may be classified in various ways. They may have different objectives and measure different attributes.

However, most of these test fall in one of the following categories: achievement, intelligence, personality, aptitude, and interest.

1.   **Achievement Test** : It is also called performance test or trade test Achievement is concerned with what one has accomplished. When candidates claim that the have done certain things and know these, the achievement test may be conducted to measure how well the candidates know these. A candidate's knowledge may be measured through his answers to certain questions or his performance at a practical test. For example, a typing test may measure the typing performance of a typist in terms of speed, accuracy, and efficiency. Performance test may be administered for selecting employees at operative level as well as at junior management level.

2.   **Intelligence Test** Intelligence test tries to measure the level of intelligence of a candidate. This test generally includes verbal comprehension, word fluency, memory, inductive reasoning, number facility, speed of perception, spatial visualisation, etc. The score on the test are usually expressed numerically as intelligent Quotient (IQ) which can be calculated as follows:

$$IQ = \frac{Mental\,age}{Actual\,age} \times 100$$

It means that the IQ is derived by converting actual age into mental age and multiplying it by 100 in order to facilitate comparison. Higher is the figure, higher is the level of intelligence. Intelligence test is designed on the basis of age - groups. Thus each age - group may have different intelligence test.

The basic idea behind intelligence is that organisation is able to get people with higher intelligence, its training and learning process will be easier because intelligent employees learn faster that dull employees.

3.   **Personality Test.** The personality testis s administered predict performance success for jobs that require dealing with people, or jobs that are essentially supervisory or managerial in character. Dimensions of personality such as interpersonal competence, dominance - submission, extroversion- introversion, self-confidence, leadership ability, patience, and ambition can be measured through personality tests. Personality test is essential a be employed by the organisation. Among the most widely used personality testis Thematic Evaluation of Management Potential (TEMP).

4.   **Aptitude Test.** Aptitude test is used for measuring human performance characteristics related to the possible development of proficiency on specific

jobs. These basic characteristics can be thought of as aptitudes. As such, aptitude test measures the latent or potential characteristics to do something provided proper environment and training are provided to the individuals. This test is more valid when the applicants have no experience or very little experience along the lines of the jobs. Specific tests have been developed for jobs that required clerical, mechanical, spatial relationships, and manual dexterity abilities and skills. However, aptitude lest does not measure motivation. Since on the job motivations is found to be more important than aptitude for the job, aptitude test is supplemented by interest tests.

5. **Interest Test.** Interest test is designed to discover a person's area of interest, and to identify the kind of jobs that will satisfy him. It s assumed that a person who is interested in a job can do much better than the person who is not interested. Interest test generally measures interest in outdoor activities, mechanical, computational, scientific, persuasive, artistic, literary, musical, clerical, social services, etc.

The above discussion shows that different tests are used for different purpose. Each of them has the usefulness and limitations in specified areas. Therefore, a combination of tests should be for selection purpose. Moreover, these tests should be released with the nature of posts to be filled up.

14.5   ADVANTAGES OF SELECTION TESTS

Various steps of selection process including selection tests are meant to solicit information about the candidates so as to arrive at a decision to select the most desirable candidates out to several available. Since only some information is available from other sources like application forms, reference, etc. selection tests are used to solicit ore information about the candidates. Therefore, the use of selection tests has many advantages.

1. Selection tests are standrdised and unbiased methods of soliciting information about the prospective employees. Thus a person who does not get selected on the basis of selection tests can not argue for the partiality in selection process. It is to be noted that in many organizations, impartiality in selection process is of prime importance like public sector organisations.

2. Selection tests can be used to weed out the large number of candidates who may not be considered for employment in the organisation. Normally, organisations receive application. They all meet the basis requirements of the jobs, but all can not be called for interview because it is very time - consuming process. Selection tests will provide the cut - off point above which candidates can be called for interview. Thus the tests will save lot of time and money.

3. The tests are able to uncover the qualities and potentials of prospective employees which can not be known by other methods including personal interview. Since the people are taken in the organsation not only for the present jobs but they are promoted over the period of time, tests provide good opportunities to test potentials for such promotions also. Thus tests are more reliable source for predicting the overall suitability of candidates for the employment.

14.6   LIMITATIONS OF SELECTION TESTS

Selection tests may provide some useful information but they suffer from some limitations also. Two such limitations are quite important which suggest that use of tests should be supplemented by other means of soliciting information about the candidates.

1. Selection tests can not make a hundred per cent prediction of an individual's on - the job success. At best, they just reveal that those who have scored above the cut-off point (other things being equal) will be more successful than those who have scored below the cut-off point. Therefore, it is desirable to use tests only as supplementary method of selection.

2. These are suitable when there is large number of candidates for limited number of jobs or positions. If the number of candidates is small, the use of tests is not economical. In such a case, it is desirable to select persons on the basis of interview only.

Besides these two limitations, many people criticise tests on the basis that these discriminate against the deprived classes because affluent classes can know better how to defect the tests. However, this limitation can be overcome by suitable design and administration of tests. A further criticism is put against the tests that these often invade privacy of people because they put many questions on the personal life of the candidates.

14.7   PRECAUTIONS IN USING SELECTION TESTS

Various limitations of selection tests suggest that these should be used cautiously. Test results can improve decision making regarding selection of employees, and as a result, organizations can select the best possible candidates if following precautions are taken in using the tests.

1. A test can be effective only when it has validity. The validity of a test is the degree to which is measures what it intends to measure. Thus a valid test is one which accurately predicts the criteria of job success. In the absence of validity of

test, it may give wrong result and the persons selected on its basis may be even inferior to those who have been rejected.

2.   Another feature which is important in a test is its reliability. The reliability of a test is the consistency with which it yields the same scores throughout a series of measurements. Thus, if a test has high reliability, a person who is tested a second or third time with the same test and under the same conditions will obtain the same result.

3.   Norms should be developed as a source of reference on all tests used in selection. Norms are standardised scores that help translate raw scores into a comparative statement. Some companies use minimum marks obtained in a test while others use cut off score for selecting candidates for further selection process. Norms can be fixed on the basis of success or failure of employees in the organisation selected on the basis of similar tests.

4.   Tests should not be used merely to decide cut-off point of weeding out the candidates. Instead the test administrators should ensure that tests have validity and therefore, these can play important role in the selection process. In order to make maximum advantages of tests, proper wightage can be given to scores in the tests. This may help in avoiding personal biases in the selection considerably.

5.   Test administration, scoring, and interpretation require technical competence and training in testing. Therefore, tests should be handled by properly trained and competent people. In fact, some of the standardised tests insist that their use be restricted to registered approved users only so that these are not used for the selection which may give horrible results.

6.   The tests should be used as an additional factor in selection a candidate. If other factors in selection like information given in application forms, references, and interviews are used alongwith tests, decision making regarding the selection of a candidate is improved to high level.

14.8   INTERVIEW

Interview is selection technique that enables the interviewer to view the total individual and to appraise him and his behaviour. It consists of interaction between interviewer and applicant. If handled properly, it can be a powerful technique in achieving accurate information and getting access to material otherwise unavailable. However, if the interview is not handled properly, it can be a source of bias, restricting or distorting the flow of communication. Interview is the most widely used selection technique because of its easeness.

There can be several types of interviews: preliminary interview, stress interview, patterned interview, and depth interview. Preliminary interview is held to find out whether the candidate is required to be interviewed in more details. Stress interview is directed to create situations of stress to find out whether the applicant can perform well in a condition of stress. Patterned interview is structured and questions asked are decided in advance. This is done to maintain uniformity in different boards of interviewers. Depth interview, also known as non-directive interview, covers the complete life history of the applicant and includes such areas as the candidate's work experience, academic qualification, health, interests, hobbies, etc, The method is informal, conversational with freedom of expression to the candidate.

14.9   PRINCIPLES OF INTERVIEWING

As indicated earlier, interview is the most frequently used technique for selection. However, it can give better results only when it is conducted properly. Following points can be taken into consideration to make and interview more effective.

1.   There should be proper planning before holding the interview. Planning may include determination of who will conduct interview, what way it will be conducted, on what basis the candidate is to be evaluated, and how much weightage will be given to interview in the total selection process. Preparation on these lines will avoid ambiguity and confusion in interviewing.

2.   There should be proper setting for conducting interview. The setting is required both of physical and mental nature. The physical setting for the interview should be comfortable and free from many physical disturbance.

      The mental setting should be one of rapport between the interviewer and the candidate. The interview should not start unless the candidate is composed and overcomes from the mental stress of the interview. It is a well known fact that the candidates feel nervous the moment they enter in the interview room. They may react badly about any showing of surprise of disapproval of their clothes or manner. In such a case, there may not be proper evaluation of the candidates.

3.   When the candidate feels at ease, the interview may be started. At this stage, the interview obtains the desired information and may provide the information sought by the candidate. The interviewer can solicit important personal information if he demonstrates a basic liking and respect of people. He should ask questions in a manner that encourages the candidate to talk. He should listen to carefully when the candidate is furnishing the information. This gives an impression to the candidate that the interviewer is quite serious about him and he will do his best.

4.   The interview of the candidate should be closed with pleasant remarks. If possible, the interviewer should given an indication about the likely end of the interview. 'Saying thanks', 'good whishes' or similar things carries much better impression about the interviewer.

5.   Immediately after the interview is over, the interviewer should make an evaluation of the candidates. At this stage the things are quite fresh in his mind. He can give remarks about the characteristics of the candidate or give grade or mark as the case may be. This will help the interviewer to make a comparative evaluation of all candidates easily.

14.10   REVIEW QUESTIONS

1.   What do you mean by selection for employment? Outline a suitable selection process for a large business organisation.

2.   Discuss the major tests that are used in selection. What are the benefits and problems in using selection tests? What precautions should be taken to make selection tests more effective?

3.   Discuss the various types of selection interviews. On what factors does the success of an interview depend?.

HUMAN RESOURCE MANAGEMENT

15.1   INTRODUCTION

Personnel management is concerned with the effective use of the skills of people. They may be sales people in a store, clerks in an office, operators in a factory, or technicians in a research laboratory. In a business, personnel management starts with the recruiting and hiring of qualified people and continues with directing and encouraging their growth as they encounter problems and tensions that arise in working towards established goals. In addition to recruiting and hiring, some of the responsibilities of a personnel manager are,

➢ To classify jobs and prepare wage and salary scales.

➢ To advice employees.

➢ To deal with disciplinary problems.

➢ To negotiate with labour unions and service union contracts

➢ To develop safety standards and practices.

➢ To manage benefit programs, such as group insurance, health, and retirement plans.

➢ To provide for periodic reviews of the performance of each individual employee, and for recognition of his or her strengths and needs for further development.

➢ To assist individuals in their efforts to develop and qualify for more advanced jobs.

➢ To plan and supervise training programs

➢ To keep abreast of developments in personnel management.

To understand the personnel management's job consider the following examples of challenging employee situations.

The firm's employee – especially the most qualified ones – can get comparable, if not better jobs with other employers.

When a firm faces a scarcity of supervisory and specialized personnel with adequate experience and job capabilities, it has to train and develop its own people. This can be time consuming and expensive.

The cost of hiring and training employees at all levels is increasing, for instance, several thousand rupees for a salesperson. A mistake in hiring or in slow and inefficient methods of training can be costly.

Personnel managers must comply with the law by employing, training and promoting women and persons from minority groups. The problem in doing so is that many of these employees have not had appropriate experience and education in the past.

Most employees, whether or not represented by labour unions, continue to seek improvements in direct compensation, employee benefits, and working conditions. All commitments must be based upon what the firm can afford, comply with current practices of other employers, and be understood and accepted by the employee. To do this, all employee policies and operating procedures should be developed and negotiated with great care.

Some employees may not perform satisfactorily simply because their firm offers competitive compensation, benefits, and working conditions. In addition to these financial or physical, compensations, they want responsibility, the opportunity to develop, and recognition of accomplishment in their jobs.

The law has requirements for pension and other benefit plans, and also mandatory retirement age. Complying with such changes presents real challenges. Personnel management works to achieve practical solutions to such problems. In large firms, it generally provides support to line management. In this staff capacity, the personnel department has the responsibility to develop and implement policies, procedures, and programs for recruitment, selection, training, placement, safety, employee benefits and services, compensation, labour relations, organization planning, and employee development.

Often, the owner – manager of a firm also has to be the personnel manager. In such a case it is necessary to have an overview of current trends and practices in personnel management. All small businesses must staff their operations. This involves brining new people into the business and making sure they are productive additions to the enterprise. Effective human resource management matches and develops the abilities job candidates and employees with the needs of the firm. A responsive personnel system assists in this process and is a key ingredient for growth.

Human resource management is a balancing act. At one extreme, we hire only qualified people who are well suited to the firm's needs. At the other extreme, we train and develop employees to meet the firm's needs. Most expanding small businesses fall between the two extremes i.e., they hire the best people they can find and afford, and they also recognize the need to train and develop both current and new employees as the firm grows.

One function of personnel management deals with how to hire and train the right people and addresses the characteristics of an effective personnel system, such as;

> Assessing personnel needs
> Recruiting personnel
> Screening personnel
> Selecting and hiring personnel
> Orienting new employees to the business
> Deciding compensation issues

Another function addresses the training and development side of human resource management. A thin function deals with how the personnel system and the training and development functions come together to build employee trust and productivity. These three functions stress the importance of a good human resource management climate and provide specific guidelines for creating such a climate.

15.2   HUMAN RESOURCE MANAGEMENT QUESTIONNAIRE

> Does the business have a plan for forecasting long- term personnel needs?
> Are there guidelines for hiring personnel, or are employees hired based on gut feelings?

- Are there job descriptions for all positions?
- What do employees like about their jobs?
- What do employees leave the organization?
- Is there an active training programme? It is based on an assessment of where the firm is now or where it should be in the future?
- Are a variety of training programmes available?
- How is morale in the firm?
- Do employees really believe what you have to say?
- Are all employees treated fairly?

15.3 DEVELOPING A PERSONNEL SYSTEM – ASSESSING PERSONNEL NEEDS

The small business owner should base the firm's personnel policies on explicit, well proven principles. Small businesses that follow these principles have higher performance and growth rates than those that do not follow them. The most important of these principles are,

- All positions should be filled with people who are both willing and able to do the job.

- The more accurate and realistic the specifications of and skill requirements for each job, the more likely it is that workers will be matched to the right job and therefore, be more competent in that job.

- A written job description and definition are the keys to communicating job expectations to people. Do the best job you can is terrible job guidance.

- Employees chosen on the basis of the best person available are more effective than those chosen on the basis of friendship or expediency or recommendation.

- If specified job expectations are clearly spelled out, and if performance appraisals are based on these expectations, performance is higher. Also, employee training results in higher performance if it is based on measurable learning objectives.

➤ The first step in assessing personnel needs for the small business is to conduct an audit of future personnel needs.

PERSONNEL MANAGEMENT MUST ASK TO HIMSELF:

➤ Can the work load I visualize be accomplished by the present work face? Will more or fewer employees be needed? Consider seasonal patterns of demand and probable turnover rates.

➤ Can any jobs be eliminated to free people for other work? What balance of full-time or part time, temporary or permanent, hourly or salaried personnel do I need?

➤ What does the labour supply look like in the future?

➤ Will I be able to fill some of the jobs I have identified? How easily?

➤ What qualifications are needed in my personnel?

Develop a method to forecast labour demand based on your answer to these questions. Once your needs are estimated, determine strategies to meet them.

The process of selecting a competent person for each position is best accomplished through a systematic definition of the requirements for each job, including the skills, knowledge and other qualifications that employees must possess to perform each task to guarantee that personnel needs are adequately specified,

1.   Conduct a job analysis
2.   Develop a written job description, and
3.   Prepare a job specification.

15.4   SCOPE OF PERSONNEL MANAGEMENT

Scope of personnel management was very limited in beginning. In those days was called "Health and happiness" department. The scope of management in general and personnel in particular has changed considerably, covering more areas and responsibilities. According to American Society for Training and Development (ASTD) it is broadly classified into nine major areas namely,

1.   Human Resource Planning (HRP)
2.   Design of Organisation and Job
3.   Selection and Staffing
4.   Training and Development
5.   Organisation Development
6.   Compensation and Benefits
7.   Employee Assistance
8.   Union / Labour Relations
9.   Personnel Research and Information Systems

Human Resource Planning (HRP)

HRP, this function is to ensure, the right type of persons at the right time at right place. It also forecast demand and supplies and identify sources.

Design of Organisation and Job

The objective of Design of organization and job is to form the organization structure, authority, relationship and responsibilities and work contents for each position in organization.

Selection and Staffing

This is the process of recruitment and selection of staff. In recruitment, process of attracting qualified and competent personnel for different jobs. This includes identification of existing sources of labour market, new development of new sources and the need for attracting a large number of potential applicants so that a good selection is possible. Selection is concerned with the development of selection policies and procedures and evaluation of potential employees in terms of job specification. Selection process includes the development of application blanks, valid and reliable tests, interview techniques, employee referral techniques, evaluation and selection of personnel in terms of job specifications, the making up of final recommendations to the line management, and the sending of offers and rejection letters.

Training and Development

Process of increasing the capabilities of individuals and groups to that they may contribute effectively to attainment of organizational goals. This includes, the determination of training needs of personnel at all levels, skill training, employee counseling, and programmes for managerial, professional and employee development. Self initiated developmental activities, (formal education) during off hours (including school/college/professional institutes) reading and participation in the activities of the community.

Organisation Development

This is an important aspect where by developing healthy interpersonal and inter-group relationship in the organization.

Compensation and Benefits

The bulk of your employee's earnings should come from a base salary competitive with the pay offered by other similar local firms. It may be possible to supplement the base salary with some form of incentive, such as a small commission or quote bonus plan. Try to relate the incentive to both your goals of your employees. Whatever plan you use, be sure each employee understands it completely.

Employee Assistance

Each employee is unique in character, Personality, expectation and temperament. By and large each one of them faces problems every day. Some are personal some are official. In either case he remains worried such worries must be removed to make him more productive and happy. Counseling is one such step.

Union / Labour Relations

This is very important for enhancing the productivity in an organization. This is one of the important areas of personnel management.

Personnel Research and Information Systems

This areas is concerned with, a systematic inquiry into any aspect of the broad question of how to make more effective an organization's personnel programmes recruitment, selection, development, utilization off, and accommodation to, human resources. Procedures and policies and findings submitted to the top executive. Data relating to quality, wages, productivity, grievances absenteeism, labour turnover, strikes, lock-outs, accidents etc., which are collected and supplied to the top management so that it may review, alter or improve existing personnel policies, programmes and procedures. Morale and Attitude surveys.

15.5 OBJECTIVES OF PERSONNEL MANAGEMENT

The following are the objectives of personnel management.

1.   Study the requirement of occupation.
2.   Development of recruitment procedure.
3.   Development of Management Information Systems (MIS)
4.   Forecasting of future requirement, recruitment, training.
5.   Periodical appraisals by means of questionnaires, interviews, seminars contests etc., to insure the most complete development and most efficient use of individual's ability.
6.   Development and use of tests and other refined techniques in the specific placement of workers and executives.
7.   Formulation of best methods of human energy.
8.   Determination of optimal conditions of work with clear cut job description.
9.   Analysis of characteristics of individual organizations for the determination of the type or types that is best adaptive to serve both the economic, social and broadly human objectives of individual organization.
10. _ Examination and control of motivating forces in the case of both workers and executive which influence the harmonious relations in the industrial situations.

15.6 TRAINING - INTRODUCTION

Training making the employees more effective and productive on their present jobs. Also it provides opportunities to employees in acquiring appropriate attitudes and in developing skills which will enable them to occupy higher places in the organization. An employee's success at a given job largely depends upon his positive response to training and his willingness to accept instruction and gain the techniques and skills required performing the job at an acceptable level of efficiency.

15.7   NEED FOR TRAINING

The need for training in part depends upon the company's selection and promotion policies. Companies that attempt to employ only people who already have the needed skills, place less emphasis on training. On the other hand, firms that stress promotion from within may have to take special steps to ensure that employee develop the skills which will be needed. Three trends have contributed, in recent years, to more attention to the development of skill. One, fewer and fewer skills are now regarded 'born' that cannot be taught. It is hoped that one can learn almost all aspects of a job by reading. That is why we find now a days almost all technical details of a job written out in the instruction manuals. Two, the accelerated rate of technological change in the plant, office, and market place - is making many skills obsolete. Workers have to be retrained to do new tasks. Three globalization is making it increasingly essential for workers and executives to be aware of diverse gaffes, life styles and attitudes of people in other countries. They need to learn many things such as how to introduce oneself before a foreign client, converse and negotiate, talk on telephone, use body language and so on.

15.8   OBJECTIVES OF TRAINING

The major objectives of training are as follows:-

a.   To train the employee in the company culture pattern.
b.   To train the employee to increase his quantity and quality of output.
c.   To train the employee for promotion to higher jobs.
d.   To train the employee to avoid social mistakes
e.   To train the employee toward better job adjustment and high morale.
f.   To reduce supervision, wastages and accidents.

15.9   IMPORTANCE OF TRAINING

Training and development programmes, help remove performance deficiencies in employees. This is particularly true when,

1.   the deficiency is caused by a lack of ability rather than a lack of motivation to perform.

2.   The individual (s) involved have the aptitude and motivation needed to learn to do the job better, and

3.   Supervisors and peers are supportive of the desired behaviors.

There is greater stability, flexibility and capacity growth in an organization. Training contributes to employee stability in a least two ways. Employees become efficient after undergoing training. Efficient employees contribute to the growth of the organization. Growth reader's stability to the work-force. Further trained employees tend to stay with the organization. They seldom leave the company training makes the employees versatile in operations. Flexibility is therefore ensured. Growth indicates prosperity, which is reflected in increased profits from year to year. Accidents, scrap and damage to machinery and equipment can be avoided or minimized through training. Further needs of employees will be met through training and development programmes?

15.10 RESPONSIBILITY FOR TRAINING

Training is the responsibility of four main groups.
1.   The top management, which frames the training policy.
2.   The personnel management department, which plans, establishes and evaluates instructional programmes.
3.   Supervisors, who implement and apply developmental procedure, and
4.   Employees, who provide feedback, revision and suggestions for corporate educational endeavors.

15.11 PRINCIPLES OF TRAINING

1.   Top management should give high priority and take personal interest and decide upon the training policy based on organizational objective.
2.   Managerial and supervisory personnel must be made to involve and should be impressed upon regarding the benefits of training.
3.   Training programme must be need oriented and be accepted to all concerned.
4.   Selection of trainees must be made on the basic of interest in the leaving and acquiring skill process.
5.   Duration must be short enough to spare the employees without hampering regular/ normal work.
6.   The number of participants limited to 15 or 20 in order that they can interact and take active part in the programme.
7.   As far as possible supervisor officers of the trainees should not be present in the training are to enable the trainees to express then ideas and opinion freely.
8.   Training must be arranged outside the industry and the participants freed mentally and physically from the routine duties.
9.   Regular follow up procedure to evaluate the usefulness of the course as well as trainees program.

15.12 TRAINING METHODS

As a result of research in the field of training, a number of programmes are available. Some of these are new methods, while others are improvements over the traditional methods. The training programmes commonly used to train operative and supervisory personnel are discussed below. These programmes are classified into on-the-job and off-the job training programmes.

ON-THE-JOB-TRAINING METHODS

This type of training, also known as job instruction training, is the most commonly used methods. Under this method, the individual is placed on a regular job and taught the skills necessary to perform that job. The trainee learns under the supervision and guidance of a qualified worker or instructor. On-the-job training has the advantage of offering first hand knowledge and experience under the actual working conditions. On-the-job training methods include job rotation, coaching, job instruction or training through step-by-step and committee assignments.

a.   Job Rotation

This type of training involves the movement of the trainee from one job to another. The trainee receives job knowledge and gains experience from his supervisor or trainer in each of the different jobs assignment. Though this type of training is common in training, managers for general management positions, trainees can also be rotated from job to job in work ship jobs. This method gives an opportunity to the trainee to understand the problems of employee on other jobs and respect them.

b.   Coaching

The trainee is placed under a particular supervisor who functions as a coach in training the individual. The supervisor provides feedback to the trainee on his performance and offers him some suggestions for improvement. Often the trainee shares some of the duties and responsibilities of the coach and relieves him of his burden. A limitation of this method of training is that the trainee may not have the freedom or opportunity to express his own ideas.

c.   Job Instruction

This method is also known as training through step by step. Under this method, trainer explains the trainee the way of doing the jobs, job knowledge and skills and allows him to do the job.

d.   Committee assignments

Under the committee assignment, group of trainees are given and asked to solve an actual organizational problem. The trainees solve the problem jointly. It develops team work.

OFF-THE-JOB TRAINING METHODS

Under this method of training trainee is separated from the job situation and his attention is focused upon learning the material related to his future job performance. Since the trainee is not distracted by job requirements, he can place his entire concentration on learning the job rather than spending his time in performing it. There is an opportunity for freedom of expression for the trainees. Off-the-job training methods are as follows:

a.   Vestibule Training

In this method, actual work conditions are simulated in a class room. Material, files and equipment those are used in actual jobs performance are also used in training. This type of training is commonly used for training personnel for clerical and semi-skilled jobs. The duration of this training ranges from a few days to a few weeks. Theory can be related to practice in this method.

b.   Role Playing

It is defined as a method of human interaction that involves realistic behavior in imaginary situations. This method of training involves action, doing and practice. This method is mostly used for developing interpersonal interactions and relations.

c.   Lecture Method

The lecture is a traditional and direct method of instruction. The instructor organizes the material and gives it to a group of trainees in the form of a talk. To be effective, the lecture must motivate and create interest among the trainees. The major limitation of the lecture method is does not provide for transfer of training effectively.

d.   Conference or discussion

It is a method in training the clerical, professional and supervisory personnel. This method involves a group of people who pose ideas, examine and share facts, ideas and data, test assumptions, and draw conclusions, all of which contribute to the improvement of job performance. Discussion has the distinct advantage over the lecture method in that the discussion involves two-way communication and hence feed back is provided. The participants feel free to speak in small groups. The success of this method depends on the leadership qualities of the person, who leads the group.

e.   Programmed instruction

In recent years this method has become popular. The subject matter to be learned is presented in a series of carefully planned sequential units. These units are arranged from simple to more complex levels of instruction. The trainee goes through these units by answering questions or filling the blanks. This method is expensive and time consuming.

15.13   STEPS IN TRAINING PROGRAMMES

Training programmes are a costly affair, and a time consuming process. Therefore, they need to be drafted very carefully. Usually in the organisation of training programmes, the following steps are considered necessary.

1.   Discovering or identifying the training needs.
2.   Getting ready for the job
3.   Preparation of the learner
4.   Presentation of operation and knowledge
5.   Performance try-out
6.   Follow-up and Evaluation of the programme.

1.   DISCOVERING OR IDENTIFYING TRAINING NEEDS

A training programme should be established only when it is felt that it would assist in the solution of specific operational problems. The most important step, in the first place, is to make a thorough analysis of the entire organisation, its operations and manpower resources available in order to find out "the trouble spots" where training may be needed.

Identification of training needs must contain three types of analyses are organizational analysis, operations analysis and man analysis.

Organizational analysis centre primarily upon the determination of the organizations goals, its resources, and the allocation of the resources as they relate to the organizational goals. The analysis of the organizational goals establishes the frame work in which, training needs can be defined more clearly.

Operational analysis focuses on the task or job regardless of the employee doing the job. This analysis includes the determination of the worker must do the specific worker behavior required, if the job is to be performed effectively.

Man analysis reviews the knowledge, attitudes and skills of the incumbent in each position and determines what knowledge, attitudes or skills he must acquire and what alterations in his behaviors he must make if he is to contribute satisfactorily to the attainment of organizational objectives.

2.   GEETING READY FOR THE JOB

Under this step, it is to be decided who is to be trained, the new comer or the older employee, or the supervisory staff, or all of them selected from different departments. The trainer has to be prepared for the job, for he is the key figure in the entire programme.

3.   PREPARATION OF THE LEARNER

Following are the steps involved in the preparation of the learner.

a.   in putting the learners at ease
b.   in stating the importance and ingredients of the job, and its relationship to work flow.
c.   in explaining why he is being taught
d.   in creating interest and encouraging questions, finding out what the learner already knows about his job or other jobs.
e.   in explaining the `why' of the whole job and relating it to some job the worker already knows.
f.   in placing the learners as close to his normal working position as possible.
g.   in familiarizing him with the equipment, materials, tools and trade terms.

4.   PRESENTATION OF OPERATION AND KNOWLEDGE

This is the most important step in a training programme. The trainer should clearly tell show, illustrate and question in order to put over the new knowledge and operations. The learner should be told of the sequence of the entire job, and why each step in its performance necessary. Instructions should be given clearly, completely and patiently; there should be an emphasis on key points and one point should be explained at a time. For this purpose, the trainer should demonstrate or make use of audio-visual aids and should ask the trainee to repeat the operations. He should also be encouraged to ask questions in order to indicate that he really knows and understands the job.

5.   PERFORMANCE TRY OUT

Under this, the trainee is asked to go through the job several times slowly, explaining, him each step. Mistakes are corrected, and if necessary, some complicated steps are done for the trainee the first time. The trainee is asked to do the job, gradually building up skill and speed. As soon as the trainee demonstrates that he can do the job in a right way, he is put on his own, but not abandoned.

6.   FOLLOW-UP

This step is undertaken with a view to testing the effectiveness of training efforts. This consists in:

a.   Putting a trainee "on his own"

b.   Checking frequently to be sure that he has followed instructions, and

c.   Tapering off extra supervision and close follow-up until he is qualified to work with normal supervision. It is worth remembering that if the learner hasn't learnt, the teacher hasn't taught.

15.14   IMPLEMENTATION OF THE TRAINING PROGRAMME

Once the training programme has been designed, it needs to be implemented. Implementation is beset with certain problems. In the first place, most managers are action oriented and frequently say they are too busy to engage in training efforts. Secondly availability of trainers is a problem. In addition to possessing communication skills, the trainers must know the company's philosophy, its objectives, its formal and informal organization, and the goals of training programme. Training and development requires a higher degree of creativity than, perhaps, any other personnel specialty.

Programme implementation involves action on the following lines:

a.   Deciding the location and organizing training and other facilities.
b.   Scheduling the training programme.
c.   Conducting the programme
d.   Monitoring the progress of trainees

15.15   EVALUATION OF TRAINING PROGRAMME

Evaluation is an essential feature of all programmes for the training of employees. The concept of evaluation is most commonly interpreted in determining the effectiveness of a programme in relation to its objectives.

Evaluation can be done for various purposes. The evaluator should be clear about why he has been asked to evaluate training. Evaluation of training programme may be done.

1.   To increase effectiveness of the training programme while it is going on.
2.   To increase the effectiveness of the programmes to be held next time.
3.   To help participants to get the feedback for their improvement and efficient.
4.   To find out to what extent the training objectives are achieved.

15.16 EFFECTIVE MANAGEMENT

The basic objective of management functions and techniques is to make one an effective manager. The organizations require effective managers because these bears cost for employing them. However, the basic question is: who is an effective manager? From this point of view, one must identify the various characteristics of effective managers so that attempts are made to correlate the various functions of management for achieving effectiveness.

Truly speaking, the concept and criteria of effectiveness are quite debatable points in management. Effectiveness is not one-dimensional concept that can be measured and predicted from a set of clear-cut criteria. However, managerial effectiveness can be defined mostly in terms of organizational goal-achieving behavior.

15.16.1 Effectiveness and Efficiency

Often a confusion arises between effectiveness and efficiency as both these terms are used quite closely and, sometimes, interchangeably, though both these denote different states of affairs. For example, Barnard has viewed that:

"Organisation effectiveness is the degree to which operative goals have been attained while the concept of efficiency represents the cost/benefit rate incurred in the pursuit of these goals".

Thus, effectiveness is related to goals which is externally focused. Efficiency is used in engineering way and it refers to the relationship between input and output. This denotes how much inputs have been used to produce certain amount of outputs. It is not necessary that both go together always. For example, Barnard says that, " When unsought consequences are trivial, or insignificant, effective action is efficient: when unsought consequences are not trivial, effective action may be inefficient". These may be three types of situations:

1. An organization may be efficient but may not be effective.
2. An organization may be effective but may not be effective.
3. An organization may both efficient and effective.

In the first situation, the organization may be efficient but it may not be effective because efficiency refers to internal conversion processes whereas effectiveness reflects external phenomenon.

In the second situation, an organization may be effective at a point of time without being efficient. It may not be efficient but because of the external environment, it may earn profit and show effectiveness.

In the third situation, an organization may be efficient and effective both at the same time. Many types of organizations may fall under this category, and this is the situation which is required for the long term survival of organization. It is in this situation that people tend to use efficiency and effectiveness interchangeably.

15.16.2 Effectiveness Manager

An effective manager is one who is positive in his personality, that is, what type of person he is, his managerial process, and results of his managerial process, although all these are interdependent.

1. **The Person.** The Basic question in this context is what types of persons are most likely to become effective managers, and what types fail? There are various such studies to suggest the possible personal qualities of a successful manager.

2. **The Process.** Managerial effectiveness depends upon the managerial process involved in managing the affairs of the organization. In this category, there is a long list, because it is not just possible to specify here the behavior of a manager as related to his various functions. However, the following are some of the important behaviors of effective managers.

1. They manager people instead of work.
2. They plan and organize effectively.
3. They set goal realistically.
4. They derive decision by group consensus but accept responsibility for them.
5. They delegate frequently and effectively.
6. They rely on others for help in solving problems.
7. They communicate effectively.
8. They are stimulus to action.
9. They co-ordinate effectively.
10. They co-operate with others.
11. They show consistent and dependable behavior.
12. They win gracefully.
13. They express hostility tactfully.

3. **The Results.** Effective managers and effective managing will lead inevitably to good things, that is, the achievement of goals for which they are working in the organization. Thus what will be the outcome depends upon the type of organizations they are working for. There may be some conflict about the organizational goals and their measurement criteria, but here it is sufficient to say that managerial actions and behaviors must contribute to the realization of organizational goals.

15.17 REVIEW QUESTIONS

1. Are management and administration different? How will you resolve their terminological conflict?
2. What is the nature of management principles? How do they contribute in effective managing? What precautions will you take while applying management principles in practice?
3. What is effective management? How does effectiveness differ from efficiency?
4. Discuss the main characteristics of an effective manager?

DIRECTING / DIRECTION

16.1 INTRODUCTION

Direction represents one of the essential functions of management because if deals with human relations. Direction is also, frequently and by some, labeled as 'actuating'. Once the organizational plans have been laid down, the structure being designed, and competent people brought in to fill various positions in organization, direction starts. Direction is the managerial function of guiding, motivating, leading, and supervising the subordinates to accomplish desired objectives. Acquiring physical and human assets and suitably placing them will not suffice; what is more important is that people must be directed toward organizational goals. Without proper direction and supervision employees become inactive, dull and inefficient and consequently the physical assets like machinery and plant will be put to ineffective use.

16.2 DIRECTION DEFINED

Direction is the essence of all operations in an organization. It is defined as the process of instructing, counseling, guiding, motivating and leading the human factor to achieve organizational goals effectively.

1.   Direction consists of the process and techniques utilizing in issuing instructing and making certain that operations are carried out as originally planned. (Haimann).

2.   Direction is a complex function that includes all those activities which are designed to encourage subordinates to work effectively and efficiently in both the short and long run. [Koontz and O'Donnell].

3.   Direction is telling people what to do and seeing that they do it to the best of their ability. (Date).

16.3 FEATURES

The basic features of 'direction' – as revealed by the above definitions – may be stated thus :

1. Direction is an indispensable managerial function because it deals with human resources and human relations.

2. Direction in aimed at maintaining harmony among employees and groups in an organization.

3. Direction is the process around which all other management function evolve. Direction, therefore, represents the 'nucleus' of an organization.

4. Direction is necessary to integrate the individual and organizational goals.

5. Direction consists of four elements, viz., communication, motivation, leadership, and supervision.

6. Direction is universal and all-pervading function in the sense managers perform this function at all levels in an organization.

7. Direction is a continuous function. It is ongoing process; not just one-shot deal.

8. Direction provides link between different functions in an organization.

16.4   IMPORTANCE OF DIRECTION

Direction is both complex and important. It is complex because it deals exclusively with people. While dealing with people a manger quite often than not performs a tight-ropewalk. It is not a simple feat for the manager to direct people at work. Direction is important because in its absence subordinates may not perceive the organizational goals. Subordinates must be communicated what the organizational goals are, what the employees should do to achieve them, how they should do their jobs etc. Direction is important because of the following reasons :

1. Directing bridges the gap between managerial decisions and actual execution by people.

2. Direction is the 'make-happen' phase of management.

3. Direction is an integrating function of management as it effectively integrates the individual goals with organizational objectives. In the absence of integration the individual goals may be incongruent with the fundamental organizational objectives. As Koontz and O'Donnell contend" …. People are not primarily interested in enterprise objectives;

they have objectives of their own." In order to manage effectively a manager should integrate the individual goals with the organizational objectives.

4.   Direction facilities the introduction of changes in an organization. People have a tendency of resisting change in organization; they need direction to accept and implement changes in the right direction for the betterment of an organization.

16.5   PRINCIPLES OF DIRECTION

(a)   **Harmony of Objectives.** Direction function must first of all resolve the conflict between individual goals and organizational objectives. A manager must try to bring harmony and fusion between individual employees, groups and organization. A manager should foster the sense of belonging to the organization among the individuals so that they can identify themselves with the company. When both the interests are integrated contribution of subordinates to the company will be maximum. It leads to efficiency and effectiveness.

(b)   **Utility of Direction.** A sound principle of direction is that the subordinates should receive orders from one and only one superior. That means to say there should not be dual subordination. Dual subordination brings disorder confusion, chaos and undermines authority superior. Any violation of this principles may be catastrophic to the organization.

(c)   **Direct Supervision.** Since direction involves motivation the employees toward work, it is almost essential for the manager concerned to have a personal touch with the subordinates and involve in face-to-face communication regarding the work-related matters. He would also develop informal relationships with the employees. Direct supervision makes the subordinates happy and boosts their morale. Since the employee will have direct access to the boss he would like to be participative. Direct supervision also ensures quick feedback of necessary information.

(d)   **Appropriate Leadership Style.** Leadership is a process of influencing the employees in the work environment. A manager should exhibit appropriate leadership style. Leadership style is a function of characteristics of leader, characteristics of subordinates, and the situation. Long back it was held that leadership is the ability to recognize and exploit the drama of the moment, hold or steal the floor, and move events in a direction that allows people to achieve their preordained destiny (great man theory). History of an organization is but the curriculum vitae of great men. Human relations oriented executives have however an obsessive interest in informal leadership i.e. particular style. But the recent contingency theories of leadership have highlighted the view that the leadership is largely situational. In some situations, the autocratic or hard-nosed leadership style is better and in some others the soft-hearted or participative style of leadership will yield fruitful results.

(e)   **Use of motivation techniques.** A manager should know how to motivate and inspire the employees. A manager should develop selective motivation techniques such as money, pay, status, job enrichment, etc, so that the productivity and the quality of the commodity produced increases. Motivation almost always leads to higher job satisfaction. To direct properly and motivate the employees an executive must have insight into how his personality works, how employees perceive the work environment, the attitudes of employees etc. Understanding others and self are important for this. Understanding self is important for understanding others; understanding other is necessary for motivating them effectively.

(f)   **Follow-up.** Successful direction is a never-ending activity. It involves constant and continuous supervision, coaching, advice, counseling and helping the employees in their respective activities. Direction is also concerned with ensuring that people do what they are told to do. This requires continuous feedback. Feedback is essential to turn or stop or adjust the wheel of management-in-action.

16.6   ELEMENTS OF DIRECTION

Direction is one of the essential functions in administration. Direction is a part of supervision, as Newman pointed out, and supervision refers to the day-to-day relationship between an executive and his immediate assistant audit is commonly used to cover the training, direction, motivation, coordination, maintenance of discipline etc. Direction involves the following elements :

a.   good instructions,
b.   follow-up of instructions,
c.   standard practice and indoctrination
d.   explanations
e.   consultative direction.

(a)   **Good Instructions.** As William Newman has rightly pointed out every instruction given by the manager in the process of directing the employees must be reasonable, complete and clear. The instructions must be in written. Written instructions are desirable when several individuals are subject to or directly affected by instructions, and execution of the instructions will extend over a considerable period to time and the matter is of such importance that special steps to avoid the possibility of misunderstanding are needed.

(b) **Follow-up of Instructions.** Another well-recognized principle is that once the orders are issued, they should be followed up to see whether they are executed properly or the instructions should be countermanded. If the executive is indifferent in follow-up, it will lead to administration lax, time schedules become insignificant and will result in efficiency. Insistence on execution of instructions is essential to ensure efficiency in direction..

(c) **Standard Practice and introduction.** The use of standard operating procedures and customary ways of doing things is an essential part of direction. Standard practice simplifies the instruction to be given by a manager. Unfortunately, a large part of inadequate direction can be traced to misunderstanding about standard practice. Another associated aspect of standard practice is the indoctrination. Indoctrination means instilling in subordinates a set of belief s and attitudes so that they look upon an operating situation in a desirable fashion.

(d) **Explanations.** While issuing instructions, the manager should explain why the order is given.

(e) **Consultative Direction.** Before an order is issued, the people responsible for executing it will be consulted about its feasibility, workability and the better ways of accomplishing the results.

16.7 MANAGING AND THE HUMAN FACTOR

By managing, here, we mean the directing function of management. Understanding the human factor is important for an excellent performance of the directing function; as selection of motivational techniques and adoption of an appropriate leadership style - will all depend on - how the manager - direction views the human nature.

The discussion about the above stated caption centres around two factors :

a)   General and considerations to be borne in mind by managers, while directing people; and
b)   Certain important models of human beings.

Let us comment on both of the above two categories of factors.

a)   **General Considerations :**

While directing subordinates, managers must keep in mind the following fundamental facts about people they are directing, leading, motivating or communicating with :

i.   People play a multiplicity of roles in society :

Individuals working in an organisation are not merely a productive factor, they are also members of families, schools, trade association, political parties etc. In fact, the behaviour of people is a complex outcome of the multiplicity of roles, they play in society; and this complex behaviour is a matter of concern for managers, while performing the directing function.

ii.   There is no average person :

Organisations develop rules, procedures, position description etc. on the implicit assumption that all people are alike. However, it is true that each individual is unique in respect of needs, ambitions, attitudes, knowledge, desire for responsibility. Unless and until this complexity and individually of people is understood; there is all the danger that motivational techniques, leaderships styles and communication systems may be misapplied, producing hopeless results.

iii.   Personal dignity is important :

Whatever be the position of an individual in the organisation (from the chief executive to first line superior and worker); the concept of individual dignity must be observed which implies that all persons must be treated with respect. In fact, each person contributes to the objectives of the enterprise in a unique manner; and hence deserves respect.

iv.   The `Whole Person' must be considered :

An individual is a total (or whole) person influenced by inputs received from external factors such as family, friends, neighbours, political links etc. People cannot divest themselves of the impact of these forces, when they come to work. In fact, the manager must view an individual's behaviour and personality from a system's perspective; and prepare himself to deal with people accordingly.

b.   Models of human beings :

In order to understand people, many models have been developed; some important of which have been described below :

(i)   Edger H. Schein's model :

Schein has developed four conceptions about people :

(1)   Rational Economic Man

This model is based on the assumption that people are primarily motivated by economic incentives. They are essentially passive and are motivated and controlled by the organisation.

(2)   Social man

This model is based on the idea that, basically, people are motivated by social needs; and social forces of peer group are more important than controls exercised by the management.

(3)   Self actualizing man

This model is based on Maslow's need hierarchy concept; according to which human needs fall into five classes in a hierarchy ranging from basic needs to needs for self-realisation (or self-actualisation). Self-actualisation requires the maximum use of a persons's potential. According to this model, then, it can be inferred that people are self motivated.

(4)   Complex - man model

This model presents Schein's own view of people. It is based on the idea that people are complex and variable and have many motives which; combine into a complex motive pattern. As such, people respond to managerial strategies in different and unique ways.

(ii)   Lyman Porter's (and his colleagues) model

Lyman W. Porter, Edward E. Lawer, III and J. Richard Hackman have identified six models of human behaviour classified into three contrasting categories, as described below :

(1)   Rational or Emotional Model

According to ration view, people behave rationally and make decisions based on an objective analysis of different alternatives. A manager having this view of people, will interact and deal with them on a rational basis; but ignoring the human side of their personalities.

According to emotional view, people are primarily ruled by their emotions; some of which are uncontrollable. A manager holding this view of people would always try to unearth (or discover) the underlying psychological causes of people's behaviour.

(2)   Behaviouristic or Phenomenological Model

According to behaviouristic view, people's behaviour is controlled by their environment. Managers holding this view of people would suggest and try to change the environment of the organisation to get desired behaviour from subordinates.

The phenomenological view is just the opposite. It suggests that people are unpredictable, unique, subjective and relative; but have potential. A manager holding this view of people would probably try to understand the complex functioning of the brain of subordinates, from where their behaviour originates - something which is not possible.

(3)   Economic or Self - Actualizing Model

According to economic view, people get satisfaction from monetary rewards, and money is the most important motivator to be applied to get maximum contribution from people. According to self-actualising view, people want to increase their competence and strive to use their potential. A manager holding this view of people should establish an environment which helps people to realise their full potential and reach upto the highest level of progress.

(iii)   Douglas Mc Gregor's Theory X and Theory Y :

Mc Gregor has given two sets of assumptions about human behaviour contained in Theory X and Theory Y.

(Please refer to chapter on motivation, for a detailed account of these theories).

(iv)   Raymod E. Miles's Model

Miles has given a theory of management which is called `dual-model theory'

Miles has suggested three models of people

-         traditional model
-         human relations model
-         human resources model

In fact, managers believe in two models at the same time; one for their subordinates (i.e. the way they manage subordinates) and the other for themselves (i.e. the way they believe they should be managed by their superiors). Hence, Mille's theory of management is called a dual model theory.

Following is a brief account of the three models of people, as suggested by Miles:

(1)   Traditional Model :

According to this model, for people work is distasteful and less important; and money which they earn by doing work is more important. Hence, managers must closely supervise and control subordinates. In fact, people can tolerate work, if the pay is decent and the boss is fair.

(2)   Human Relations Model :

According to this model, social needs of people are more important than money, in motivating them to work. Satisfying social needs will improve morale and reduce resistance to formal authority on the part of subordinates.

(3)   Human Resources Model

According to this model, people want to contribute to meaningful goals; which they have established for themselves. They desire to exercise self-direction and self control. Manager's basic task is to make use of 'untapped' human resources; by creating an environment in which people may contribute to the limits of their ability.

16.8   CREATIVITY AND INNOVATION

An important factor in managing people is creativity. A distinction can be made between creativity and innovation. The term creativity usually refers to the ability and power to develop new ideas. Innovation, on the other hand, usually means the use of these ideas. In an organization, this can mean a new product, a new service, or a new way of doing things. Although this discussion centers on the creative process, it is implied that organizations not only generate new ideas but also translate them into practical applications.

16.8.1 The Creative Process

The creative process is seldom simple and linear. Instead, it generally consists of four overlapping and interacting phases : (1) unconscious scanning, (2) intuition, (3) insight, and (4) logical formulation.

The first phase, unconscious scanning, is difficult to explain because it is beyond consciousness. This scanning usually requires an absorption in the problem which may be vague in the mind. Yet managers working under time constraints often make decisions prematurely rather than dealing thoroughly with ambiguous, ill-defined problems.

The second phase, intuition, connects the unconscious with the conscious. This stage may involve a combination of factors that may seem contradictory at first. For example, in the 1920s Donaldson Brown and Alfred Sloan of General Motors conceived the idea of a decentralized division structure with centralized control - concepts which seem to contradict each other. yet the idea makes sense when one recognizes the underlying principles of

(1) giving responsibility for the operations to the general manager of each division, and

(2) maintaining centralized control in headquarters over certain functions. It took the intuition of two great corporate leaders to see that these two principles could interact in the managerial process.

Institution needs time to work. It requires that people find new combinations and integrate diverse concepts and ideas. Thus, one must think through the problem. Intuitive thinking is promoted by several techniques such as brainstorming and synectics, which will be discussed shortly.

Insight, the third phase of the creative process, is mostly the result of hard work. For example, many ideas are needed in the development of a usable product, a new service, or a new process. Interestingly, insight may come at times when the thoughts are not directly focused on the problem at hand. Moreover, new insights may last for only a few minutes, and effective managers may benefit from having paper and pencil ready to make notes of their creative ideas.

The last phase in the creative process is logical formulation or verification. Insight needs to be tested through logic or experiment. This may be accomplished by continuing to work on an idea or by inviting critiques from others. Brown and Sloan's idea of decentralization, for example, needed to be tested against organizational reality.

16.8.2 Techniques to Enhance Creativity

Creativity can be taught. Creative thoughts are often the fruits of extensive efforts, and several techniques are available to nurture those kinds of thoughts, especially in the decision – making process. Some techniques focus on group interactions; others focus on individual actions. As illustrative of the various techniques, two popular ones are brainstorming and synectics.

Brainstorming One of the best – known techniques for facilitating creativity has been developed by Alex F. Osborn, who has been called "the father of brain storming." The purpose of this approach is to improve problem solving by finding new and unusual solutions. In the brainstorming session, a multiplication of ideas is sought. The rules are as follows :

1.   No ideas are ever criticized.
2.   The more radical the ideas are, the better.
3.   The quantity of idea production is stressed.
4.   The improvement of ideas by others is encouraged.

Brainstorming, which emphasizes group thinking, was widely accepted after its introduction. However, the enthusiasm was dampened by research which showed that individuals could develop better ideas working by themselves than they could working in groups. Additional research, however, showed that in some situations the group approach may work well. This may be the case when the information is distributed among various people or when a poorer group decision is more acceptable than a better individual decision which, for example, may be opposed by those who have to implement it. Also, the acceptance of new ideas is usually greater when the decision is made by the group charged with its implementation.

Synectics Originally known as the Gordon technique (named after its creator, William J. Gordon), this system was further modified and became known as synectics. In this approach, the members of the synectics team are carefully selected for their suitability to deal with the problem, a problem which may involve the entire organization.

The leader of the group plays a vital role in this approach. In fact, only the leader knows the specific nature of the problem. This person narrows and carefully leads the discussion without revealing the actual problem itself. The main reason for this approach is to prevent the group from reaching a premature solution to the problem. The system involves a complex set of interactions from which a solution emerges – frequently the invention of a new product.

16.8.3 Limitations of Traditional Group Discussion

Although the techniques of brainstorming and synectics may result in creative ideas, it would be incorrect to assume that creativity flourishes only in groups. Indeed, the usual group discussion can inhibit creativity. For example, group members may pursue an idea to the exclusion of other alternatives. Experts on a topic may not be willing to express their ideas in a group for fear of being ridiculed. Also, lower-level managers may be inhibited in expressing their views in a group with higher-level managers. Pressures to conform can discourage the expression of deviant opinions. The need for getting along with others can be stronger than the need for exploring creative but unpopular alternatives to the solution of a problem. Finally, because they need to arrive at a decision, groups may not make the effort of searching for data relevant to a decision.

16.8.4 The Creative Manager

All too often it is assumed that most people are noncreative and have little ability to develop new ideas. This assumption, unfortunately, can be detrimental to the organization, for in the appropriate environment virtually all people are capable of being creative, even though the degree of creativity varies considerably among individuals.

Generally speaking, creative people are inquisitive and come up with many new and unusual ideas; they are seldom satisfied with the status quo.

Although intelligent, they not only relay on the rational process but also involve the emotional aspects of their personality in problem solving. They appear to be excited about solving a problem, even to the point of tenacity. Creative individuals are aware of themselves and capable of independent judgment. They object to conformity and see themselves as being different.

Unquestionably, creative people can make great contributions to an enterprise. At the same time, however, they may also cause difficulties in organizations. Change – as may manager knows – is not always popular. Moreover, change frequently has undesirable and unexpected side effects. Similarly, unusual ideas, pursued stubbornly, may frustrate others and inhibit the smooth functioning of an organization. Finally, creative individuals may be disruptive by ignoring established policies, rules, and regulations.

As a result, the creativity of most individuals is probably underutilized in many cases, despite the fact that unusual innovations can be of great benefit to the firm. However, individual and group techniques can be effectively used to nurture creativity, especially in the area of planning. But creativity is not a substitute for managerial judgment. It is the manager who must determine and weigh the risks involved in pursuing unusual ideas and translating them into innovative practices.

16.8.5 Innovation and Entrepreneurship

Recently, innovation and entrepreneurship have received considerable attention. When hearing these terms, one thinks immediately of the success stories of people such as Steven Jobs of Apple Computers and Ross Perot of Electronic Data Processing (acquired by General Motors). It may be an appealing thought to get rich and get rich quick, often by establishing new companies.

Peter Drucker suggests that innovation applies not only to high-tech companies but equally to low-tech, established businesses. Worthwhile innovation is not a matter of sheer luck; it requires systematic and rational work, well organized and managed for results.

What does entrepreneurship imply? It suggests dissatisfaction with how things are and awareness of a need to do things differently. Innovation comes about because of some of the following situations.

1.   The unexpected event, failure, or success
2.   The incongruous – what is assumed and what really is
3.   The process or task that needed improvement
4.   Changes in the market or industry structure
5.   Changes in demographics
6.   Changes in meaning or in the way things are perceived
7.   Innovation based on knowledge.

Innovations based solely on bright ideas may be very risky and are, at times, not successful. General Electric's ambitious plans for the "factory of the future" may have been a costly mistake. These plans may have been based on unrealistic forecasts and GE's unrealistic expectations to automate industry. The concept of the new factory expressed the wish of the chairperson, who wanted to promote entrepreneurship in an organization that was known to be highly structured.

The most successful innovations are often the mundane ones. Take the Japanese, who make minor innovations (providing, for example, little conveniences that customers like) in their cars or in their electronic equipment. James Brain Quinn found in his research that successful large companies are listening carefully to the needs of their customers. They establish teams that search for creative alternatives to serve their customers – but within a limiting framework and with clear goals in mind.

Innovation is not only relevant to high-tech firms but also crucial for old line, traditional companies which may not survive without the infusion of innovation. Managers in those companies must create an environment that fosters entrepreneurial spirit and actions.

16.9   HARMONIZING OBJECTIVES : THE KEY TO LEADING

Understanding the human factor in enterprises is important for the managerial function of leading. How a manager views human nature influences the selection of motivational and leadership approaches. A number of models presenting various conceptions of the nature of people have been proposed; however, no single view is sufficient to understand the whole person. Therefore, an elective view of the nature of people is suggested.

People do not work in isolation; rather, they work to a great extent in groups toward the achievement of personal and enterprise objectives. Unfortunately, these objectives are not always harmonious. Likewise, the goals of sub-ordinates are not always the same as those of the superior. Therefore, one of the most important activities of managers is to harmonize the needs of individuals with the demands of the enterprise.

Leading bridges the gap between, on the one hand, logical and well considered plans, carefully designed organization structures, good programs of staffing, and efficient control techniques, and, on the other hand, the need for people to understand, to be motivated, and to contribute all they are capable of to enterprise and department goals. There is no way that a manager can utilize the desires and goals of individuals to achieve enterprise objectives without knowing what these individuals want. Even then, managers must be able to design an environment that will take advantage of these individual drives. Managers must know how to communicate with and guide their subordinates so that they will see how they serve their own interests by working creatively for an organization.

16.10   REVIEW QUESTIONS

1.   Define Direction?
2.   Explain the Principles involved in Direction?
3.   List out the elements of direction.
4.   Write short notes on human factor?
5.   Define the term managing?
6.   Differentiate creativity and innovation.
7.   Write briefly about the term Harmonizing objective?

LEADERSHIP

17.1   MEANING

Leadership is too complex a term to be defined in a simple and straight manner. There are many factors involved in successful leadership and it is not possible to identify or measure all of them. The presence of successful leadership can only be felt in terms of the results of group working i.e., profits, quality of output, employee morale, consumer satisfaction, enterprise image, and so on.

The following definitions refer to different aspects of leadership be,

Chester Barnard: Leadership is the "ability of a superior to influence the behavior of his subordinates and persuade them to follow a particular course of action".

Koontz and O' Dannel: "Leadership is the ability of a manager to induce subordinates to work with confidence and zeal".

Allen: "Leaders is one who guides and directs other people. He must give effective direction and purpose".

George R.Terry: "Leadership is "the activity of influencing people to strive willingly for mutual objectives".

Robert C. Appleby: Leadership is "a means of direction is the ability of management to induce subordinates to work towards group ideas with confidence and keenness".

17.2   NATURE OF LEADERSHIP

Leadership may be viewed variously as (a) a status group (b) a focal person; (c) a functions; and (d) process.

Leadership as a Status Group

It refers to a situation where as person acquires leadership by reason of his heredity (as when he is a descendant of a royal family), or election, or appointment to a position.

Leadership as a Focal Person

According to this view, leadership vests the in people who are traditionally regarded as leaders by virtue of managerial positions held by them, such as in the case of directors, executives, administrators, managers, chiefs, etc.

Leadership as a Function

The leadership function consists in facilitating the achievement of group goals. The person who performs this function is regarded as the leader. As a result, while there are several people involved in working towards accomplishment of group goals and many complex factors, including a sheer luck, which may affect the outcome, the credit of discredit for success or failure of the collective endeavor is attributed to the leader of the group.

Leadership as a Process

According to this view, leadership is an interactive process in which leadership and followers exchange influence, i.e. the leaders influence the followers by his ideas, direction and support, and the followers influence the leader by their contribution to the achievement of group goals. And because there is positive balance of influence in favor of the leader, the followers accept his power in the case of an informal group, and his authority in the case of a formal group. In this sense, a person can be an effective leader only so long as his followers accept his power of authority.

17.3   NEED FOR LEADERSHIP

An organization needs leadership on a continuous basis. The following reasons highlight the need for leadership.

   1.   **Imperfect organization structure:**   It is not possible for any organisation structure to provide to all kinds of relationships. This explains the existence of informal group within the framework of a formal organisation. With effective

leadership, imperfection of a formal organisation structure may be corrected and the formal and informal groups may be made to work in unison.

2. **Technological, economic and social changes**. In the face of rapid technological economic and social changes, the organisation is required to effect suitable changes in its operations and style. For example, in the event of a fall in demand, it may discontinue production of certain goods and services, or take up production of alternative goods and services. Only and effective leadership can enable it to meet the challenges posed by environmental factors.

3. **Internal imbalances inspired by growth:** As an organisation grows in size and complexity, it may develop certain imbalances. For example, increase in organizational activities may lead to increase in the levels of management, thus adding to complexity of the organisation structure, and problems of command, co-ordination and control of work at all levels. Only an effective leadership can steer the organisation through such situations.

4. **Nature of human memberships**. Persons working in an enterprise come from different backgrounds and have different interests, values, beliefs and intellectual and temperaments make-up.

Again, each member is a part of different social groups, e.g., the family, neighborhood group, etc. which are external to the organisation and beyond its control. The influence of these groups on the attitudes and behavior of the individual members may at times create a conflict between individual goals and group interest.

An effective leadership can create a suitable motivational framework which provides for satisfaction of different needs and motives of the organisation members as also resolution of individual - group conflicts.

17.4 DISTINCTION BETWEEN LEADERSHIP AND HEADSHIP OR DOMINATION

Leadership is different from headship or domination. Headship refers to people who are placed in their positions by virtue of official authority or historical accident, with little control over circumstances. For example, the head of a family or educational or military organisation may exercise authority, but may not necessarily be the leader of his subordinates because he may not be in position to significantly influence their activities.

Leadership is essentially an influence process, and the leader may be defined as the one who significantly influences the activities of a group toward achievement of stated goals. While it is true that is a group, every member exercise some influence over the others in the group, the influence exercised by the leader is quite significant and the group quite willingly allows him this authority, as it sees him as an effective instruments for fulfillment of its own goals. Thus, it may be said that a group only accepts a person's leadership on its own terms.

To conclude, it may be said that while headship refers to the exercise of legal and formal authority at all levels in the organisation, leadership is concerned with the use of non-formal authority at the emotional - motivational level.

17.5   LEADERSHIP THEORIES

Many of the research studies, particularly by behavioral scientists, have been carried on to find out the answer to the question: what makes leader effective? Is his success due to his personality, or his behavior, or the types of followers he has, or the situation in which he works, or a combination of all these? These researchers, however, could not give a satisfactory answer of the question. Instead these researches have resulted in various theories or approaches on leadership, the prominent among these being trait theory, behavioral theory, and situational theory. Each theory has its own contributions, limitations, assumptions, and frame work of analysis. The understanding of the various theories of leadership will provide a guideline to judge as how a leader emerges.

1.   Trait Approach

Trait is defined as relatively enduring quality of an individual. The trait approach seeks to determine 'what makes a successful leader' from the leader's own personal characteristics. From the very beginning, people have emphasized that a particular individual was successful leader because of his certain qualities or characteristics. Trait approach leadership studies were quite popular between 1930 and 1950. The method of study was to select leaders of eminence and their characteristics were studied. It has the hypothesis that the persons having certain traits could become successful leaders. Various research studies have given intelligence, attitudes, personality, and biological factors. A review of various research studies has been presented by Stodgily. According to him, various trait theories have suggested these traits in successful leaders. (i) Physical and constitutional factors (height, weight, physique, energy, health, appearance);(ii)Intelligence;(iii)Self-confidence (iv) sociability (v) will (initiative, persistence, ambition,)(vi)dominance; and (vii) surgency (talkative, cheerfulness, geniality, enthusiasm, expressiveness, alertness, and originality). In a later study, Giselle has found supervisory ability, achievement motivation, self - actualizing, intelligence, self-assurance, and decisiveness as the qualities related with leadership success. One summary of leadership research found intelligence in ten studies, initiative in six, extroversion and sense of humor in five, and enthusiasm, fairness, sympathy, and self-confidence in four. The various studies show wide variations in leadership traits. The various traits can be classified into innate and acquirable traits, on the basis of their source.

Innate qualities are those which are possessed by various individuals since their birth. These qualities are natural and often known and God-gifted. On the basis of such qualities, it is said that 'leaders are born and not made'. These qualities cannot be acquired by the individuals

Acquirable qualities of leadership are those which can be acquired and increased through various processes. In fact, when child is born, he learns many of the behavioral patterns through socialization and identification processes. Such behaviors patterns are developed among the child as various traits over a period of time. Many of these traits can be increased through training programmes.

Critical Analysis

The trait theory is very simple. However, this fails to produce clear - cut results. It does not consider the whole environment of the leadership, of which trait may be only one factor. Moreover, no generalization can be drawn about various traits for leadership as these were considerable variations in traits established by various researches. Jennings has concluded, "Fifty years of study has failed to produce a one - personality trait or set of qualities that can be used to discriminated leaders and non-leaders". In brief, this approach presents the following problems:

1.   There cannot be generalization of traits for a successful leaders. This was evident by various researches conducted on leadership traits.

2.   No evidence has been given about the degree of the various traits because people have various traits with different degrees.

3.   There is a problem of measuring the traits. Though there are various tests to measure the personality traits, however, no definite conclusion can be drawn.

4.   There have been many people with the traits specified for leaders, but they were not good leaders.

This approach, however, gives indication that leader should have certain personal characteristics. This helps management to develop such qualities through training and development programmes.

2.   Behavioral Approach

This approach emphasizes that strong leadership is the result of effective role behavior. Leadership is shown by a person's acts more than by his traits. Though traits influence acts, these are also affected by followers, goals, and the environment in which these occur. Thus, there are four basic elements - leaders, followers, goals and environment - which affect each other in determining suitable behavior. Leadership acts may be viewed in two ways. Some acts are functional (favorable) to leadership and some are dysfunctional (unfavorable). The dysfunctional acts are also important in leadership because they demotivate employees to work together. As such a leader will not act in this way. The dysfunctional acts are inability to accept subordinates' ideas, display of emotional immaturity, poor human relations, and poor communication.

A leader uses there skills - technical, human, and conceptual - to lead his followers. Technical skill refers to a person's knowledge and proficiency in any type of process or technique. Human skills are the ability to interact effectively with people and to built team - work. Conceptual skill deals with ideas and enables a manager to deal successfully with abstractions, to set up models and devise plans. Behavior of a manager in a particular direction will make him good leader while opposite of this would discard him as a leader. Setting goals, motivating employees for achieving goals, raising the level of morale, building team spirit, effective communication, etc, are the functional behavior for a successful leader.

Critical Analysis

The basic difference between trait approach and behavioral approach is that former emphasizes some particular trait to the leader while latter emphasizes particulars behavior by him. It is true that favorable behavior provides greater satisfaction to the followers and the person can be recognized as a leader. However, this approach suffers from one weakness, that is, a particular behavior at a time may be effective, while at other times may not be effective. This means the time factor becomes a vital element which has not been considered here.

3.   Situational Approach

The prime attention in this approach is given to the situation in which leadership is exercised. Since 1945, much emphasis in leadership research is being given to the situations that surround the exercise of leadership. The contention is that in one situation leadership may be successful while in others it may not.

For the first time, this approach was applied in 1920 in armed forces of Germany with the objective to get good generals under different situations. Winston Churchill was treated to be the most efficient Prime Minister during the Second World War. However, he was flop afterworlds when situation changed. Ohio State University research has given four situations a variable that affect the performance of leadership.

These are:

i.   The cultural environment
ii.   Differences between individuals
iii.   Differences between jobs
iv.   Differences between organisations.

i.   The Cultural environment. Culture is a man-made social system of belief, faith and value. Many aspects of life have a significant influence upon behavior and any understanding of employee's behavior requires the understanding of culture in which he lives. Culture may interfere with rational production efficiency by requiring actions unnecessary or unrealistic from a national point of view, but necessary from the cultural point of view. Thus, leadership should be directed to influence behavior of followed in the context of the culture.

ii.   Differences between individuals. Human behavior is caused by some combination of antecedent factors. Besides for any given aspect of behavior, there may be many contributing factors, not causative in nature. There are a variety of such factors which affect behavior in different ways such as aptitudes, personality characteristics, physical characteristics, interests and motivation, age, sex, education, experience, etc. Within this framework, individuals in the leadership process may be classified as (a) leaders, and (b) follower. The individual's characteristics affect the leadership process . Thus, some persons may perceive a particular leadership style suitable while others may have a different perception. For example, followers with authoritarian personality tend generally to be more comfortable where influence is being exercised.

iii.   Differences between jobs: People in the organisation perform different types of jobs. The importance of placing individuals in jobs which they can perform at a satisfactory levels stems from four different considerations - economics, legal, personal and social. Different job conditions influence leadership behavior differently. It is because of the fact that demands of job almost inevitably force a leader into certain kinds of activities. Such requirements do much to set the framework within which the leader must operate. It means the number of leadership options available to the individual is thereby reduced.

iv.   Differences between organisations. Various organizations differ on the basis of their size, age, ownership pattern, objective, complexity, managerial pattern, cultural environment, etc. In different types of organizations, leadership process tends to differ. For example, in military or government administration, leadership behavior will be different as compared to business organization.

Critical Analysis

The situational theory of leadership gives the analysis how leadership behavior differs with situational variables. Thus the questions, why a manager in a particular situation is successful while in the other situation is unsuccessful, is answered by this theory. However, this approach is not free certain limitations which are as follows:

i.   This theory emphasizes leadership ability of an individual in a given situation. Thus, it measures his present leadership potentialities. Whether this individual will fit in another situation is not answered by this theory.

ii.   Organizational factors become helpful or constraints to a great extent to an individual leaders in exercising the leadership. Thus, it is difficult to measure his personal abilities as a good leader.

iii.   The theory does not emphasis the process by which good leaders can be made in the organisation. Thus, it puts a constraint over leadership development process.

17.6   IMPORTANCE OF LEADERSHIP IN MANAGEMENT

By analyzing the functions of leadership, the importance of leadership in management can be stated under the following five heads:

1.   **Motive Power to group efforts:** Managements, for getting the work done by others, is to supply leadership in the organisation. As group efforts and teamwork are essential for realizing organizational goals, leadership, becomes vital for the execution of work. Through the exercise of leadership, managers can influence any group of human work accomplishment. Leadership pulls up the group to a higher level of performance through its work on human relations.

2.   **Aid to authority:** Managers exercise authority in managing people of the organization and their task becomes easy wherever they are aided by leadership. There are serious limits to the use of authority and power in obtaining high performance. Authority alone can never generate the initiative and resourcefulness required in many jobs. But leadership can obtain tangible and improved results of human efforts because of its main reliance on influence. Leadership contains all the essential ingredients of direction for inspiring people and providing the will-to-do for successful work accomplishments.

3.   **Emphasis on human performance:** Effective leadership is needed at different levels of management from top management down process through its leadership action. It is the social skill of leadership that accomplishes objectives by mobilization and utilization of people. The best of the plans can be foundered and the ideal organization structure can be shelved by the deliberate restriction of human efforts at the operating level. High performance of working people is the focal point in managerial work. And this high performance can be secured by leadership of supervisory management.

4.   **Integration of formal with informal organizations:** If management fails to provide competent leadership, informal leadership will prevail over management in controlling and regulating the behavior of employees. Being confronted with such a situation, management fails to influence workers, to improve their performance and to stop employee unrest. Leadership is the natural accompaniment of all associations of human beings. For their personal and social contentment, workers are performed to rely mostly on informal leadership if management cannot provide effective leadership. Competent leadership can, however, integrate informal organizations with formal organization and utilize them constructively for achieving company objectives.

5.   **Basis for Co-operation:** Leadership provides the basis for co-operation in several ways. Good two-way communication, man-to-man personal relationship, use of participation and creation of opportunity for need satisfaction are meant for increasing understanding between the leader and his subordinates of their mutual viewpoints. This increased understanding obtained through the interactions of individual personalities promotes favorable feelings and attitudes among them.

17.7   FUNCTIONS OF LEADERSHIP

a.   **Motivating and guiding personal.** Leadership provides the vital spark to motivation of human beings. Motivation has its roots in human relations which, in turn, can be fostered and toned up by leadership. Whenever a group of human beings desires to accomplish a common objective, the situation calls for the assistance of leadership. It is the leadership that guides, inspires and directs group members for achieving a unity of purpose and effort. Leadership alone can elevate men's visions to higher thinking and raise their capacity to a higher standard of performance. It infuses such will-to-do into the group working as to secure the best contribution of human energy. Without leadership, a group disintegrates, destroys its team spirit and fritters away its energy.

b.   **Influencing and shaping the social system.** Leadership is the concomitant of all human associations in our society. Leadership emerges as a natural process in any grouping of human beings. If there is a lack of formal and recognized leadership in the group, informal leadership is bound to develop from the rank and file members of the group. After its emergence leadership persuades the group to have an identity of interest, outlook and action. Leadership provides imagination, foresight, enthusiasm and initiative to the group. It exhibits an imitable code of conduct and responsibility, prescribes a high standard of performance and stresses the importance of respect for the individual. Unsatisfactory human performance in any organization can be primarily attributed to poor leadership.

c.   **Understanding followers and securing their co-operation.** Not only the leader influences his followers, but he also is influenced by their problems and feelings. On the basis of information, response and operational facts secured from followers, leader's behavior and action are modified and made ready for their voluntary co-operation. To grasp followers' problem and feelings properly, however, leadership requires a skill of sympathetic contact, careful listening, correct diagnosing and winning their confidence. A true spirit of co-operation grows principally out of the manner in which the leader deals with his followers.

d.   **Creating a climate for performance**. For enabling the followers to apply their full capabilities for work accomplishment and to extend their unselfish support, the leader is required to create a climate for performance. With this end in view, the leader must know what motivates his followers and how these motivators operate. The more thoroughly the leader understands the process of motivation, the more effective he is likely to be in getting the work successfully done by his follows:

17.8   TYPES OF LEADERS

Leadership cannot exist without followers. The characteristics of the followers and the conditions, under which they follow, are materials to the exercise of leadership. The maturity levels of the followers, namely their ability (job maturity) and willingness or motivation (psychological maturity) with to a great extent determine the behavior of the leader vis-à-vis his follower. Thus, in respect of the followers with low maturity who are neither able nor willing to perform, the leader will have to adopt task behavior, i.e he will have to tell them what, how, when and where the given task is to be performed. Similarly, the leader will have suitably to adjust his behavior with followers who are able but not willing, or willing but not able, or both able and willing.

Based on the types of leader behavior, leaders may be classified as follows:

1.   Autocratic Leader
2.   Laissez Faire or Free Rein Leader
3.   Democratic Leader
4.   Intellectual of Functional Leader
5.   Institutional Leader
6.   Paternalistic Leader

1.   Autocratic Leader

An autocratic leader is one who tends to run the show all by him. He specifics the goals which he requires his followers to perform, organizes the work situation, sets the time - frame within which the task is to be accomplished, provides specific directions and requires the followers to keep him regularly posted with the progress of the task.

The autocratic leader views his followers as having little or no maturity as regards skills or willingness with which the job is to be accomplished. As such, he will neither have any discussion with them as to any aspect of job accomplishment, nor delegate to them any authority. To extract the required performance from his follower, he exercise close supervision and control and uses his reward and coercive power to that end. Thus, if the followers comply with the leader's expectations as regards performance, he rewards them. If they are lacking in performance, he uses coercive power to induce performance and holds out the threat of punishment by way of inconvenient work assignments, fines, or dismissal.

An autocratic leader believers in the "X" theory of motivation and firmly believes that without close supervision, control and fear of punishment, followers will not work since they are inherently lazy, unambitious, and averse to accept responsibility, or take any initiative.

An autocratic leader is in fact no leader. He is merely the formal head of his organisation. Workers under him feel harassed and disturbed, and prepare themselves sooner or later to offer resistance. With the emergence of indiscipline among his staff, the autocratic leader fails to obtain unquestioned compliance from his workers because they begin to assert themselves, and the result is that they gradually stop obeying his orders. After a time, there is total loss of his authority to demand compliance.

2.   Laissez faire or free rein leader

A laissez faire or free rein leader permits his followers to do whatever they want to do. He does not formulate any policies or procedures and does not lay down guidelines within which the followers could accomplish their jobs. Thus, his followers are left to fend for themselves.

Since in a laissez faire set up, there is no attempt on the part of anyone to influence any one else, there is a vast scope and opportunity for an extensive range of behavior, though it may often be at cross - purposes. There is a near total abdication of formal leadership according to the needs of each situation.

Obviously, laissez faire leadership can be successful only where the followers have a high degree of maturity, i.e they are both able and willing to perform. In the case of followers with less than high maturity, such leadership is not likely to succeed because, in the absence of suitable task behavior on the part of the leader, they would merely grope in the dark, not knowing that, how, when and where to perform. Besides, deprivation of socio-emotional support from the leader may make them feet insecure and vulnerable.

3.   Democratic Leader

Democratic style of leadership is based on the assumption that the leader derives his power by consent of the followers whom he is to lead and that, give proper motivational environment; they can direct themselves and be creative on their respective jobs. In other works, while the followers have the requisite ability to perform the jobs, they are lacking in willingness to do so.

The democratic leaders encourage his followers to participate in decision-making and implementation. However, decisions are made only within the limits established by the policies and procedures which, again, are formulated after elaborate group discussion. Of course, the leader is present all along to guide and control the discussion but the followers are allowed to express their points of view without any let or hindrance. The decisions formulated during these discussions represent the consensus of all participants.

Democratic leadership seeks to evolve a self -regulating and self disciplining mechanism. If any member of the group does anything which is in any manner opposed to the interests of the group, he is promptly checked and controlled by the other members of the group, and this is done by means of a system of rewards and punishment devised by the group.

Participation, consultation and agreement of the group remember are important features of a democratic leadership. Democratic functioning can at times be dilatory and subject to various pulls and pressure from different groups, or individuals, representing opposite viewpoints. Moreover, participative leadership is based on the assumption that the followers are all able, though not willing to perform the tasks assigned to them. In the even, it poses the problem of working out a system of proper motivational support that would be equally acceptable to all.

4.   Expert or Functional Leader

An expert of functional leader does not command; any formal authority in the literal sense of the term. He only stands out because of his special qualifications for the job handled by the him. Which is also the main reason why followers look up to him for guidance and control?

The expert leader is essentially task-oriented, and most of his time is spent thinking about doing things faster and better. He has his eyes firmly fixed on what he intends to achieve and pursues his goal single - mindedly. However, since his success depends not only on his own work, but also on the activities of his followers, he may not be as effective as he plans. If his followers are not as serious and painstaking as he is, he may behave is demanding fashion, in the process relying more and more on the "X" theory of motivation. In the event, his followers may feel frustrated as they are prevented from maximizing their own potential. Over time the situation may get from bad to worse, because the expert leader is by definition quite poor on the human relations front.

5.   Institutional Leader

The institutional leader is one who wields power over his followers due to the position of office occupied by him in the organizational hierarchy. At times, he may also derive power from his personality and behaviors. By virtue of such positional and personal power, he manipulates and controls are activities of others to accomplish the group objectives.

The institutional leadership may or may not be an expert in his field of activity. When he, lacks the expertise, he may suffer from a sense of inadequacy, leading to an inferiority complex, and to compensate for it, he may exert to an exceptional extent to achieve his objectives. In the process, he may engage more and more in task behavior and less and less in relationship behavior, such that the followers may develop a feeling of frustration and alienation.

6.   Paternalistic Leader

A paternalistic leadership is characterized primarily by loyalty of followers in a warm and cohesive setting. The leader is much concerned with the well being of his followers and comes to their rescue ever so often.

Since a paternalistic leader is concerned more with relationship behavior, it can be successful only in cases where the followers possess job maturity and are only lacking in psychological maturity. In any other case, such leader may only produce an atmosphere of a country - club which may display social warmth and cohesion but can do little way of a accomplishment of tasks. Even otherwise, under a paternalistic leader the followers, particularly the competent and achievement - oriented among them, feel frustrated due to lack of opportunity for showing initiative. This is because while the leader, like a banyan tree, gives protection to all, the unwittingly creates conditions under which no follower can grow and be able to realize his potential.

17.9   QUALITIES OF LEADERSHIP

To be able to prove effective leadership to his subordinates, a leader needs to have certain qualities. According to Orway Tead, a leader must posses, "physical and nervous energy, a sense of purpose and direction, enthusiasm, friendliness and affection, integrity, technical mastery, decisiveness, intelligence, teaching skills, and faith". According to Henry Fayol the qualities that a leader must possess are:

a.   health and physical fitness
b.   mental vigor and energy
c.   courage to accept responsibility
d.   steady, persistent, thoughtful determination
e.   sound general education, and
f.   management ability embracing foresight and art of handling men.

The more important qualities of a leader may be summarized as follows:

1.   **Physical and mental vigor:** The leader has to put in hard mental and physical work, which requires tremendous stamina and vigor to sustain long and irregular hours of work.

2.   **Emotional stability:** The leader should not be unduly moved by emotion or sentiment. He should be able rationally and logically to analyze the various problems before him and reach a decision without any fear or favor. He should not lose his temper or show indecision even in the face to heavy odds.

3.   **Sense of judgments:** The leader should be a master of human psychology. He should possess deep understanding of human behavior, emotions sentiments, needs, motives, etc. This would enable him to anticipate the response to his decision and actions.

4.   **Balance:** The leader should be rational and objective in his approach. He should be free from bias, prejudice and pre-conceived notions. Only then he would be able to decide issues on their merits.

5.   **Understanding or empathy**: The leaders should show understanding for others viewpoints. If he tends to have his own way in all matters, he might lose their goodwill.

6.   **Motivation:** Only a person who is himself well motivated can motivated others. The desire to lead people should come from within. If person is forced to do his job under fear of punishment, he would behave more like a follower than a leader.

7.   **Communicating Skills:** The leader should be good at communicating ideas, feelings, decisions, orders, etc. He should be good and effective speaker and writer. Then alone he would be able to persuade, inform stimulate and direct his subordinates.

8.   **Agility to guide:** The leader should help his subordinates to learn. Both by word and deed, he should demonstrate to them the best ways of accomplishing the jobs.

9.   **Sociability:** The leader should show keen interest in his subordinates. He should try to meet them often and encourage them to discuss their problems and difficulties with him. He should be friendly, helpful and easily accessible to all his subordinates.

10.   **Technical competence:** The leader should possess a thorough knowledge of the theory and practice of his job. Besides, he should be quite familiar with the jobs done at different work points in his department.

11.   **Other personal abilities:** The leader should have an attractive and pleasing personality. He should possess optimistic and cheerful outlook. He should have sound physical and mental health. His subordinates will accept his leadership only when they find him full of youthful vigor, energy, vitality, endurance and creativity.

Besides, he should be honest, sincere, fair and reasonable in his dealings with his subordinates. If he is a man of integrity and behaves with his subordinates in a dignified manner, his leadership will be cheerfully and enthusiastically accepted by one and all.

17.10 REVIEW QUESTIONS

1.   What is meant by leadership?
2.   How is leadership different from headship?
3.   Discuss the reasons that make leadership necessary
4.   Describe the various approaches to the study of leadership
5.   What are the various functions of a leader?
6.   Describe the types of leaders
7.   Write a note on the qualities of a leader.

MOTIVATION

18.1 INTRODUCTION

A worker is basically a human being. He is a person first and then only a worker. Every manager has to understand that a worker cannot be considered a mechanical system. A worker has to be inspired and actuated to accomplish the objectives of an organization. To accept an order and to execute it with interest and vigour requires an element of actuating or motivating.

As management is the art of getting things done by the workers, this art of getting work done will depend mainly on whether a person has been motivated properly or not. Motivation creates a sense of responsibility and special interest in the work. It increases the desire to work; it is enthusiasm to work.

To motivate means to provide a motive; to impel people to action; and to create incentives to work. Motivation inspires people to work efficiently and effectively. Technically speaking, motivation is an energizer of human behavior; It is a special urge to move in a particular direction. Motives are also the expression of the needs of a person. With motivation, a person can be made to work willing with zeal and enthusiasm.

A manager has a job not with the products, but with people. He can handle them only when he can understand their motives and motivate them to take the desired actions. So the skill of motivation is vital for successful management in an organization. A manager has to bring the ability of the workers to expression.

18.2 DEFINITIONS

MICHAEL, J. JULIUS: Motivation is the act of stimulating someone or oneself to get the desired course of action.

KOONTZ AND O'DONNELL: Motivation is a general terms applying to the entire class of drives, desires, needs, wishes, and similar forces.

DUBIN: Motivation refers to the complex of forces starting and keeping a person at work in an organization. To put it generally, motivation starts and maintains an activity along a prescribed line. Motivation is something that moves the person to action and continues him in the course of action already initiated.

MARCH AND SIMON: Motivation is the process or the reaction which takes places in the memory of individuals. It refers to the combination of forces or motives maintaining human activity.

18.3   IMPORTANCE OF MOTIVATION

Motivation results in creating a favorable work environment within an organization. It adds the will to work along with the ability to work for a worker. Motivation will act as an activator and energizer by directing the behaviour of persons towards the accomplishment of goals. Understanding of motives and motivation theories provides a great deal of insight into the reasons why different individuals exhibit different behavioural patterns. It also helps in understanding why the same person exhibits different reactions to the same stimulus at different times.

Motivation helps in securing voluntary cooperation from workers. It creates the will to work, and confidence in the work force. Motivation helps to satisfy the needs of workers, naturally there will be a sense of belongingness and total involvement on the part of the workers in the achievement of organizational goals. The knowledge and skill of the workers can be used to the best advantage of the organization and there will be increased efficiency.

All this will result in increased productivity and quality of work. Motivated people are the most satisfied people. They will function with a sense of responsibility and commitment to the organization. Naturally, it results in a low rate of labour turnover and absenteeism. A property motivated team will not have unnecessary friction with the management and with its fellow workers. This will help in maintaining very good industrial relations.

Motivation is the drive to satisfy a want or goal, and satisfaction is experienced when the outcome has been achieved. A person might have high job satisfaction, but a low level of motivation for the job, or the reverse.

18.4 PROCESS OF MOTIVATION

In management parlance, motive and need are used interchangeably. In fact, need is a good point to begin discussion on motivation. A need represent the lack, or absence, or deficit of something within the system or organism. When an individual experiences lack or deficit of something, he looks around his work environment to see if there are any incentives or reward for performance of a task which would lead to satisfaction of that need. Thus, a need is personal or internal to a person, while incentives are external. He acts or behaves in a particular manager. But it is not a random act or unguided behavior. His behaviour is motivated or caused. It is directed towards a goal, i.e. satisfaction of his need, or achievement of what he is lacking. With the satisfaction of his need, or achievement of what he is lacking, the mechanism of motivation is complete. Satisfaction of a need restores the balance or equilibrium in the organism, which remains upset and disturbed until the need is unsatisfied.

18.5 ELEMENTS OF MOTIVATION

In any motivational system, there are three elements, namely: (a) the individual who is being motivated; (b) the job; and (c) the work situation.

The individual: Every individual, whether a top ranking manager or a lower-level worker, is a unique being. Workers may differ from one another in several respects, such as, age, sex, education, intelligence, personality, physical characteristics, experience, heredity, and social and cultural background. These differences will determine the needs attitudes of workers. They will also determine how each worker will react to motivational devices such as monetary and non-monetary incentives.

The job: Every job within the set-up of an organisation prescribes different requirements and holds a different level of attractiveness for each worker. Routine jobs are not liked by many because of the monotony and dullness involved in doing them. But sometimes even challenging jobs may not hold attraction for some people. This means there will rarely be a job which is regarded as a source of enjoyment and pride by one and all.

The work situation: The environment within which work is to be performed also creates motivation. This includes (a) organisational goals and values which help to identify desired outcomes or results, and the nature of behaviour that will help to achieve them (b) the type of technology (c) leadership style in terms of participation in decision - making and (d) the rewards such as salary, perquisites, benefits, promotional prospects, status, etc.

18.6   NATURE OR CHARACTERISTICS OF MOTIVATION

It is difficult to describe the nature of motivation. However, the following points about it deserve to be noted:

1.   A Psychological concept

Motivation deals with workers on the psychological plane. Even workers with extraordinary abilities will not be able to perform as desired until they are effectively motivated.

Effective performance on the part of workers can be said to be the result of their abilities backed by proper motivation. Thus, Performance = Abilities Opportunity x Motivation.

While motivation has the capacity to secure desired performance form workers, it can be effective only upon an accurate analysis of workers needs for the satisfaction of which they may be induced to work in the desired manner.

2.   Motivation is total, not piecemeal

A worker cannot be motivated in parts. For successful motivation, he should be treated as an indivisible unit, taking into account all his urges and aspirations.

A motivational device which promises fulfilment of some needs of workers and not others will fall short of its objective of evoking total commitment of workers.

3.   Motivation is determined by human needs

A worker will perform the desired activity only so long as he sees his action as a means of continued fulfilment of his strongly - felt needs. Once a particular need is satisfied for good, he may lose interest in the activity that provides him satisfaction of the said need. In such a case, he will have to be provided awareness of satisfaction of his other needs so that he continues to be inclined to pursue the said activity.

4.   Motivation may be financial or non-financial

Motivation may be provided in several ways depending upon the needs, emotions and sentiments of workers. But broadly speaking, it may be classified as financial and non-financial.

Financial motivation seeks to satisfy physiological and security needs and it is by way of wages, allowances, bonus, prizes and other perquisites. On the other hand, non-financial motivation which seeks to satisfy social, recognition and creative needs may be way of appreciation for the work done, higher status and greater responsibility, or increased participation in decision - making.

5.   Motivation is a constant process

Human needs are infinite. No sooner a person has satisfied one need than he seeks to satisfy another. As very aptly put by McGregor, "Man is a wanting animal - as soon as one of his needs is satisfied, another appears in its place. This process is unending...."

Motivation cannot be a time-bound process. Nor can it be a touch - and - go affair. To keep the workers continuously engaged in the planned activities, they must be kept in a state or continued animated tension by means of unfolding before them ever new avenues for the satisfaction of their limitless needs.

18.7   THEORIES OF MOTIVATION

Workers should be persuaded, inspired and motivated for contributing their best efforts in achieving the objectives of the organization. To motivate people effectively, managers should prepare certain plans. There are various plans, strategies or theories of motivation. All of them are grouped under two categories: (a) Traditional theories of motivation, (b) Modern theories of motivation.

Traditional Theories

"Be strong" theory or "fear and punishment" theory: The Philosophy of might is right, characterized the thinking of aggressive and authoritarian managers. Managers developed a strategy of forcing people to work by threatening to punish or dismiss them or to cut their rewards if they did not work well. This theory is based one the military principle, "Neither make reply nor question why but do nor die", and the assumption is that people would work efficiently and with interest if they were driven by fear and punishment. There was tight control and rigid supervision over workers. This strategy was successful in the early days of the Industrial Revolution. But in the present circumstances, this theory is not practicable. It is resisted and condemned by workers as it is authoritarian.

Efforts and rewards theory: This strategy or approach tried to establish a direct relationship between efforts and rewards. F.W. Taylor conceived this idea in his piece - rate system of wages. Management through that people could perform and contribute better to the extent they were rewarded. To practise this theory, managers should establish the standards or performance, monitor the behavour of employees and decide about the rewards and penalties based on the degree of performance.

Monastic theory: This is almost like the efforts and rewards theory. Here, the management assumes that people work for money only. This theory seeks a single cause of behaviour. It assumes that all the activities of men are directed only towards earning money. More effective will provide more wages, which will further encourage the workers to more effort. This is also known as the "Effort - Reward - Effort Theory". But this theory is criticised on the basis that rewards can serve as motivator's upto a particular point only, and not beyond that.

Carrot and stick theory: This theory suggests a judicious combination of both rewards and penalties for motivation. This theory is based on the strategy of putting a carrot in front of a donkey and hitting it with a sick from behind so that it has to run. The carrot refers to incentives like money and other inducements, and the stick refers to penalties, fear of dismissal, demotion, etc.

Be good or paternalistic theory: After experiencing the 'Be strong' theory and its limitations, some managers implemented a new strategy. They were kind, generous and had the interests of the employees at heart. They functioned much as parents towards their children. But they expected loyalty, demanded respect and provided their employees what they though were good for them. They were fair but firm. Employees in many cases responded to this strategy favourably. As a result, the paternalistic theory was successful in its approach and effectively competed with the "Be strong" and "fear and punishment" theories. High wages, job security, good facilities for education, health, recreation and good work environments were provided to gain loyalty and increase efficiency and productivity. But this theory was disliked by some people on the ground that they had to depend on the employers for everything, as children on their parents.

Modern Theories

McGregor's theory: Douglas Murray McGregor classified the basis assumptions on human behaviour into two parts and called these sets of propositions Theory X and Theory Y.

McGregor's theory X: This theory was indirectly conceived and applied by F.W. Taylor. But it was McGregor who stated Theory X in very clear terms. In his own words, Theory X states, that:

Management is responsible for organising the elements of productive enterprise - money, materials, and equipment's people in the interest of economic ends.

With respect of people, this is a process of directing their efforts, motivating them, controlling their action, modifying their behaviour to fit the needs of the organistion.

Without the active intervention by management, people would be passive even resistant - to organisational needs. They must therefore be persuaded, rewarded, punished, and controlled. Their activities must be directed. This is management's task. We often sum it up by saying that management consists of getting things done through people.

The average man is by nature lazy and he works as little as possible.
He lacks ambition and dislikes responsibility
He is inherently self-centered, indifferent to organisational needs
He is by nature resistant to change and he is not very bright.

So this theory assumes that authority should be clear and flow directly from the superiors to subordinates without any reservation. It implies that management should be hard and strong. Close supervision and tight control over individual behaviour has to be introduced as work by nature is distasteful and people will try to shirk work and responsibility. But if the management believes in this theory, it will result in a lot of problems.

McGregor's theory Y: In view of the above misleading assumptions and practical difficulties, McGregor declares, "We require a different theory of the task of managing people based on more adequate assumptions about human nature and human motivation. I am going to be so bold as to suggest the broad dimension of such a theory. Call it Theory Y if you will",. His observations or Theory Y are as follows:

> Management is responsible for organizing the elements of productive enterprise - money, materials, equipment, and people - in the interest of economic ends.

> People are not by nature passive or resistant to organizational needs. They have become so as a result of experience in organization.

> Motivation, the potential for development, the capacity for assuming responsibility, the readiness to direct behaviour toward organizational goals, are all present in people. Management does not put them there. It is the responsibility of management to make it possible for people to recognize and develop these human characteristics for themselves.

> The essential task of management is to arrange organizational conditions and methods of operation so that people can achieve their own goals best by directing their own efforts towards organizational objectives.

They Y is basically a process of creating opportunities, releasing potential, removing obstacles, encouraging growth and providing guidance. It also provides for two way communication, participate management, decentralization and delegation of authority, emphasis on self-control, self-responsibility and self-discipline, emphasis on satisfaction of higher - level needs and maximum scope for management development programmes. Theory Y also assumes that work is as natural as play, provided the conditions are favorable.

Ouchi's Theory Z: William Ouchi proposed Theory Z as an alternative theory of organizational behaviur. Theory Z organizational culture comprises three major characteristics (a) Trust, (b) Subtlety, and (c) Intimacy.

Theory Z outlines a complete transformation of the motivational principles underlying high - performance organizations and implies a revolutionary change in management practices. The main characteristic features of the theory are as follows.

> Long-term employment
> Emphasis on training
> Seniority - based rewards
> The Ringi System of collective decision making
> Emphasis on self-discipline
> Holistic concern for employees and their families

Maslow's Theory

Human needs can be classified into: (a) basic physiological needs or primary needs and (b) social and psychological needs or secondary needs. Abraham Maslow states that individuals have these and they are motivated to satisfy these unsatisfied needs. If they are satisfied, they do not motivate individual behaviour. Needs are arranged according to a hierarchy of importance from the basic physiological to the complex self-actualization needs. The need at any level of the hierarchy will emerge only when the lower level needs is full satisfied.

Maslow states that individual needs arranged in a hierarchy from the lower - level physiological needs to the higher needs for self-actualization.

Basic physiological needs are the primary needs of an individual. The survival of an individual depends upon the satisfaction of these needs, namely, food clothing, shelter, sex, air, water and other necessaries of life. The organization helps an individual to satisfy their basic needs by providing reasonably good salaries, benefits and working conditions. Once these needs are satisfied, the individual will get an idea - about the higher level needs.

Safety and security needs are considered immediately after satisfying the psychological needs of individuals. These needs can be satisfied from job security, income, provision for old age, insurance, and safer working conditions.

Social needs are also called belonging needs. When basic needs and safety needs are satisfied, social needs become important. Social affiliation will make the job interesting. These needs are: love and affection, friendship, and so on.

Esteem needs or ego needs or status needs develop a concern for getting recognition, status, importance and respect from others. These needs are independence, achievements, competence, skills, knowledge, initiative and success. A very good organizational climate and more opportunity for development, responsibility, praise and promotion can play a vital role in satisfying esteem needs.

After the satisfaction of the esteem needs, the highest level of needs, self - actualization, will become an important needs. It involves realizing one's potentialities, capabilities for continued self - development and self-fulfilment. It is a personal achievement. Such challenges and achievements provide more satisfaction to a person.

The above hierarchy of needs stated by Maslow proves the fact that the second and subsequent needs do not dominate until the first and the previous needs are reasonably satisfied. Wants are continuous in nature and there cannot be an end satisfaction. The speciality of Maslow's theory is that the needs arise in a certain order of preference.

Even though Maslow's theory of hierarchy of needs has become popular, it is still subjected to a lot of criticism. The experience in continental European countries and Japan has shown that this theory does not apply effectively to their executives. Most of the American workers do not very much bother about their esteem needs are better satisfied than their security and social needs. Money can be a good motivator only for physiological and social needs, but not for satisfying higher - level needs. Some people may remain contented with the satisfaction of physiological needs only, without developing any further needs.

Herzberg's hygiene - motivation theory: Frederick Herzberg and his associates conducted research based on the interview of 200 engineers and accountants working in 11 different firms in the Pittsburg area. Herzberg developed a theory with two factors. They are hygiene factors and motivational factors. The dissatisfiers are known as hygiene factors because they support the mental health of the workers. Another set of job conditions operates primarily to build strong motivation and high job satisfaction. They are called as motivational factors.

Hygiene factors as stated by Herzberg are related to the work environment and are external to the job. They include wages, fringe benefits, status, job security, working conditions, company policy, administration, and interpersonal relations. The presence of these factors at a satisfactory level prevents job dissatisfaction, but they do not provide motivation to the workers. Even though they are not motivators, they will prevent the individual from becoming dissatisfied. Motivational factors are the motivators which are essential to increase the productivity of the employees. They are also known as satisfiers and they are concerned with job itself rather than the environment. These factors are recognition, feeling of achievement, responsibility, advancement, opportunity for growth, and so on.

Herzberg stated that it is also necessary to pay special attention to the motivational factors of satisfiers rather then concentrating on the traditional hygienic factors.

McClelland's three need theory: David C.McClelland developed further needs namely, the need for achievement, the need for power, and the need for affiliation. His observation is that businessman and particularly the entrepreneur managers, have more achievement motivation than other groups is society. Such people are goal - oriented, seek a challenge and desire perfect feedback in the performance. People with high affiliation needs value interpersonal relationships and are sensitive to other people's feelings. They want to be liked by others. They seek company by joining clubs and associations. On the other hand, people with a strong power need seek to dominate, influence and control others. Such power may be positive or negative. McClelland concludes that the need for achievement is one of the key factors of economic growth.

Vroom's expectancy theory: Vroom, while attacking Herzberg's two -- factor theory, offered an expectancy approach to the understanding of motivation. His theory explains three concepts of valence, instrumentality, and expectancy. Valence represents the value or significance of an outcome for a person, e.g. increased salaries, promotion. Instrumentality refers to the person's perception of the relationship between first-level outcomes. It is the extent to which a person will feel that performance is instrumental in getting him increased salaries or promotion. Expectancy refers to the extent to which such efforts will lead to the first - level outcome. Vroom's theory explains how the goals of individuals influence their efforts and that the behaviour individuals select depends upon their assessment of the probability that behavour will take with success towards the goal. To conclude, Vroom emphaized the significance of individual perceptions and assessments or organizational behaviour

18.8   REVIEW QUESTIONS

1.   Define motivation. Bring out the importance of motivation.
2.   What are the traditional theories of motivation?
3.   Discuss Theory X and Theory Y
4.   Explain Maslow's Hierarchy of Needs theory
5.   Discuss Herzberg's theory of motivation
6.   Explain Theory Z of management.

COMMUNICATION

19.1   INTRODUCTION

Communication is essential to minimize conflict, confusion and chaos. It eliminates friction, frustration and helps in motivating people. Communication is a vital link, a process of linking executives to workmen and workers to superiors. It is a dynamic interactive process of connecting people to people. As Raymond V.Lesikar states in his Business Communication, 70 per cent of our active hours are spent in communicating verbally, listening, speaking, reading and writing - in that order.

The term communication is derived from the original Latin word communize, which means "common". It involves the act of imparting a common idea or understanding to another person and covers any behavior that affects an exchange of meaning. Communication basically refers to the meaningful transmission of ideas to others, either orally or in writing. It can also take the form of symbols, codes, electronic impulses or even silence. Communication has become a very significant subject today not only for management experts, but also for technicians, engineers, psychologists, sociologists and organizational theorists.

19.2   DEFINITIONS

CYRIL L. HUDSON: Communication in its simplest form is conveying of information from one person to another.

LOUIS A. ALLEN: Communication is the sum of all the things one person does when he wants to create understanding in the mind of another. It is a bridge of meaning. It involves a systematic and continuous process of telling, listening and understanding.

THEO HAIMANN: Communication is the process of passing information and understanding from one person to another......... It is the process of imparting ideas and making oneself understood by others.

CHARLES E. REDFIELD: Communication is the broad field of human understanding and interchange of facts and opinions and not the technologies of telephone, telegraph, radio and the like.

KOONTZ AND O'DONNELL: Communication is an exchange of facts, ideas, opinions or emotions by two or more people.

KEITH DAVIS: Communication is the process of passing information and understanding from one person to another. It is essentially a bridge of meaning between people. By using this bridge of meaning, a person can safely cross the river of misunderstanding that separates all people.

NEWMAN AND SUMMER: Communication is an exchange of facts, ideas, opinions or emotions by two or more persons.

Careful scrutiny of the above definitions will reveal that communication essentially involves at least two people: only one person cannot communicate. Communication is both information and understanding. It includes all possible means by which matter is conveyed from person to person. Communication is directed towards a response.

19.3   IMPORTANCE OF COMMUNICATION

Importance of communication could be brought into limelight, through the following points:-

i.   Communication is the basis of organizational functioning

Communication is the basis of organizational functioning. It is only when necessary communications are made to subordinates and operators; about their jobs that action on their part is possible. In fact, communication is the petrol which drives the vehicle of the organization.

ii.   Communication as an aid to planning

Communication is an aid to the process of decision - making in general; and planning, in particular. Any type of decision - making (including planning decisions) requires, among other things, basic information about the enterprise resources and limitations, and the external environmental factors; which must be supplied i.e.

communicated to the management by suitable agencies. In fact, much of the accuracy of planning would very much depend on the accuracy of information communicated to the management, in this regard.

iii.   Communication as an aid to leadership

Communication is very basic to the process of exercising interpersonal influence, through leadership. A leader communicates the objectives, policies, rules and procedures of the enterprise to followers and also communicates the necessary work-orders, instructions and guidance to them, for the proper execution of the intended jobs, to be performed by the group. The members of the group i.e. followers would communicate their problems, needs and performance to the leader. The better is the communication system existing between the leader and his followers; the better are likely to be the results, produced by the group, during the process of exercising leadership.

iv.   Communication as an aid to co-ordination

Co-ordination is greatly facilitated when persons doing similar work or related aspects of work, are in perfect mutual understanding with one another - as to the manner and approach to work-performance. Such mutual understanding among people interest, is largely an outcome of free communication allowed to exist among them; through which they can reconcile their differences and agree on a common approach to work performance. Hence, communication is a good and great aid to achieving co-ordination of individual efforts.

v.   Communication helps overcoming resistance to changes and ensures their implementation

People, in general, resist to changes when changes are either not properly communicated to them or the purpose behind introducing such changes is not explained to them. Through communication, the management can convince people of the desirability of introducing organizational changes, overcome resistance to them and prepare a base for their implementation.

vi.   Communication as the basis of good human relations

Communication promotes good human relations, in the organizational life. Apparently communications is transfer messages; while intrinsically it is transmission of understanding among the sender and the recipients of messages. A free flow of communication, through facilitating transmission of understanding, paves the way for the development of good human relations in the organization.

In particular, communication helps to resolve differences; helps in redressal of grievances and becomes the basis for

-      Sound manager subordinate relations
-      Sound labor management relations

vii.   Communication helps building good public relations

Good public relations comprise relations of the enterprise with outside agencies, particularly consumers and the public at large. Many business enterprises, now-a-days, maintain a separate public relations department; which basically entertains problems, complaints of the public and assures them of their solution. What process the public relations department follows in building good public relations, is largely a process of entering into communication with the public-communicating to the public and being communicated by it.

viii.   Communication as an aid to controlling

The essence of controlling is the remedial action initiated by management to correct deviations in actual performance, as against the planned standards. Such remedial action is possible, only when the actual performance of people and the deviations from standards are communicated to management, for controlling purposes.

ix.   Communication facilitates delegation of authority

Delegation of authority is entirely based on the process of communication. A superior communicates the job assignment, necessary instructions etc. to the subordinate; and the latter, in turn, communicates his problems, difficulties and progress of work to the former. Maintaining open lines of communication between the superior and the subordinate, is a prerequisite for successful delegation of authority.

x.   Communication as pervading all walks of organizational life

Communication is needed in personnel matters, like recruitment, selection, training, orientation, and placement etc. of employees. It is needed for purposes of motivating subordinates. Enforcement of discipline, in the organization, requires communication of the rules of organization to all members of the organization. As a matter of fact, communication pervades all walks of organizational life.

19.4   PROCESS OF COMMUNICATION

The process of communication consists of the following steps or stages:

i.   Message

This is the background step to the process of communication, which, by forming the subject matter of communication necessitates the start of a communication process. The message might be a fact or an idea, or a request or a suggestion, or an order or a grievance.

ii.   Sender

The actual process of communication is initiated at the hands of the sender; who takes steps to send the message to the recipient.

iii.   Encoding

Encoding means giving a form and meaning to the message through expressing in into-words, symbols, gestures, graph, drawings etc.

iv.   Medium

It refers to the method or channel, through which the message is to be conveyed to the recipient. For example, an oral communication might be made through a peon or over the telephone etc; while a written communication might be routed through a letter or a notice displayed on the notice-board etc.

v.   Recipient (or the Receiver)

Technically, a communication is complete, only when it comes to the knowledge of the intended person i.e. the recipient or the receiver.

vi.   Decoding

Decoding means the interpretation of the message by the recipient; with a view to getting the meaning of the message, as per the intentions of the sender. It is at this stage in the communication process, that communication is philosophically defined as, 'the transmission of understanding'.

vii.   Feedback

To complete the communication process, sending feedback to communication, by the recipient to the sender is imperative. 'Feedback' implies the reaction or response of the recipient to the message, comprised in the communication.

19.5   PRINCIPLES OF COMMUNICATION

In order to be effective and meaningful, the managerial function of communication must be guided by the following principles:-

i.   Principle of understanding

Communication must be such, as transmits understanding of the communication message to the recipient; as per the intentions of the sender.

A practical application of this principle requires that the message must be clearly expressed - whether made orally or in writing. Further, the message must be complete - leaving no scope for any doubts likely to confuse the recipient and compel him towards a misinterpretation of the message.

ii.   Principle of attention

Communication must be made in such a manner; that it invites the attention of the recipient to it.

For a practical application of this principle, it is imperative that not only must the message be expressed in a pleasant and sound manner; but also the purpose of the sender in making communication, must be absolutely clarified.

iii.   **Principle of Brevity**

The message to be communicated must be brief; as usually the recipient, specially an executive, would not have much time to devote to a single piece of communication.

However, brevity of the message must not be sought at the cost of clarity or completeness of the message. The sender must strike a balance among these three forces - brevity, clarity and completeness.

iv.   **The principle of timeliness**

The communication must be timely i.e. must be made at the high time, when needed to be communicated to the recipient. An advance communication carries with it the danger of 'forgetting', on the part of the recipient, while a delayed communication loses its purpose and charm, and becomes meaningless, when the right time for action on it has expired.

v.   **The principle of appropriateness (or rationality)**

The communication must be appropriate or rational, in the context of the realization of organizational objectives.

Communication must be neither impracticable to act upon; nor irrational, making no contribution to common objectives.

vi.   **Principle of feedback**

Communication must be a two-way process. The feedback (or reaction or response) of the recipient to the message, must be as easily transferable to the sender, as the original communicable made by the sender.

The idea behind emphasizing on the feedback aspect of communication is that it helps the sender to modify his subsequent communications in view of the reactions of the recipient - making for better and improved human relations.

vii.   Principle of the constructive and strategic use of informal groups

The management must not hesitate in making a constructive and strategic use of informal groups; for ensuring and facilitating speedier communications in emergency situations. Such as a use of informal groups would also help develop good human relations - by upgrading the status of informal groups and their leaders.

However, management must assure itself that rumors are not spread by informal groups. And for this, a guard over the manner of functioning of informal groups, while transmitting a formal communication, is but imperative.

19.6   COMMUNICATION METHODS

There are three important methods of communication: (a) Verbal Communication, (b) Written Communication and (c) Gesticulation.

Verbal Communication

It is a face-to-face type of communication involving conversation. Conversation is a natural human activity, and a more effective method of communication. It provides clarity, accuracy, certainty and nearness for communication. Verbal communication can also be made through mechanical devices like telephones, intercoms, dictating machines, etc. In organizations, verbal communication is popular both for downward and upward communication. Instructions, lecturers, orders and counseling are done through verbal communication. It helps in getting quick responses and good feedback. It develops a friendly environment, cooperation and team spirit. In emergency situations, it is the best method of communication. But the problem is distance or misunderstanding. It creates legal difficulties also as there will not be any documentary evidence.

Written Communication

It is the most important medium of communication. Orders, instructions, circulars, manuals, handbooks, etc., are provided only through written communication. It can be transmitted simultaneously to numerous persons. Workers can also give their suggestions and grievances in writing. Written communication serves as a permanent reference; it is official and more effective; it should be drafted clearly, correctly, completely and convincingly to make it effective.

Gesticulation

Gesticulation is a method supplementary to verbal communication. A handshake, a pat on the back, can be effective gesticulation, communicating appreciation or praise.

19.7 ESSENTIALS OF GOOD COMMUNICATION

1. **Have clarity of thought:** The idea to be communicated should be clear and complete without any conflict or confusion; Employee communication in particular should be specific, meaningful and clear, without any abstract ideas and vagueness. The language spoken should be common and understandable.

2. **Communication should be functional:** A superior who states that he will trust the workers and then proceeds to make unnecessary or too many checks on the workers will fail in communication. He must say what he means, and he must mean what he says. A manager who insists on the punctuality of workers can make the communication functional, and when he is punctual. This is essential because it is human psychology to discount a message when the attitude and actions behind it contradict it.

3. **Develop participation:** Communication cannot be a one-way traffic. Both the communication channels should be kept open. Workers are not mere listeners; they also will have something to say. Managers should encourage participative communication so as to have an objective and perfect understanding of situations.

4. **Plan the transmission:** A communicator has to plan carefully about what to communicate. One has to plan about the media and channels to make the communication most effective. A harmonious blend of both formal and informal channels will make the communication more effective.

5. **Develop listening systems:** Listening plays a vital role in the perfect understanding of a communication. It is an art which can be developed by continuous practice. There is a tendency on the part of managers not to listen to workers with real interest, which should be avoided. Good listening is good understanding.

6.   **Maintain cordial superior - subordinate relationship:** Effective communication is possible only when the employer-employee relationship is cordial. There must be mutual trust, faith and perfect understanding on both sides. Coordination on the part of managers and cooperation on the part of workers will help in making the communication more effective.

7.   **Regulate the flow of information:** Communication flow should be optimum without any shortage or overloading. Communication should not create a gap because of shortages, or be a burden because of overloading. Top management need not go through all the incoming messages. Only exceptionally important messages can be handed over to the top management and the remaining routine matters can be decided at the lower level itself.

8.   **Use feedback effectively:** Feedback will give a suitable response to the sender of the communication. Immediate and prompt feedback will make the communication very clear.

19.8   BARRIERS TO COMMUNICATION

There are various barriers to good and effective communication. But the main barrier is the fact that many organizations really do not provide or encourage two-way communication. There are other barriers causing breakdowns, distortion or rumours. If these barriers are removed, a considerable degree of effectiveness and accuracy can be achieved in communication. The following are the important barriers to communication.

1.   **Barriers in organizational structure:** A rigid and ultra-formal organizational structure creates problems of re-communication. Ulrich and Booz have stated that good communication exists where anyone in the organization is free to contact whoever can help him with his problems. Long lines of communication, great distance of subordinates from superiors, lack of proper and regular instructions, and overloading of work at certain levels of authority may also create barriers of communication.

2.   **Semantic barriers:** Semantics is the science of meaning. The receiver of the message should perceive and understand the message in the same sense in which the sender has communicated it. As words will have different meanings, they may be understood in different senses by different people.

3.   **Difference in status or rank:** Difference in rank and status is always a source of mis-understanding. The placing of persons in superior and subordinate relationships may inhibit a free flow of information, ideas, suggestions and questions. What the superior sees in his position as responsibility, the subordinate sees as power. Sometimes, mild criticism or a small piece of advice given by a superior to help a subordinate may be taken as a strong reprimand. The greater the rank difference, the greater will be the distortion. Factors which increase the rank barriers are unavailability at short notice, special executive chambers, elaborate offices, etc. The superior with his status may feel that he cannot fully admit to his subordinates those problems, conditions or results which may reflect adversely on his ability and judgment.

4.   **Badly expresses messages:** Messages which are vague, abstract, lack coherence, have poor sentence formation, are repetitive, etc. may affect the quality of the communication.

5.   **Faulty translation:** Language is an important barrier. Every type of information has to be translated into understandable pieces of information.

6.   **Loss by transmission and retention:** In oral communication, 30 percent of the information is lost in each transmission. Even in written communication, there may be poor retention.

7.   **Distrust of the Communicator:** If a superior has no trust and confidence in his employees, he will tend to listen to them in a prejudiced or biased manner. Ultimately, this may result in inaccurate responses and ineffective communication.

8.   **Faulty listening:** Telling will be meaning unless someone is listening to it. Listening requires thinking, processing and understanding the message. One must have patience, interest and active participation in listening.

9.   **Emotional approach:** When a communication is packed with emotion, there will not be any objectivity in it.

10. **Resistance to change:** When new ideas are introduced, they may not be welcomed by employees as they may prefer to maintain status quo. Change in timing or methodology may not be received immediately and accepted well.

11.   **Overloading of communication:** Overloading of communication channels may create a traffic jam in the channels resulting in noise and irrelevant messages, as happens often in telephones.

One can overcome all such barriers by planning the communication system properly, and by recognizing the human elements involved in it. Messages must be direct and simple; the language should be understandable; provision for a good feedback system has to be made; listening should be proper and effective; and there must be coherence, clarity and consistency in communication.

19.9   METHODS OF OVERCOMING COMMUNICATION BARRIERS

➢ Each and every employee in an organization should take responsibility for sending message.
➢ For communicating a particular message, the management has to follow the upward, downward or horizontal systems.
➢ The management has to inform all employees about the need for communication.
➢ The message should be sent in a simple and clear language.
➢ A good information system should be established.
➢ If necessary, communication should be sent informally.
➢ Employees must send correct information.

19.10 EFFECTIVE COMMUNICATIONS

For effective communication, the American Management Association (AMA) has identified the following points:

➢ A clear message
➢ Advantage of communication
➢ Understanding the physical and human environments
➢ Consultation with other experts in preparing the information
➢ Discussion on important aspects of communication
➢ The values of the receiver
➢ Importance of the communication
➢ Follow-up action
➢ Completing the job as per the communication
➢ Possessing good listening skills

19.11   TEN COMMANDMENTS OF GOOD COMMUNICATION: AMA (1961)

1.   Seek to clarify your ideas before communicating

The more systematically we analyze the problem or idea to be communicated, the clearer it becomes. This is the first step towards effective communication. Many communications fail because of inadequate planning. Good planning must consider the goals and attitude of those who will receive the communication and those who will be affected by it.

2.   Examine the true purpose of each communication

Before you communicate, ask yourself what you really want to accomplish with your message - to obtain information, to initiate action, to change another person's attitude or behavior. Identify your most important goal and then adapt your language, tone and total approach to serve that specific objective. Don't try to accomplish too mush with each communication. The sharper the focus of your message, the greater its chances of sources.

3.   Consider the total physical and human setting whenever you communicate

Meaning and intent are conveyed by more than words alone. Many other factors influence the overall impact of a communication and you must be sensitive to the total setting in which you communicate. Consider, for example, your sense of timing - i.e. the circumstances under which you make an announcement or render a decision; the physical setting - whether you communicate in private, for example, or otherwise; the social climate that pervades work relationships within the company or a department and sets the tone of its communications; custom and past practice - the degree to which your communication conforms to, or departs from the expectations of your audience.

Be constantly aware of the total setting in which you communicate. It is essential that communication adapts to its environment.

4.   Consult with others, where appropriate, in planning communications

Frequently, it is desirable to see the participation of others in planning a communication or developing the facts on which to base it. Such consultation often helps to lend additional insight and objectivity to your message. Moreover, those who have helped you plan your communication; will give it their active support.

5.   Be mindful, while you communicate, of the overtones as well as the basic content of your message

Your tone of voice, your expression, your apparent receptiveness to the responses of others - all have tremendous impact on those you wish to reach. Frequently overlooked, these subtleties of communication often affect a listener's reaction to a message even more than its basic content. Similarly, your choice of language - particularly your awareness of the fine shades of meaning and emotion in the words you use - predetermines in large part - the reactions of your listeners.

6.   Take the opportunity, when in arises, to convey something of help or value to the receiver

Consideration of the other person's interests and needs - the ability to look at thinks from his point of view will frequently create opportunities to convey something of immediate benefit or long-range value to him. People on the job are the most responsive to the managers whose messages take their own interests into account. This is called empathy in communication.

7.   Follow up your communication

Our best efforts at communication may be wasted, and we may never know whether we have succeeded in expressing our true meaning and intent, if we do not follow up to see how well we have put our message across.

This you can do by asking questions, by encouraging the receiver to express his reactions, by follow-up contacts, by subsequent review of the performance. Make certain that every important communication has a feedback so that complete understanding and appropriate action result.

8.   Communicate for tomorrow as well as today

While communications may be aimed primarily at meeting the demands of an immediate situation, they must be planned with the past in mind, if they are to maintain consistency in the receiver's view; but, most important of all, they must be consistent with long-range interests and goals. For example, it is not easy to communicate frankly on such matters as poor performance or the shortcoming of a loyal subordinate - but postponing disagreeable communications makes them more difficult in the long run and is actually unfair to your subordinates and your company.

9.   Be sure your actions support your communications

In the final analysis, the most persuasive kind of communication is not what you say but what you do. When a man's actions or attitudes contradict his words, we tend to discount what he has said. For every manager, this means that good supervisory practices - clear assignment of responsibility and authority, fair rewards for effort, and sound policy enforcement - serve to communicate more than all gifts of oratory.

10.   Seek not only to be understood but to understand: be a good listener

When we start talking, we often cease to listen - in that larger sense of being attuned to the other person's unspoken reactions and attitudes. Even more serious is the fact that we are all guilty, at times, of inattentiveness when others are attempting to communicate with us. Listening is one of the most important, most difficult - and most neglected - skills in communication. It demands that we concentrate not only on the explicit meanings another person is expressing but on the implicit meanings, unspoken words and undertones that may be far more significant. Thus, we must learn to listen with the inner ear, if we are to know the inner man.

19.12 ELECTRONIC MEDIA IN COMMUNICATION

Managers have studied and are gradually adopting various electronic devices that improve communication. Electronic equipment includes mainframe computers, mini computers, personal computers, electronic mail systems, and electronic typewriters, as well as cellular telephones for making telephone calls from cars and beepers for keeping in contact with the office. Let us first look at telecommunication in general and at the increasing use of teleconferencing in particular.

Telecommunication

Although telecommunication is just emerging, a number of companies have already effectively utilized the new technology in a variety of ways, as shown by the following examples.

1. A large bank supplies hardware and software to its customers so that they can easily transfer funds to their suppliers.
2. Several banks now make bank-by-phone services available even to individuals.
3. Facsimile mail service ensures delivery of a document across the country within hours.
4. The computerized airline reservation system facilitating making travel arrangements.

5. One large medical supply company gained a competitive edge by providing hospital purchasing agents with opportunity to enter supply orders directly at the computer terminal.

6. Many firms now have detailed personnel information – including performance appraisals and career development plans – in a data bank.

As you can see, there are many applications of telecommunication. But to make telecommunication systems effective, the technical experts must make every effort to identify the real needs of managers and customers and to design systems that are useful. Let us now turn to a specific application of the new technology: teleconferencing.

Teleconferencing

For some time now companies such as IBM, Bank of America, and Hughes have used teleconferencing. However, due to the wide variety of systems, including audio systems, audio systems with snapshots displayed on the video monitor and live video systems, the term "teleconferencing" is difficult to define. In general, most people think of a teleconference as a group of people interacting with each other by means of audio and video media with moving or still pictures.

Full-motivation video is frequently used to hold meetings among managers. Not only do they hear each other, but they can also see each others expressions or discuss some visual display. This kind of communication is, of course, rather expensive, and audio in combination with still video may be used instead. This method of communicating may be useful for showing charts or illustrations during a technical discussion.

Advantages

Some of the potential advantages of teleconferencing include savings in travel expenses and travel time. Also, conferences can be held wherever necessary, since there is no need to make travel plans long in advance. Because meetings can be held more frequently, communication is improves between, for example, headquarters and geographically scattered diverts.

Disadvantages

There are also drawbacks to teleconferencing. Because of the easier arranging meetings in this manner, they may be held more often than necessary. Moreover, since this approach uses rather new technology, the equipment is subject to breakdowns. Most important, perhaps, teleconferencing is a poor substitute for meeting with other persons face-to-face. Despite these limitations, an increased use of teleconferencing is likely in the future.

19.13   REVIEW QUESTIONS

1.   Explain the importance of communication.
2.   What are the modes of communication?
3.   What are the types of communication?
4.   What are the various barriers to communication?
5.   How can one overcome the communication by barriers?
6.   Explain the essentials of good communication.
7.   What is the role of electronic media in communication?
8.   Write down the advantages and disadvantages of teleconferencing?

CONTROL PROCESS

20.1 INTRODUCTION

Control is a fundamental managerial function or process which measures current performance and guides it towards some predetermined objectives. The essence of control lies in checking progress against plans, setting up individual and organizational performance standards, and seeing that they are achieved as per the plan. Henry Fayol states that in an undertaking, control consists of verifying whether everything occurs in conformity with the plan adopted, the instructions issued and the principles established. Its object is to point out weaknesses and errors in order to rectify them and prevent their recurrence. It operates on everything: things, people and actions.

The process of control also involves assessment of present or recent operations to identify desirable changes when performance is found to be unsatisfactory. The essence of control is action, which adjusts operations to predetermined standards, and its basis is information in the hands of managers. There are various possibilities like confusion, mistakes, delay, loss of effort and friction which may result in deviation from the original plans and programmes. So mere planning may not be adequate. Control highlights all such deviations as soon as they appear between the performance and the standards prescribed.

20.2 DEFINITIONS

KOONTZ AND O'DONNELL: Control is measurement and correction of the performance of activities of subordinates in order to make sure that enterprise objectives and plans devised to attain them are being accomplished.

ERNEST DALE: Control is a system which not only provides a historical record of what has happened to the business as a whole, but also pinpoints the reasons why it has happened and provides the data that enable the chief executive or the departmental head to take corrective steps if he is on the wrong track.

GEORGE R. TERRY: Control is determining what is being accomplished, that is, evaluating the performance, and if necessary, applying corrective measures so that the performance takes place according to plans.

20.3   CONTROL VERSUS CONTROLS

In the normal course, controls are conceived as plural of control. But this is a misconception. As 'rent' in economics has a different meaning, so is the term 'controls' having a surprisingly different meaning in management and organizational behavior literature. In management, controls means measurements, whereas controlling is a process of gathering and feeding back information about performance so that decision makers can compare actual results with planned results and decide what to do about any apparent discrepancies or problems.

Peter F. Druker, a well-known authority on management, brings out the distinction between the term 'control' and 'controls', in the following fashion :

(i)   Controls refer to measurement and information whereas control is related to 'direction'.

(ii)   Controls pertain to means and control pertains to an end.

(iii)   Controls deal with facts and with the events of the past; control on the other hand, deals with expectations, i.e. with future.

(iv)   Controls are analytical and concerned with what was and what is. Control is normative and concerned with ought to be.

Thus controls are means to an end, 'end' being control.

20.4   IMPORTANCE

Control encourages top management for more and more delegation and decentralization. It spots the areas of weaknesses and the range of deviations from the original plans. It stimulates action which will gear up all the departments. McFarland says that "Control is vital to the strength and morale of company employees" - workers will never like a situation to go out of control. Control will help in taking correct and clear-cut decisions. It can make planning effective and meaningful.

20.5   LIMITATIONS

1.   It is very difficult to establish standards for intangible activities.
2.   Control cannot be effectively exercised over external factors which are basically uncontrollable.
3.   Intensive control measures may be resisted by employees.
4.   Control may not function effectively with untrained and unqualified subordinates.

5.   Control may be resisted on the ground that it interferes with freedom of individual thinking and action.

20.6   CHARACTERISTICS

Control and planning are inseparable. No business can exist without these twin concepts in some form or other. Control cannot exist without planning and therefore, the planning has to be designed to fit the specification of control. A standard is a type of plan which guides in evaluating performance.

Control is a continuous process. Control is a process of constant revision and analysis of standards, and understanding of the variation between the plans and the performance.

Control is forward looking. One cannot exercise any control over the past. One can only review the past events. Control is possible only of future performance.

Control is all-pervasive. Even though the scope of control varies, control as such functions at all levels of responsibility to execute plans.

Control has a positive approach. Control can never be negative, and it is not an obstacle or a bottleneck; it is a managerial necessity and will help the management in getting positive and successful results.

20.7   ELEMENTS OF CONTROL

There are six elements in control system. An executive exercising control has to understand each element in the context of its necessity. These elements are :

1.   Authority
2.   Knowledge
3.   Guidance
4.   Direction
5.   Constraint
6.   Restraint

All these elements are absolutely essential to exercise an effective control.

20.8   ESSENTIALS OF A GOOD CONTROL SYSTEM

The following are broad considerations which are essential to have an effective control system:

1.   **Suitability.** The nature and need of the activity will help in determining a good system of control. Controls in a production department will be different from those used in marketing departments. Control for the production manager will be different from control for a supervisor.

2.   **Prompt reporting**. If there are any deviations from the plans and standards, they must be reported promptly and immediately.

3.   **Forward-looking**. A good control system should avoid the possibility of getting similar deviations in future. All potential deviations should be corrected.

4.   **Focus on strategic points**. A good system of control not only points out the deviations or exceptions but also pinpoints where they are vital or strategic.

5.   **Flexible**. A good control system should remain workable even when the plans are changed or standards are altered.

6.   **Objective**. To have effective control, there should be objective, precise and suitable standards. They should be definite and determinable.

7.   **Economical**. The cost of installation and operation of a control system should be justified by its benefits.

8.   **Understandable**. A control system should be clear and easily understandable to the people who will use it, so that control becomes easy, smooth and meaningful.

9.   **Remedial action**. A good control system not only detects deviation, but also suggests practical corrective action. Koontz and O'Donnell state that an adequate system of control should disclose where failures are occurring, who is responsible for them and what should be done about them.

10.   **Human factor**. A good control system should be worker-centred rather than work-centered. Accountability for major deviations and assistance for improvement should be organized.

        To conclude: planning is the basis of control, action is essence, delegation is the key; and information is the guide.

20.9   TYPES OF CONTROL

        Depending on the 'time' at which control is applied, controls are of three types - historical (feedback), concurrent, and predictive (feed-forward).

Historical control

Traditionally, control was viewed as historical. It is because most of the control methods measure results after the performance. Control provides informaton as to how the goals of organization are met or not met Income statements and position statements are examples of this type of control. Here control is seen as a postmortem of events the purpose of which is to improve in the future.

Another name for historical controls is the feedback controls. Feedback control (or post-action control) is largely historical. In other words, the measured activity has already occurred, and it is impossible to go back and correct performance to bring it up to the standard. Instead, correction must occur after the fact. Examples of feedback controls are disciplinary action, performance appraisal interviews, financial and budgetary results and final inspections.

Concurrent Control

It is also called 'real time' control. Concurrent control techniques immediately consider any problem and analyze it to take necessary and corrective steps before any major damage is done. Control chart is an example of this control.

Concurrent controls are also known by another name 'steering controls' and occur while an activity is taking place. The navigator of an aircraft who adjusts the aircraft's movements is an example of concurrent control. When you ride a bicycle, you must adjust your steering constantly, depending on the turns in the road, obstacles, and changes in the terrain to keep your vehicle upright and move toward your destination.

Predictive control

Here the control system anticipates problems the management encounters in future. Cash budget is an example of this type where the finance manager is in a position to estimate the next year's flow of cash. If there is a shortage of funds in a particular month, he can arrange for bank loan or some other alternative. Predictive control is also frequently termed as 'feed forward control'. Predictive control attempts to anticipate problems or deviations from the standard in advance of their occurrence. It is, thus, a more aggressive, active approach to control, allowing corrective action to be taken in advance of the problem. One notable characteristic of feed forward control is that it anticipates problems and permits action to be taken before a problem occurs.

Feed forward and concurrent controls are sufficiently timely to allow management to take corrective changes and still achieve objectives. But there are several other factors to be considered such as:

(i)   Despite their appeal, they are costly.

(ii)   Many activities do not lend themselves to frequent and continuous monitoring.

(iii)   At some point, excessive control becomes counter-productive.

20.10 THE CONTROL PROCESS

K. Boulding states that the barest essential of any organization is a control mechanism. Control is the key factor. If the control mechanism fails, plans and programmes will also fail. A control mechanism or control process has five basic elements. They are as follows.

- ➢ Establishment of standards of performance
- ➢ Measurement of actual performance
- ➢ Comparison of actual performance with the original standards
- ➢ Taking corrective action
- ➢ Feedback

Establishment of standards: A standard is a criterion against which future results can be measured. Such standards may be tangible or intangible. A standard should be tangible, for better evaluation. It should be clear and meaningful. Performance standards are expressed in terms of cost, quality, quantity and time. Standards like employee morale, discipline, public relations, image of the concern, etc. cannot be easily quantified, as they are intangible. Quantitative standards can be determined by statistical methods such as sampling.

Measurement of actual performance: The very purpose of control is to check or measure the actual performance. If the standards prescribed are tangible, it is easy to measure the performance in similar units. If the standards are intangible, it is difficult to measure the performance. Work, operations and turnout should be observed, measured and facts collected. Statistical data, reports, opinions, accounting information, etc. will help in measuring the actual performance.

Comparison of actual performance with the original standards: After measuring the actual performance, it has to be compared with the original standards. The comparison may disclose either agreements or deviations from the standards established. But the manager has to be very clear about the concept of deviation: minor or negligible deviations may be ignored, but major and significant deviations should be correctly understood. For this, the manager must have his own range of tolerance, which he can fix with his knowledge and experience.

Taking corrective action: As soon as deviations are reported, the concerned manager should take steps to correct the action. This is essential because measurement of performance should not become just a ritual or post mortem of past events. If the deviation is significant, then the original standard itself has to be rechecked. Corrective action should be taken immediately, without any loss of time. Corrective action may be improving the methodology, techniques, organizational structure, proper selection, training and remuneration of workers, or even effective communication and successful motivation. Corrective action may be either to cure or to prevent such deviations. Wherever possible, automatic, self-regulating mechanisms should be introduced to bring back performance in line with the original plan.

Feedback: Feedback is an important element in the control process. It ties together all the elements of the control mechanism. The controller will receive feedback information regarding actual performance in comparison with the original standards. If the feedback is positive and reveals accomplishment, the manager must encourage and appreciate the subordinates. If the feedback brings negative results, the manager has to take corrective action and alter the operations accordingly. Feedback will help in getting information well in time about the work performance, and it also motivates people.

20.11 REVIEW QUESTIONS

1.   Define control. Explain the importance of control in a modern business enterprise.
2.   Discuss the characteristics of the controlling function.
3.   What is meant by a control process? Discuss its basic elements.
4.   Discuss the requirements of an effective control system.
5.   What are the essentials of good control system?

CONTROL TECHNIQUES

21.1 TRADITIONAL TECHNIQUES OF CONTROLLING

21.1.1 Budgeting (or Budgetary Control System)

(a) Introductory observations

A budget is both - a method of planning and an instrument (or device) for controlling. It is a plan in so far as the numerical expression of the standards of performance (i.e. anticipated results) is concerned. However, when the actual operational performance is judged against these standards; the budget assumes the role of a control technique. As such, a budget is properly called a budgetary control; the suffix 'control' usually being omitted.

(b) The concept of 'budget'

A budget might be defined as the expression of a management plan into numerical terms (financial, quantitative or time); being a statement of anticipated results expected of the working of a particular aspect of organizational operational life, for a specific future period of time, say a month, a quarter, a half year, a year or so.

(c) Types of business budgets

Some important types of business budgets are described below:

(i) Sales Budget

One most important aspect of the revenue budgets of business enterprises is the sales budget.

A sales budget is a statement of an expected volume of sales, flowing to a business enterprise over a specific future period of time.

(ii)   **Production Budget**

An important budget concerning the operational life of a business enterprise is the production budget.

A production budget is a statement of anticipated production to be done by an industrial enterprise during a specific future period of time; in view of the resource availability for production purposes.

Production budget might be expressed in terms of -

Man-hours; where most of production work is done by manual labor.

or   **Machine-hours ;** where production activities are mechanized.

(iii)   **Production-facilities budgets**

Based on the need and requirements of the overall production budget; budgets for various productions facilities are prepared - as branches of the production budget. Some of such ancillary budgets are as follows:

(a)   **Materials budgets** i.e. a budget for direct material needed for the budgeted output.

(b)   **Labor budget** i.e. a budget for direct labor needed for the budgeted output.

(c)   **Factory overheads budget** i.e. a budget for factory overheads likely to be incurred, during the production process, to produce the targeted output.

(d)   **Administrative (or office) overheads budget** i.e. a budget for office overheads likely to be incurred, during the handling of the targeted output, at the 'office-stage'; in the industrial enterprise.

(e)   **Selling and distribution overheads budget,** i.e. a budget for selling and distribution overheads likely to be incurred, at 'the selling and delivery stage', during the budget period.

(iv)   **Cash Budget**

A cash budget is an important branch of the overall Finance Budget. This budget assumes great significance in the operational life of any business enterprises; as cash is needed for various purposes, quite off and on.

A cash budget is a statement of anticipated cash receipts and cash disbursements; occurring during a specific future period of time - to find out the likely surplus or shortage of cash, during that period.

(v)   Capital Expenditure Budgets

A major aspect of financial budgeting concerns with designing capital expenditure budgets, for items like plants, machines, equipments, furniture, etc.

(vi)   Balance-sheet budgets

Balance-sheet budgets are statements of forecast of capital account, liabilities and assets.

In fact, sources of changes in Balance Sheet items are the outcome of the functioning of budgetary control system, as a whole. Hence, Balance Sheet budgets prove the accuracy of all other budgets.

(d)   The Budget Organization

For the best designing and functioning of the budgetary control systems, there is the need for a separate 'budget-organization'.

The 'budget-organization' implies the formulation of a Budget Committee extended into various sub-committees. The main task of the budget committee is to finalize and co-ordinate the planning and implementation of the budgetary control system.

The Budget Committee, headed by the Chief Executive, consists of various functional heads like the Production Manager, the Purchase Manager, the Finance Manager, the Marketing Manager, the Personnel Manager, the Engineer, the Accountant, the Cost Accountant and other functional experts. In this Budget Committee, there is a usually a provision for a 'budget-officer' who acts as the secretary of the committee; and makes preparations for arranging the meetings of the Budget Committee.

(e)   Advantages of the Budgetary Control System

Some important advantages of the budgetary control system are as follows:

(i)   Expression of planning in definite terms

Since budgets are a numerical expression of business plans; the budgetary control system - built around the concept of budgeting - expresses plans in definite terms. This way, it is easier for managers to communicate plans more precisely to subordinates and operators. Further, people understand plans in a better manner, and can easily take actions for the realization of plans.

(ii)   Comprehensive managerial technique

Budgetary control system is a comprehensive managerial technique of managing an enterprise. It is both, a method of planning and an instrument of controlling. Planning and controlling are two extremes of budgetary control; and other managerial functions viz. organizing, staffing, direction naturally fit into the budgetary control structure at their appropriate places.

(iii)   Communication of jobs (or duties) though budgets

The budgetary control system is the mouthpiece of management; as budgets convey to people what jobs are assigned to them or what role they are supposed to play, in the organizational life.

(iv)   Instrument of co-ordination

Budgetary control system is an instrument of co-ordination. Through budgets, the functioning of functional departments, management levels and actions of individuals throughout the enterprise are all endeavored to be co-ordinated.

(v)   Profit-maximization attempted through cost-control

Through emphasizing on cost minimization and expenditure control; the budgetary control system helps management to strive for the profit-maximization goals in a legitimate manner.

(iv)   Fixation of responsibility facilitated

Budgetary control system judges the organizational operational efficiency; by locating the spots where weaknesses are occurring. Thus, responsibility for weaknesses or shortfalls in performance can be easily fixed through the budgetary control system.

(f)   Limitations of the Budgetary Control system

Budgetary control system is a rose, full of thorns. Some significant limitations of this system can be stated as follows:

(i)   Not comprehensive

Budgetary control system is a lop-sided managerial device; in as much as the qualitative aspects of managing cannot be fully and precisely made a part of it. In fact, despite intelligent quantification of qualitative aspects; the real intentions of these aspects cannot be incorporated into the budgetary control system.

(ii)   Difficulty in setting rational standards

Usually, while devising a budgetary control system, it is difficult to set rational standards of performance. Despite the adoption of the best scientific approaches to setting rational standards; prejudices, bias and personal opinions of managers enter the budgetary control system, through the back door.

(iii)   Danger of over-budgeting

Regulating the organizational operational life through the budgetary control system, might carry a danger of over-budgeting i.e. too much emphasis on details of minor items and light emphasis on major heads, requiring strict-control.

(iv)   Lack of departmental co-operation and co-ordination

There might be a lack of departmental co-operation and co-ordination, while designing and implementing the budgetary control system. In fact, some managers might not be willing to co-operate with one another into the making of the system; due to personal differences and conflicting approaches. As such, departmental co-ordination, which is the heart of the budgetary control system, might be unavailable or unobtainable, because of lack of co-operation among departmental managers. As a result, the budgetary control system becomes faulty or misleading, and a mere theoretical exercise in managing.

(v)   Umbrella for inefficiency

Budgetary control system may become an umbrella for hiding organizational inefficiency; as many people might act within budgets - though remaining highly inefficient otherwise.

21.1.2 Non-Budgetary control techniques

Some of the non-budgetary control techniques are described below:

(i)   Direct personal observation and supervision

Direct personal observation and supervision by a manager is, perhaps, the oldest techniques of controlling. In this technique, control is exercised by a manager through a face-to-face contact with employees; by directly observing their performance e.g. by taking rounds in the plant where workers are performing or in any other manner.

This technique of controlling has the obvious advantage that corrective action by the manager could be taken on the spot. Moreover, this technique of direct observation has psychological impact on workers; as they are motivated to work as per standards of performance due to the fear of the manager.

However, direct personal observation and supervision technique of controlling has certain disadvantages, like the following:

(i)   It is a time-consuming technique. The manager is left with little time for attending to his official duties.
(ii)   Direct personal supervision cannot be exercised all the time over all the employees.
(iii)   Due to this technique of controlling; there may be interference in the smooth flow of work of employees.
(iv)   This technique has a negative impact on self-motivated and enlightened workers; and they often resist to it.

(ii)   Written Reports

Under this technique of controlling; each manager prepares written reports on the performance of his subordinates; and submits these to higher authorities. Lower management submits reports to middle management to top management and the top management (i.e. Board of Directors) to the body of members.

The written report method of controlling has a psychological impact on workers. In fact, the fear of likely adverse remarks in the report makes workers discharge their duties efficiently.

However, this technique of controlling has certain limitations, as described below:

(i)   This technique carries an element of subjectivity, in that a manager may deliberately favor or disfavor particular employees while drafting reports.

(ii)   It is an imperfect technique of controlling, as the manager may not include all aspects of workers' performance, in his reports.

(iii)   Drafting of written reports is a time-consuming process.

(iv)   Some managers may not to competent enough to draft reports.

(iii)   Statistical Reports and Analysis

Under this technique of controlling, a special staff of specialists prepares statistical reports and presents them in form of tables, ratios, percentages, correlation analysis, graphs, charts, etc. to higher management levels. Such reports are prepared in areas like production, sales, quality, inventory etc; and these reports usually become the basis of managerial decision-making and action.

(iv)   Break-even analysis

Break-even analysis is a technique of Marginal costing. It is based on a classification of costs into fixed and variable categories. The key-concept in break-even analysis is that of contribution, defined as:

Contribution = Selling price per unit – Variable cost per unit

With the help of this concept of contribution the management is first interested in a full recovery of fixed costs. After recovering the fixed costs fully; the business enterprise reaches a point of break-even i.e. a point at which there is neither a profit nor losses. Break-Even-Point (i.e. B.E.P.) is calculated as follows:

Suppose fixed costs	=	Rs. 1, 00,000
Selling price per unit	=	Rs. 20
Variable cost per unit	=	Rs. 12
∴ Contribution per unit	=	Rs. 8 (i.e. 20 - 12)

$$\text{B.E.P.} = \frac{\text{Fixed costs}}{\text{Contributed per unit}} = \frac{1,00,000}{8}$$

$$= 12,500 \text{ units}$$

A B.E.P. of 12,500 units indicates that if that business produces and sells 12,500 units; it will recover fixed costs fully; and will have neither profits nor losses.

After reaching B.E.P., business can earn a profit of Rs.8 per unit (i.e. equal to contribution per unit); on selling each additional unit. (as fixed costs have already been recovered).

The technique of break-even analysis is helpful in profit planning and controlling - by predicting behavior of fixed and variable costs.

(v) Ratio analysis

Ratio-analysis is a tool of Financial Accounting and Management Accounting. Under this technique, the financial analyst analyses financial statements (i.e. the Income Statement and the Position Statement) by computing appropriate ratios.

In fact, figures do not speak. Ratios make them speak. The useful and meaningful accounting data give important clues to management for decision-making purposes - speaking through the media of accounting ratios.

Accounting ratios are usually divided into the following categories:

- Liquidity ratios
- Solvency ratios
- Activity or performance ratios
- Profitability ratios

21.2 MODERN TECHNIQUES OF CONTROLLING

Some popular modern techniques of controlling are described below:-

(i) Management audit

Management audit is a modern technique of controlling; in which the aim is to examine the efficiency of the management's philosophies, policies, techniques etc. in successfully running an enterprise.

It may be defined as follows:

Management audit is an independent, overall and scientifically critical examination of the entire management process - with a view to discovering quality of management; and judging its success and failures in running and managing an enterprise.

Conducting Management Audit

Management audit may be conducted either by an internal agency in the form of Management Audit Cell (MAC); or by an external agency such as management consultants. A growing tendency in the U.S.A. in regard to conducting management audit is to have certified management auditors for this purpose; so that a more objective view of management's efficiency could be presented.

Point of Comment

The scope of management audit is very wide. Management audit may cover areas like the following:

-        an appraisal of managers
-        economic functioning of the enterprise
-        fulfillment of major social responsibilities
-        functioning of the Board of Director
-        Soundness of organizational structure
-        intensity of sales promotion efforts
-        emphasis on research and development etc.

Evaluation of Management Audit

Management audit, by identifying, deficiencies in management's principles and practices helps in effecting structural improvements in the entire managerial system. Moreover, the fact of conducting management audit makes management more alert and progressive in its approach.

However, the scope of management audit is ill-defined. There is a lack of well-defined principles and procedures for conducting management audit.

(ii)   Internal Audit (or Operational audit)

An effective modern technique of controlling is the internal audit, now coming to be called operational audit.

The scope of internal audit is wider that external audit. It not only concerns with ensuring a true and fair recording of the accounting information; but also offers comments on various operational aspects of enterprise-life. Hence called operational audit.

Internal audit (or operational audit) may be defined as follows:

Internal audit is vouching and verification of accounting information by a staff of internal auditors; and is also concerned with examining the overall operational efficiency of the enterprise.

Point of comment

In a way, internal audit also encompasses elements of management audit.

Scope of internal audit

Internal audit, besides, including financial audit as the core aspect of it; includes consideration of the following:

- appraisal of financial controls
- compliance with policies and procedures
- efficiency in utilizing resources
- appraising quality of management performance etc.

Evaluation of internal audit

Internal audit recommends improvements in the operational life of the enterprise, and provides managerial with a perennial supply of control information. It keep a moral check on all the members of the organization.

However, installation and operation of internal audit system is much costly and time-consuming. Moreover, internal audit people have a lop-sided approach to their work; in that they have a tendency to look at every aspect of business operations form the accounting point of view.

(iii)   Social audit

Social audit may be defined as follows:

Social audit is concerned with the measurement of social performance of an organization in contrast to it economic performance.

The concept of social audit was first developed by Howard R. Bowen in the U.S.A. in the fifties. The application of the concept of social audit may be attributed to an increasing awareness of social responsibilities by business enterprises.

Some time back, the Tata Iron and Steel Company Limited conducted a social audit in its organization; though the audit report was not made available to the general public.

(iv)   Responsibility Accounting

Responsibility accounting is a technique of controlling borrowed from Management Accounting.

It is a system of controlling, whereby, the performance of managers is judged by assessing how far they have achieved the targets set for their departments or sections; for whose performance they are responsible.

Responsibility accounting may be defined as follows:

Responsibility accounting consists in dividing a business organization into responsibility centres, whereby, a distinct manager is assigned responsibility for achieving the predetermined target for his centre; and his success is judged by his ability in controlling the 'controllable costs' of his centre.

Points of comment

   (i')   Under responsibility accounting system, costs are assigned to responsibility centres; rather than to products.

   (ii')   Costs incurred by a responsibility centre are divided into two categories - controllable and uncontrollable. The head of the centre is directly responsible for the control label costs of his centre.

(v)   Human Resource Accounting (HRA)

Rensis Likert and D.E. Bowers have undertaken experiments in human resource accounting.

HRA might be defined as follows:

HRA is accounting for people in an organization; which involves a measurement of costs incurred by an enterprise to recruit, select, hire and train human assets and a measurement of the economic value of people to the enterprise.

Point of comment

Other techniques of controlling emphasize on profits, costs, performance etc; but ignore the value of the human asset which makes for all the difference in organizational performance.

Approach to measuring the value of human assets

There are two approaches to measuring the value of human assets:

- Original costs of human assets i.e. costs incurred in acquiring, compensating and training people.
- Replacement costs i.e. the costs required to replace a specific person.

An individual's value to an organization is the present worth of the set of future services that he/she is expected to provide during the period of his/her stay in the organization.

Evaluation of HRA

HRA helps management by providing valuable information for effective planning and managing human resources. With the help of measurement of costs of human assets, management can select persons with highest expected realizable value.

However, the biggest limitation of HRA is the basic problem involved in measuring the value of human assets - whether it should be based on original costs or replacement costs.

Many organizations, particularly, in the U.S.A. are following HRA.

(v)   Management Information System (MIS)

Management Information system (also known as MIS) is an integrated technique for gathering relevant information from whatever source it originates and transferring it into unusable form for the decision-makers in management. It is a system of communication primarily designed to keep all levels of organizational personnel abreast of the developments in the enterprise that affect them. MIS provides working tools for all the management personnel in order to take the best possible action at the right time with respect to the operations and functions of the enterprise for which they are largely responsible. The emphasis of MIS is on information for decision-making. MIS facilitates control from several angles:

1.   MIS performs a useful triple service function to management. Actually MIS itself is a three stage process - data generation, data processing and information transmission. MIS enhances the management's ability to plan, measure and control performance, and taking necessary and corrective action.

2.   Facilitates total performance. MIS provides more specialized and technical kind of information for the concerned managers. MIS provides multiple types of information for all management levels on a baffling variety of organizational matters.

3.   Takes into account several critical dimensions. MIS takes into account - the real time requirements, frequency of requirement, accuracy requirement, data reduction requirement, storage requirement etc. MIS objectively determines what information is needed by whom, and with what frequency.

4.   MIS reduces overload of information. MIS stresses the information that is most useful to the decision-maker. Any firm, large or small, that uses a formalized approach or electronic data processing system for its daily business has foundation of MIS. But normally, the larger the organization the more likely that MIS can be used by top management in establishing company policies and plans, monitoring the company performance and adapting the company strategies in response to changing circumstances.

(vi)   Network analysis techniques - PERT/CPM

(a)   Introduction:

PERT (Programme Evaluation and Review Technique) was developed by the special project office of the U.S. Navy in 1958. Almost at the same time, engineers at the Du Pont Company U.S.A. developed CPM (Critical Path Method). Though there are some differences between PERT and CPM; yet both these techniques utilize the same principles.

(b)   Application in PERT/CPM

Some of special areas for the application of PERT/CPM are given below :

(i)   Building/construction projects
(ii)   Ship building
(iii)   Airport facilities building
(iv)   Installation of computer systems
(v)   Publication of books

(c)   Steps in PERT/CPM

The application of PERT/CPM involves the following steps :

(i)   Identification of components

The first step towards the application of PERT/CPM is an identification of all key activities or events necessary for the completion of the project.

The term activity may be defined as an operation or a job to be carried out; which consumes time and resources. It is denoted by an arrow, in the network diagram.

The term event may be defined as the beginning or completion of an activity. It is denoted by a circle in the network diagram.

(ii)   Sequencing of activities and events

A network diagram is prepared to show the sequence of activities and events. It has a beginning and a terminal point for the project. It also depicts a number of paths of activities from the beginning to the completion of the project. For sake of convenience, each event is given a serial number.

(iii)   Determination of estimated time

For completion of the project during the contract period; it is essential to determine the expected time required to complete each activity.

Under PERT, three time estimates for the completion of each activity are made -

-      Optimistic or the shortest time
-      Pessimistic or the longest time
-      Normal or most likely time

(iv)   Determination of the critical path

At this stage, it is required to identify the sequence of those activities whose completion is critical for the timely completion of the project. Once the critical path is known; the management will be in a position to deploy resources more fruitfully; to spot troubles early and apply controls where these are most essential.

Point of comment

There must be no delay in the completion of activities which lie on the critical path; otherwise the entire project will be delayed.

(v)   **Modification in the initial plan**

The initial plan may be modified by resequencing some activities that lie along the critical path. When this is possible, it will result in a shorter time for the completion of the project.

(d)   **Distinction between PERT and CPM**

Though basic principles involved in PERT and CPM are the same; yet some differences between the two may be expressed as follows:

(i)   PERT is event oriented; whereas CPM is activity oriented.

(ii)   In CPM it is assumed that the duration of every activity is constant; and hence only one time estimate is given for each set of activities. On the other hand, PERT allows for uncertainty in the duration of activities; and hence three time estimates optimistic (or the shortest time), pessimistic (or the longest time) and normal (or the most likely time) are given.

(iii)   CPM requires some previous work experience for the completion of each activity; which is not necessary in PERT.

(iv)   CPM is used where cost is the main consideration; while PERT is used where time is the main consideration.

(e)   **Evaluation of PERT/CPM**

Merits

Following are the main advantages of PERT/CPM

(i)   PERT/CPM provides an analytical approach to the achievement of project objectives which are defined clearly. It thus facilities better utilization of time, efforts and capital.

(ii)   It identifies most critical elements and pays more attention on these. It, thus, facilitates 'control by exception' and increases effectiveness in handling projects.

(iii)   PERT/CPM brings all the components of a project together in the flow chart and permits simultaneous performance of different parts of the project.

(iv)   PERT/CPM forces managers to analyze all possibilities and uncertainties. It, thus, helps to minimize time and cost overruns.

(v)   It provides a kind of feed forward control; because delay in one activity affects all succeeding activities. Management can take action in advance, by effecting modifications of future activities.

Limitations

Major limitations of PERT/CPM are as follows:

(i)   It is not possible to accurately estimate time and cost involved in various activities of a project. Errors in estimation can make PERT/CPM erratic and unreliable.

(ii)   PERT/CPM is time-consuming and expensive. As such, small firms cannot afford to take advantage of these techniques.

(iii)   PERT/CPM cannot be applied with regard to assembly line operations, in which scheduling of operations is more guided by the speed of machines.

(iv)   PERT/CPM lays stress on time and cost control; overlooking other aspects of the project like quality and design of the project.

(vii)   Self-control

People often resist to externally imposed control. The best controlling system is that in which people opportunity for exercising self-control has.

Situation creating conditions for exercising self-control.

Some of the situations providing opportunities for self-control may be:

(1)   Management By Objectives (MBO)

Under MBO, there is a great possibility that people will exercise self-control; because they have their own hand in setting objectives for themselves; and are more likely to be committed to those objectives.

(2)   Delegation of Authority

Successful delegation of authority requires attitudes of mutual trust and confidence between the superior and the subordinates. A superior may not like to impose controls on a responsible and competent subordinate; and may allow him to exercise self-control - as a measure to motivate him.

(3)   Assignment of Challenging Work

When some challenging nature of work is assigned to an individual; the job itself creates situations in which only self-control could be exercised by the individual on himself.

(4)   Highly Dedicated Employees

In case of highly dedicated employees, there is not much need to impose controls over them; as they could be assumed to be self-starters. They may be left to exercising self-control.

Points of Comment

1.   Even in situations of externally imposed controls; there is provision for exercising self control. In fact, minute-to-minute control by a manager over subordinates' performance is never possible.

2.   People must not be left entirely to exercising self-control. There must be an ideal mix of externally imposed controls and self-controlling philosophy.

21.3   REVIEW QUESTIONS

1.   "Despite the emergence of many modern techniques of controlling, the budgetary control system maintains its unique place in the word of controlling." In the light of this observation, give an overview of the process, merits and limitations of the budgetary control system.

2.   Give an account of some popular non-budgetary control techniques, with special reference to break-even analysis and ratio analysis.

3.   What is management audit? How is it conducted? How does it differ from interval audit?

4.   Give a brief account of responsibility accounting and human resource accounting, as modern techniques of control.

5.   "Both PERT and CPM utilize the same principles; yet there are differences between the two."Comment. State the steps involved in designing PERT/CPM, and make a mention of the merits and limitations of PERT/CPM.

6.   What is self-control? Is it the best form of controlling? What are the situations which provide opportunities for exercising self-control?

7.   Write notes on:
      (a)   Social audit
      (b)   Statistical Reports and analysis
      (c)   Operational audit.

INFORMATION TECHNOLOGIES IN CONTROLLING

22.1   INFORMATION TECHNOLOGY

The systems model of management shows that communication is needed for carrying out the managerial functions and for linking the organization with its external environment. The management information system (MIS) provides the communication link that makes managing possible.

The term management information system has been used differently by various authors. It is defined here as a formal system of gathering, integrating, comparing, analyzing and dispersing information internal and external to the enterprise in a timely, effective, and efficient manner.

The management information system has to be tailored to specific needs and may include routine information, such as monthly reports, information that points out exceptions, especially at critical points, and information necessary to predict the future. The guidelines for designing a management information system are similar to those for designing systems and procedures and other control systems. Since they have been discussed elsewhere, they need not be elaborated here.

Electronic equipment permits fast and economical processing of huge amounts of data. The computer can, with proper programming, process data toward logical conclusions, classify them, and make them readily available for a manager's use. In fact, data do not become informatino until they are processed into a usable form that informs.

22.1.1 Expanding Basic Data

The focus of attention on management information, coupled with its improved processing, has led to the reduction of long-known limitations. Managers have recognized for years that traditional accounting information, aimed at the calculation of profits, has been of limited value for control. Yet in many companies this has been virtually the only regularly collected and analyzed type of data. Managers need all kinds of nonaccounting information about the external environment, such as social, economic, political and technical developments. In addition, managers need nonaccounting information on internal operations. The information should be qualitative as well as quantitative.

While not nearly enough progress has been made in meeting these requirements, the computer, plus operations research, has led to an enormous expansion of available managerial information. One sees this especially in relation to data on marketing, competition, production and distribution, product cost, technological change and development, labor productivity, and goal accomplishment.

22.1.2 Information Indigestion

Managers who have experienced the impact of better and faster data processing are justly concerned with the danger of "information indigestion". With their appetite for figures whetted, the data originators and processors are turning out material at an almost frightening rate. Managers are complaining that they are being buried under printouts, reports, projections and forecasts which they do not have time to read or cannot understand or which do not fill their particular needs.

22.1.3 Intelligence Services

One attempt at solving the information overload is the establishment of intelligence services and the development of a new profession of intelligence experts. The service would be provided by specialists who know (or find out) what information managers need and who know how to digest and interpret such information for managerial use. Some companies have established organizational units under such names as "administrative services" or "management analyses and services" for making information understandable and useful.

22.2 THE USE OF COMPUTERS IN HANDLING INFORMATION

The computer can store, retrieve and process information. Often a distinction is made between kinds of computers. The mainframe is a full-scale computer, often costing millions of dollars, that is capable of handling huge amounts of data. Some of these "supercomputers" are used for engineering, simulation, and the manipulation of large data bases. The minicomputer has less memory and is smaller than the mainframe. This kind of computer is often connected with peripheral equipment. The microcomputer is even smaller and may be a desk computer, home computer, personal computer, portable computer, or small computer for a business system. Increasingly, however, minicomputers are used by large organizations either as stand-alone computers or as parts of a network.

But the distinction between the various classes of computers is disappearing. With the introduction of th new microcomputers based on the 80386 microproessor these computers have become very powerful. However, th full utilization of the hardware (the computers) depends to a considerable degree on the lagging development of the software programs.

Among the many business applications of the computer are material requirements planning, manufacturing resource planning, computer-aided control of manufacturing machinery, project costing, inventory control and purchasing. The computer also aids design and engineering, an application which made the U.S. space program possible. Then there are the many uses in processing financial information such as accounts receivable and accounts payable, payroll, capital budgeting and financial planning.

22.2.1 the Impact of Computers on Managers at Different Organizational Levels

Information needs differ at various organizational levels. Therefore, the impact of computers will also be different.

At the supervisory level activities are usually highly programmable and repetitive. Consequently, the use of computers is widespread at this level. Scheduling, daily planning, and controlling of the operation are just a few examples.

Middle-level managers, such as department heads or plant managers, are usually responsible for administration and coordination. But much of the information important to them is now also available to top management if the company has a comprehensive information system. For this reason, some people think that the need for middle-level managers will be reduced by the computer. Others predict that their roles may be expanded and changed.

Top-level managers are responsible for the strategy and overall policy of the organization. In addition to determining the general direction of the company, they are responsible for the appropriate interaction between the enterprise and its environment. Clearly, the tasks of CEOs are not easily programmable. Yet top managers can use the computer to retrieve information from a data base that facilitates the application of decision models. This enables the company to make timely responses to changes in the external environment. Still, the use of the computer will probably affect the jobs of top managers less severely than it will affect the jobs of those at lower levels.

22.2.2 The Application and Impacts of Microcomputers

The personal computr (PC) is becoming increasingly appealing to managers because it is flexible and relatively inexpensive and can be used more quickly than the mainframe computer. Its applications include the following:

Budget preparation	Simulation models
Graphic presentation	Forecasting
Electronic spreadsheets	Electronic mail
Financial analyses	Tapping into data bases
Word processing	Time-sharing

The implications of the increasing use of the microcomputer are manifold. There is a need for specialized staff support, education for managers and nonmanagers, and a redefinition of jobs. For example, the distinction between line and staff is becoming less clear. The information that was formerly gathered by staff can now be obtained with ease by other managers by accessing a common data base. On the other hand, information that was the preogative of upper-level managers can also be made available to personnel at lower levels, possibly resulting in the shift of power to lower levels in the organization. But not all information should be accessible to all people in the company. Thus, one of the problems currently faced by many firms is maintaining the security of information.

22.3   CHALLENGES CREATED BY INFORMATION TECHNOLOGY

Eliminating the unauthorized use of information is just one of many challenges. Others include reducing resistance to the use of computers, adapting to speech recognition devices and telecommuting, and implementing computer networks.

22.3.1 Resistance to Computer Application

While high school students may feel comfortable using the computer, some managers fear it. One study revealed that the typical executive affected by this phobia is male, is about 50 years old, and has worked most of his life for the same company. This fear might explain why certain managers are reluctant to use the computer. They are afraid of looking unskilled if they are not able to understand the new technology or do not have the typing skills often necessary for inputting data to the computer. In the past, typing was considered the task of the secretary, not the manager.

A survey of CEOs in Fortune 500 companies showed that over 50 percent of the respondents never used the computer and over 70 percent of them did not have a computer in their office. On the other hand, a majority of the top executives thought that computers assist managers in doing their jobs, which suggests that computers are considered useful below the level of the CEO. Those not favourably inclined to the use of computers made variouis comments, such as that their time is too valuable to be spent learning computer skills.

The application of graphics can help overcome the resistance to computers. Instead of being buried in reams of computer printouts, information is displayed as easy-to-understand graphics. Pepsi Co, for example, invested $250,000 in decision support graphics over 3 years, generating 80,000 charts and slides. At any rate, as more sophisticated technology makes the use of the computer easier, its acceptance is likely to increase.

22.3.2 Speech Recognition Devices

Another way to encourage the use of computers is through speech recognition devices. The aim is to input data into the computer by speaking in a normal manner, rather than by using the keyboard. Several companies are working on such devices, but it may still take several years before they can be widely applied, although simple speech recognition has been in limited use for some time. Merely expanding the vocabulary through larger memory is not enough. Imagine the program sophistication needed to distinguish between similar sounds such as "then" and "than", and "too" and "two". Despite the complex problems, some people think that the efforts made in this area will result in products that may revolutionize office operation.

22.3.3 Telecommuting

The widespread use of computers and the ease of linking them through telephone lines to a company's mainframe computer has led to telecommuting. This means that a person can work at a computer terminal at home instead of commuting to work. Some of the advantages claimed include greater flexibility in scheduling work, the avoidance of traffic congestion, and a reduced need for office space.

The futurist Alvin Toffler envisioned an "electronic cottage" with computer terminals installed at home. But John Naisbitt, in his book Megatrends, is skeptical of the idea and suggested that after telecomuting for some time, workers will miss the office gossip and the human interactions with coworkers. Some companies that have contracted work to telecommuters have been criticized for not providing the benefits usually given to office workers. At Pacific Bell, however, participants in the voluntary program are considered full-time employees. Moreover, some employees go to the office atleast once a week to check their mail and to mingle with coworkers.

With the increasing traffic congestion, especially in metropolitcan areas, one may see a somewhat greater use of telecommuting. But it is doubtful that it will replace the office as we know it today.

22.3.4 Computer Networks

The widespread use of stand-alone computers often results in duplication of efforts. The data base in the mainframe or the minicomputer, for example, may not be accessible from the desktop computer. Therefore, computer networks have been developed that link workstations with each other, with larger computers, and with peripheral equipment.

Persons at several workstations can communicate with each other as well as access other computers. Moreover, workstations can be connected to costly hardware that may be underutilized by a single user. For example, several users can share laser printers or tape backup units that ensure saving of the data files. There are many other applications of computer networks, such as electronic mail and the gathering and disseminating of industry data future trends. Although computer networking is still in its infancy, new technological developments are rapidly changing the system of information handling.

22.4   REVIEW QUESTIONS

1.   What are the challenges created by I.T. in controlling ?
2.   Explain the role of computers in handling the information.

PRODUCTIVITY AND OPERATIONS MANAGEMENT

The scheme of discussion under the above stated caption is as follow:-

23.1 PRODUCTIVITY

    a.   Introductory observations
    b.   Productivity defined
    c.   Problems in measuring productivity of knowledge workers

23.2 AN OVERVIEW OF PRODUCTION / OPERATIONS MANAGEMENT

    a.   Meaning of operations management
    b.   Significance of operations management
    c.   Process of operations management

23.3 TECHNIQUES EMPLOYED IN PLANNING AND CONTROLLING OPERATIONS MANAGEMENT

    a.   Operations Research (O.R)
    b.   Other tools and techniques

Let us commence discussion about productivity and operations management, as per the above suggested scheme of discussion.

23.1 PRODUCTIVITY

a. Introductory Observations

Productivity is one of the major concerns of managers of today; and will be more of a matter of concern for managers of tomorrow all over the world. In fact, productivity is something which accounts for profitable operations of an enterprises, and provides opportunities to an enterprises for remaining competitive and successful, in an era of global competition.

b.   Productivity defined

In fact, there is no general agreement on a universal meaning of the term productivity. However, it may be defined as the output - inputs ratio, within a given time period and with due consideration for quality of performance.

c.   Problems in measuring productivity of knowledge workers

Measurement of the productivity of skill workers (like brick-layers, mechanics, butchers etc.) is easier; but it becomes more difficult to measure the productivity of knowledge workers (like managers, engineers, programmers). Skill workers mainly operate on the basis of their technical skills; whereas knowledge workers mostly use their knowledge while discharging their jobs. Technical skills of knowledge workers are subordinate to their knowledge, which is their basic asset.

Productivity of knowledge workers is more difficult to measure, because of the following reasons;

    i.   Knowledge workers contribute indirectly to the final product e.g. engineers.

   ii.   Knowledge workers provide assistance to other organizational units. For example, it is difficult to say how much improvement in the sales is due to the efforts of the advertising manager or how much improvement is there in labor management relations, because of the efforts of the personnel manager.

  iii.   It is difficult to measure the quality of the actions of the knowledge workers. For example, the success of a strategy formulated by the General Manager may not be known for years; as the success of failure of a strategy depends on many external factors, over which the manager has no control.

Despite the limitations of measuring productivity of knowledge workers, it is a fact that greatest scope for increasing productivity lies in the work performed by knowledge workers eg. Managers, engineers, cost accountants etc.

23.2   AN OVERVIEW OF PRODUCTION / OPERATIONS MANAGEMENT

a.   Meaning of operations management:

Operations management may be defined as follows.

Operations management is the designing, operating and controlling of production systems; whereby, products / services are produced / delivered, through a process of conversion from inputs to output.

According to Johnson, Newell and Vergin, "Operations Management is the design and operations of systems".

Point of comments:

Production of goods and services is a system; since the organizational components interact with each other as well as with outside environment. Production management is an open-adaptive system.

b.   Significance of operations management

Introduction of operations management improves organizational efficiency. According to studies conducted, the surgical unit of a hospital showed considerable improvement in operational efficiency, when the concept of operations management was introduced. The hospital under observation had surgical unit with a capacity of 5 patients and a recovery room with a capacity of 12 patients. The hospital had been using a random input policy of scheduling patients for surgery, without any order of priority. On the basis of computer simulation, the scheduling policy was changed; so that patients requiring the longest surgery were scheduled first. This resulted in higher utilization rates for operation rooms and recovery rooms and more timely completion of surgical and recovery schedule. Similarly, banks can use operations management techniques in expediting services to customers. Be it an industrial organizations or a service organization; operations management techniques lead to efficient utilization of space, technology etc, and consequently better service to society and more profitability for the organization itself.

c.   Process of operations management

Operations management is an open-adaptive system; and in constant interaction with external environment. The basic working of the operations management is depicted, through the following chart:

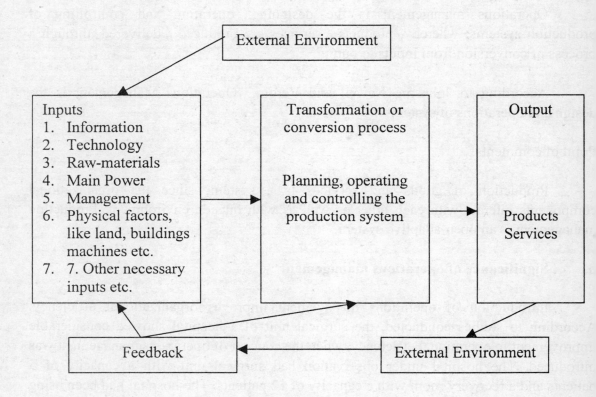

The above chart shows that the production system obtains its inputs (as described in the input box) from the external environment i.e. the society which is the supra system. These inputs are transformed into output, through the conversion process which consists of planning, operating and controlling the production system. The output (goods, services) are transferred to external environment from where the management gets a feedback i.e. response or reaction. On the basis of this feedback, necessary modifications, corrections and adjustments are made in the inputs and the transformation process - to better operate the production system and to better serve the society.

Steps involved in operations management

Steps involved in operations management are described below under three categories;

(a).   Planning the system
(b).   Operation the system
(c).   Controlling the system

a.   Planning the system:

The sub-steps of operations management in this category are as follows:-

(i)   Search for and selection of the product or service:

This step requires exploration. Exploration is the search for new ideas which may come from many sources like,

-           Research and development section
-           Salespersons, who are constantly in touch with consumers?
-           Competitors, who may be in the process of developing some substitutes

All the ideas the tested for feasibility and profitability. The selected ideas must be consistent with the objectives, strategies, programmes of the organization.

(ii)   Production design

The production design, the following steps may be recommended:

1. Prepare a preliminary design by evaluating various alternatives, taking into account reliability, quality and maintenance requirements.
2. Reach a final decision by developing, testing and simulating the processes, to see if they work.
3. Select the process for producing the product; considering the technology and methods available.

(iii)   Determination of production layout

There are several kinds of production layouts

1. Arrange the layout, in the order in which the product is produced / assembled.
2. Lay out he production system, according to process employed.
3. In the fixed position layout, the product stands in one place for assembly (e.g. layout for printing press, ships)
4. Lay out the production system, according to nature of project (e.g. layout for building a bridge or tunnel to fit specific geographic requirements)
5. Lay out the production process to facilitate sale of products
6. Lay out the production process to facilitate storage or movement of goods.

(b)   Operating the system: ˙

Operating the production systems required

-    Setting up an organizational structure
-    Staffing positions and training people
-    Supervising workers, so that they product desired goods/ services
-    Motivating and leading people, to get best performance out of them.

Operating involves scheduling work operations and allocating work in such a manner as to meet short-term as well as long-term levels of output, which are consistent with forecasted demand. The operational decisions require use of operational research tools to ensure optimum smooth output.

Point of comment:

Operating the system also involves updating, which means continuous revision of operating methods and system to meet the ever changing and dynamic social and technological environment. This revision is necessary in response to-

-    changes in customer demand and preferences
-    changes in technology
-    changing competition scenario
-    changes in organisation objectives
-    changes in personnel etc.

(c)   Controlling the system

The controlling mechanism is to be developed at the same time as the designing of operating systems and most be integrated with the system.

Controlling process ensures that the operating systems are attaining the desired results. These controls are in areas of - quantity and quality of output, utilization of raw - materials and wastage, price and quality of raw - materials purchased, inventory levels of raw - materials and finished goods etc.

Controlling operations are done with emphasis of information systems. With the development of computer hardware and software, it is now possible for virtually any measurable data to be reported as events occur. Systems are available for quick collection of data; keeping data readily available and reporting without delay, the status of any project, at any instant.

23.3   TECHNIQUES EMPLOYED IN PLANNING AND CONTROLLING OPERATIONS MANAGEMENT

Techniques employed in planning and controlling operations management are classified into two categories:

a. Operations Research (OR)
b. Other tools and techniques.

Let us first take O.R, as planning and controlling technique for operations management

Meaning and essential characteristics of OR

Various quantitative techniques are integrated into a new discipline, normally known as "Operations Research" (OR)

Operations research, to a considerable extent, is a product of World War II. It involves the application of the methods of the physical scientist and the engineer to economic and commercial problems, made possible by the development of rapid computing machines.

Following is cited a simple and logical definition of OR:

OR is the application of specific methods, tools and techniques to operations of system with optimum solution to the problems.

In simple words, OR might be defined as quantitative common sense for obtaining optimum solution to business problems.

The essential characteristics of OR as applied to decision - making are as follows:

i.   OR emphasizes on mathematical models - the logical presentation of a problem.
ii. It incorporates in the model those variables in a problem that appear to be most important to its solution.
iii. It quantifies variables to the extent possible; since only quantifiable data can be inserted into the model to yield measurable results.
iv. OR emphasizes on goals in a problem area and develops measures of effectiveness in determining whether a given solution shows promise of achieving those goals.

Special tools or techniques of OR

Construction of mathematical models is the central tools or OR. However, OR, in itself, includes many techniques which are briefly described below.

(i)   Linear Programming (LP)

The problem confronting any management is to decide the manner in which the limited resources of the organization are to be allocated among different uses - so as to maximize the attainment of organizational objectives.

Linear programming is a mathematical technique used for the purpose of allocation of limited resources in an optimum manner. The word linear means that relationships handled are those which are represented by straight - lines; and the word programming means making decisions systematically.

Therefore, LP is the maximization (or minimization) of a linear function of variables subject to a constraint of linear inequalities.

The technique is applicable in production planning, transportation, warehousing, location etc, as these are problem creating areas.

ii.   Inventory Planning and Control

The key concept in inventory planning and control is the calculation of Economic Order Quantity (EOQ) which is given by the following formula:

$$Q = \sqrt{\frac{2U \times P}{S}}$$

Where, Q   = economic order quantity
        U   = quantity (units) purchased, in a year
        P   = cost f placing on order
        S   = Annual cost of storage of one unit

Suppose   U   = 1600 units a year; p = Rs.100;
           S   = Rs.8; then

$$R = \sqrt{\frac{2 \times 1600 \times 100}{8}}$$

= 200 units

Economic order quantity refers to the size of the order, which gives maximum economy in purchasing any material.

iii.   Just-In-Time Inventory System: (JIT)

JIT inventory method also known as zero inventory or stockless production is very popular in Japan. In this system, the supplier delivers the components and parts to the production line, Just-in-time to be assembled.

For the JIT method to work, the following requirements must be fulfilled:

1. The quality of parts must be very high; as a single defective part could hold up the assembly line.
2. There must be dependable relationships with suppliers.

3. The suppliers should be located near the company, with dependable transportation being available.

iv.   Distribution Logistics

Distribution logistics treats the entire logistics of a business - from sales forecasting to shipping finished goods - as a single system. The goals is to optimize the total costs of the system in operation; while furnishing a desired level of customer service and meeting the constraint of limited inventory levels.

By optimizing total costs in a broad area of operation, the system might show that it would be cheaper to use more expensive transportation on occasion, rather than to carry high inventories.

(Logistics means the practical organization that is needed to make a complicated plan successful, when a lot of people and equipment is involved).

Limitation of Operations Research

Despite its utility in solving managerial problems, OR suffers from the following limitations.

i.   OR calls for a high order of mathematics. Managers are long away from fully using the mathematics that is available.

ii. OR has limited usefulness in decision making areas which involve a large number of qualitative factors.

iii. There is usefully lack of information which is needed to make OR useful in practice. People find that the information which they need about certain variables is not available.

iv. There is a gap between practicing managers and trained operations researchers. Managers lack knowledge of mathematics; operations researchers lack an understanding of managerial problems.

v.   OR Techniques are costly and many problems are not important enough to justify this cost.

b.   Other tools and techniques

Besides OR and its applications; some other techniques employed in planning and controlling operations management are described below.

i.   PERT/CPM

A detailed account of PERT/CPM is given in chapter 26.

ii.   Value Engineering

A product can be improved and its cost lowered through value engineering; which consists of

-        analyzing the operation of the product or service;
-        estimating the value of each operation;
and   -   attempting to improve that operation by trying to keep cost slow at each step.

iii.   Work Simplification

Work simplification is the process of obtaining the participation of workers, in simplifying their work. Training sessions are conducted to teach concepts and principles of techniques such as time and motion studies, work-flow analyses, and the layout of the work situation.

iv.   Quality circles

The concept of quality control circles or quality circles was developed in Japan during early 1960 and widely used in the U.S.A. during later 1970 and early 1980.

A quality circle is a small group of employee (say five to ten) belonging to the same work unit; who meet frequently with their supervisor (known as quality circle leader) to identify, discuss and solve work related problems of their work unit.

Point of comments

There may be a number of quality circles in an organization; with a coordinator to co-ordinate the working of various quality circles.

Quality circles provide opportunities for interaction among people. People given suggestions for effective improvements in their work - unit performance. The excellent work performed by quality circles is also rewarded.

v.   CAD / CAM and MAP

Product design and manufacturing have changed greatly in recent years because of the application of computer technology.

CAD (Computer Aided Design) CAM (Computer Aided Manufacturing) help engineers to design products much more quickly than they could do with the traditional paper and pencil approach.

Automobile companies have developed what is called MAP (Manufacturing Automation Protocol), which is a network of machines and various office devices hooked together.

23.4   REVIEW QUESTIONS

1. "Productivity is one of the major concerns of managers today, everywhere is the world". Comment. Define productivity and identify the problems involved in measuring productivity knowledge workers.

2. "Operations management is an open - adaptive system. In the light of this statement, define operations management and state the basic steps involved in operations management system.

3. "OR might be defined as quantitative common senses". Comment. What are the special took of OR relevant for operations management?

4. What is JIT inventory? What are the requirements for successful implementation of JIT method?

5. Write notes on:
    a.   Limitations of OR
    b.   Quality circles
    c.   Economic order quantity

OVERALL AND PREVENTIVE CONTROL

24.1 INTRODUCTORY OBSERVATIONS

From the viewpoint of approach to controlling; controlling techniques are of two broad types - direct control and preventive control. Direct control may again be partial or overall, as depicted below:

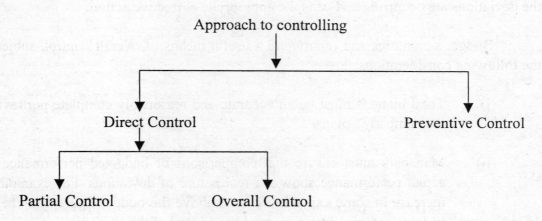

Direct controls are based on feedback, by measuring deviations from standards analyzing the causes of deviations and taking the necessary corrective steps to bring performance on the right track.

Direct controls may be partial in nature, designed for specific things like policies, wages / salaries, cash, cost, capital expenditure etc.

Overall controls are designed to measure the success of organization as a whole, against organizational objectives.

Preventive controls are based on the philosophy of preventing undesirable deviations from occurring, by developing and maintaining a highly qualified managerial staff.

24.2   AN OVERVIEW OF OVERALL DIRECT CONTROL TECHNIQUES

Some popular techniques of overall direct control are described below:

a.   Budget Summaries and Reports

A budget summary is a resume (short account) of all individual budgets and reflects company's plans in terms of - sales volume, costs, profits, utilization of capital etc. It shows to the top management as to how well the company, as a whole, is successful in achieving its objectives.

Budget summaries provide an effective means for overall control, in situations of decentralized authority. Top management has a convenient means of finding out where the deviations are occurring and can take appropriate corrective action.

Budget summaries and reports are a useful means of overall control, subject to the following considerations:

(i)   Total budgets must be an accurate and reasonably complete portrayal of the company's plans.

(ii)   Managers must ensure that comparisons of budgeted performance and actual performance show the real nature of deviations. For example, an increase in some expenditure head above the budget figure, may be due to some external factor, beyond the control of the manager.

(iii) While comparing budgeted performance and actual performance, attention must be paid to important variations. Minor discrepancies should receive little attention.

(iv)   Many-a-times, managers must forget the budget and take special action to meet unexpected events; because budgets are servants of managers and not their masters.

b.   Profit and Loss Control

Profit and Loss or the Income Statement for an enterprise as a whole serves important control purposes; because it is useful in determining revenues and related expired costs during a given period; which account for success or failure of a business.

Many companies use profit and loss technique for division / departmental control. In fact, when the purpose of the entire business is to make a profit; each department must contribute to this purpose.

How is Profit and Loss Control Exercised?

In profit and loss control, each major department details its revenues and expenses; including a proportionate share of the company overheads and calculates its profit / loss periodically.

However, profit and loss control is not practicable for small departments; as the paper - work involved in building up profit and loss statements for smaller departments tends to be too heavy. Further, profit and loss control is not applied to control staff and service departments.

Limitations of Profit and Loss Control

Some of the limitations of profit and loss control may be stated to be as following:

(i) **The is a lot of paper work involved** for recording intra-company transfer of costs and revenues. Whether intra-company transfers to be made at costs or at a figure above costs; require careful decision and appropriate and accurate recording.

(ii) **Profit and loss control is inadequate** for overall control purposes, till it is coupled with a good budgetary control system.

(iii) When profit and loss control is carried very far in the organization; departments may come to compete with each other; which phenomenon may be dangerous for enterprise co-ordination.

(c) Return On Investment (ROI)

ROI is one of the most successfully used overall control techniques; which measure the success of a company by the ratio of earnings to investment of capital. This approach has been an important part of the control system of the Du-Pont Company, USA, since 1919.

ROI is computed according to the following formula:

$$ROI = \frac{\text{Profits before interest, tax and dividends}}{\text{Capital employed}} \times 100$$

Where, capital employed refers to the total long-term investment in a company. (We may also take average capital employed i.e, capital employed in the beginning + capital employed at the end ÷ 2)

Capital employed is calculated as the summation of fixed assets ÷ net working capital (i.e. current assets - current liabilities).

Point of Comment

With the help of ROI, a company can compare its present performance with its past performances; and can also compare itself with other companies having similar investment and being similarly situated.

Evaluation of ROI

Merits:

(i)   **ROI gives an overall assessment of business functioning.** It guides management in increasing profits through a better utilization of capital invested. It, in fact, focuses managerial attention on the central objective of the business i.e. making best profits possible on capital available.

(ii) **ROI is effective; where authority is decentralized.** When departmental managers are furnished with a guide to efficiency that applies to the company as a whole; they develop a keener sense of responsibility for their departments and top management can easily hold subordinate managers responsible.

Limitations:

Some limitations of ROI are as follows:

(i)   **There is a problem of valuation of assets.** If assets are jointly used or costs are common, what method of allocation between departments should be used? Should a manager be charged with assets at their original costs or their replacement costs or their depreciated values? Setting up of a ROI system as control device is not an easy task.

(ii)   ROI preoccupies with financial factors; and overlooks environmental factors such as social and technological. Qualitative factors which are scarce (like competent managers, good employee morale, good public relations) and equally significant or rather more significant than capital employed are totally neglected in ROI calculation.

(iii)   There is no standard ROI available for inter-firm and intra-firm comparison purposes.

24.3   ASSUMPTION UNDERLYING DIRECT CONTROL SYSTEM

Some of the assumptions of direct control system, which are often criticized, are described below:

(i)   Assumption that performance can be measured

Once major assumption underlying direct control system is that performance can be measured. Factors like inputs, output, cost, price, time etc. can be measured. However, there are factors which vitally affect an organization's success but which are qualitative in nature and cannot be measured e.g. potential of managers to develop, effectiveness of research, creativity of manpower, soundness of managerial decisions etc. Hence, direct controls are lop sided in nature.

(ii)   Assumption that personal responsibility exists for deviations

Sometimes this assumption is valid; sometimes it fails. For example, no manager is responsible for undesirable deviations caused by uncertainties of external environment e.g. increase in interest rates, scarcity of a particular fuel, obsolescence of existing technology etc.

(iii) Assumption that cost of investigation in terms of time, efforts, money etc. is justified

It takes time and efforts to undertake an analysis of deviations. In direct control system which is based on feedback analysis; recalling facts may be difficult as time has passed. In most of the cases, the cost of investigation into causes of deviations may exceed the benefit, likely to arise, from the controlling exercise.

(iv)   Assumption that mistakes can be discovered in time

Discovery of deviations from plan may often come too late for effective corrective action. Much information for control purposes depends on historical data - which are available to managers quite late; and then managers take time to interpret the data. As such, true control can be applied only to future actions; not current actions.

(v)   Assumption that the person responsible will take corrective steps

Fixing responsibility for deviations may not lead to corrective action; when the manager involved is one of hight-ups in the organization. Subordinate manager dare not ask their superiors to correct themselves; to whom they report for their own performance.

24.4   PRINCIPLE OF PREVENTIVE CONTROL SYSTEM

The basic philosophy of preventive control system is that best way to correct deviations is not to let these take place at all.

The basic tool of preventive control system is to develop better managers; who will look at managing and managerial problems from a wider and intelligent perspective; so that undesirable deviations caused by poor management are eliminated. Highly qualified managers will make fewer mistakes; thus reducing (but certainly not eliminating) the need for direct controls.

The principle of preventive control, thus, is that the higher the quality and caliber of managers; the lesser will be the need for direct controls.

Point of Comment

Under preventive control system, the responsibility for negative deviations can be fixed, by applying fundamentals of management i.e. whether managers act in accordance with established principles, in carrying out their functions.

24.5   ASSUMPTIONS UNDERLYING PREVENTIVE CONTROL SYSTEM

Following one the basic assumptions underlying preventive control system:

(i)   Assumption that qualified managers makes a minimum of errors.

It appeals to logic that more qualified the managers are the lesser is the probability that they will make mistakes. In fact, qualified managers are likely to make a minimum of errors. However, while evaluating the quality of the decisions made by a manager; emphasis must be laid so much not on the quantity of errors, but on the quality of errors. A manager could be wrong in only 2% of the decisions made by him; but the quality of wrongness may be such as to seriously endanger the survival of the company.

(ii)   Assumption that management fundamentals can be used to measure performance

Application of managerial concepts, principles, theory, techniques (i.e. fundamentals of management) is much dependent on the state of knowledge concerning managing, possessed by a manager. Fundamentals of management are useful and can be applied in measuring managerial performance i.e. while analyzing negative deviations, it could be discovered whether the manager applied the established principles, techniques, etc. of management in the right way and with the right perspective.

(iii)   Assumption that the application of management fundamentals can be evaluated

This assumption is different from the preceding one in that here we are interested in the measurement of the skill with which managers apply management fundamentals to their five functions of planning, organizing, staffing, directing and controlling. For instance, in a scheme of MBO, the ability to set and achieve verifiable objectives reveals some measure of a manager's performance. Such performance (as revealed e.g. by MBO programmes) is a reflection on the knowledge and skill of a manager and his competence to occupy the particular managerial position.

24.6   ADVANTAGES OF PREVENTIVE CONTROL

A preventive approach to controlling, offers the following advantages to an organization.

(i)   A basis for managerial training / development

An evaluation of manager, under the philosophy of preventive control is likely to uncover deficiencies in managers. On the basis of the results of managerial evaluation and appraisal, top management can design programmes of managerial training / development to overcome those deficiencies.

(ii)   Encouragement of Self-Control

Preventive control system encourages what may be called `control by self-control'. This is so because managers know that their mistakes will be uncovered in their evaluation process; and owning responsibility for mistakes in their hearts, will start making voluntary corrections. In fact, a feeling of self-control turns managers into more responsible personalities.

(iii)   Managerial Burden Lightened

Preventive control lightens managerial burden caused due to efforts in correcting deviations, as a result of direct controls. Preventive control, as the name implies prevents deviations from occurring and much saves managerial time and efforts; which, otherwise, would have been wasted in correcting deviations had those occurred.

(iv)   Better Superior - Subordinate Relationships

Under preventive control system, subordinate managers know what is expected of them, understand the nature of managing; and feel a close relationship between performance and measurement. Intelligent superior managers will reciprocate this feeling by recognizing what they are expected to evaluate in subordinates and develop techniques for doing so. Anyway, superior-subordinate relationships are likely to improve under the philosophy of preventive control.

24.7   DEVELOPING EXCELLENT MANAGERS - THE KEY TO PREVENTIVE CONTROL

The key to preventive control lies in developing excellent managers; whose behavior, actions and direction to subordinates will minimize the chances of the occurrence of deviations.

Discussion about developing excellent managers could be analyzed into two categories:

(a)   Efforts required on the part of managers themselves; and
(b)   Efforts required on the part of the organization.

Let us describe the major factor towards developing excellent managers comprised in both these categories.

(a)   Efforts required on the part of managers themselves

Efforts required on the part of managers themselves towards developing excellent managers may be as follows:

(i)   Willingness to Learn

Managers should not base too much of their / learning on experience; and they must be aware of the dangers of experience as events or programmes of the past may not work in future - entirely different from the past conditions. Mangers must be willing to learn new concepts, principles, theories and techniques of management to avoid what is called managerial obsolescence. In fact, there is no end to new learning in management discipline; which is growing at a very fast pace.

(ii)   Planning for Innovations and Inventions

The idea here is two-fold-planning of innovations, and planning for inventions.

(1)   Planning for Innovation

Managers are required to be innovative. New product ideas, new processes of production or new marketing ideas do not just occur, by chance or luck. Managers must constantly keep themselves involved in creative thinking; which will not only help them come out with innovations for the enterprise but also help themselves in turning into excellent management personalities.

(2)   Planning for Inventions

Managers must try to develop more managerial inventions. Some historical managerial inventions have been : the Gantt chart, variable budgeting technique, PERT / CPM etc. Managers can give rise to inventions; if they take interest in management research and devote their time, efforts, creativity and skill towards planning for better and better managerial techniques.

(iii)   Tailoring Information

Managers usually worry over the inadequacy of data on which they one forced to act. There is then a need for tailoring information i.e. obtaining the right information, in the right form and at the right time, for which managers must have their own designs. Information design must not be confused with the clerical work of information gathering and summarizing.

(b)   Efforts required on the part of the organization

Efforts required on the part of the organization towards developing excellent managers may be:

(i)   Acceleration of Management Development Programmes

To avoid managerial obsolescence, it is necessary that the organization must design and implement schemes of managerial development; so as to transmit new knowledge and tools in the field of management in a simple and useful way to practicing managers.

Sending managers to attend seminars and conferences may be a useful means of managerial development in this context. Making available latest books and articles on new management knowledge to managers and motivating them to digest the same, is, yet another way to bring manager up-to-date on specific areas of new knowledge and techniques of management.

(ii)   Measuring managerial performance and rewarding it

As a measure to motivate managers to develop into excellent personalities; the organization must design schemes for measuring managerial performance and rewarding those managers who successfully accomplish their targets. Schemes of MBO, delegation of authority for challenging works etc. are some of the means, at the disposal of organization, in this context.

(iii)   Need for management research and development

There is a great need to conduct more research into developing new tools and techniques of management. The level of research in the field of management is rather low; particularly because management research is complex and controlled laboratory experimentation is not possible. Further management research is expensive. However, organization must provide all facilities, funds and motivation to researchers. Perfection of analysis to include all kinds of variables in a research project must not be insisted on; as small contributions by researchers may provide building blocks for great researches, subsequently.

(iv)   Need for Intellectual Leadership

There is a need not just for technically sound leadership; but intellectual leadership (based on imagination, foresight, human skills, conceptual skills etc.) to drive the vehicle of a productive organization towards its mission and goals. The enterprise top management must help create in environment in the enterprise which may be instrumental in developing intellectual leadership in managers. Intellectual leaders will help develop intellectual followers (i.e. subordinates); and a time may come when the entire organization will be full of intellectuals, in all walks of organizational life.

24.8   REVIEW QUESTIONS

1.   What is the difference between direct control and preventive control? Which is better? Give an overview of popular overall direct control measures.
2.   Compare the assumptions underlying direct control and preventive control systems.
3.   What is the principle of preventive control? What are its advantages for the organization?
4.   "The key to preventive control lies in developing excellent manager." In the light of this observation, suggest guidelines for developing excellent managers.
5.   Write notes on:
      (a)   ROI
      (b)   Management Fundamentals
      (c)   Self-control.

GLOBALIZATION AND LIBERALIZATION

25.1 INTRODUCTION

The trend towards globalization has gathered more momentum after the political and economic changes that swept across the Communist countries, the economic reforms in other countries and the latest multilateral trade agreement which seeks to substantially liberalize international trade and investment.

We may consider globalization at two levels, viz., at the macro level (i.e., globalization of the world economy) and at the micro level (i.e., globalization of the business and the firm).

Globalization of the world economy is achieved, quite obviously, by globalizing the national economies. Globalization of the economies and globalization of business of are very much interdependent.

25.2 GLOBALIZATION OF WORLD ECONOMY

The world economy has been emerging as a global or translational economy. A global or transnational economy is one which transcends the national borders unhindered by artificial restrictions like government restrictions on trade and factor movements. Globalization is a process of development of the world into a single integrated economic unit.

The transitional economy is different from the international economy. The international economy is characterized by the existence of different national economies, the economic relations between them being regulated by the national governments. The translational economy is a borderless world economy characterized by free flow of trade and factors of production across national borders.

Peter Drucker in his New Realities observes that in the early or mid seventies with OPEC and president Nixon's floating of the dollar the world economy changed from being international to translational. According to Drucker, the transnational economy is characterized by inter alia, the following features.

i)   The transnational economy is shaped mainly by money flows rather than by trade in goods and services. These money flows have their own dynamics. The monetary and fiscall

ii)   In the transnational economy management has emerged as the decisive factor of production and the traditional factors of production, land and labour, have increasingly become secondary. Money and capital markets too have been increasingly becoming transnational and universally obtainable. Drucker, therefore, argues that it is management on which competitive position has to be based.

iii)   In the transnational economy, the goal is market maximization and not profit maximization.

iv)   Trade, which increasingly follows investment, is becoming a function of investment.

v)   The decision making power is shifting from the national state to the region (i.e., the regional blocks like the European Community, North American Free Trade Agreement, etc.)

vi)   There is a genuine and almost autonomous world economy of money, credit and investment flows. It is organized by information which no longer knows national boundaries.

vii)   Finally, there is a growing pervasiveness of transnational corporatioins which see the entire world as a single market for production and marketing of goods and services.

There are thus many factors which tend to promote the transnationalization of the world economy. The multilateral trade negotiations under the auspices of GATT/WTO have been liberalizing trade and investment.

A growing proportion of the world output is traded internationally. Since 1962, world-wide exports have increased from 12 percent to more than 30 percent of world GNP[2]. For many countries, the foreign trade GDP-ratio has been rising. This implies that a growing proportion of the national output is for the consumption of people in other countries and that a growing proportion of the domestic consumption is met by goods and services produced in other countries. This is one of the indications of the increasing interdependence between nations.

The global trade integration that took hold in the mid-1980s is expected to become more pronounced in future. The integration of developing countries in world trade would proceed much more rapidly than was true before the start of this decade. Their rate of merchandise trade-integration (i.e., the excess of international trade over output growth) was negative in the fifteen years prior to 1985. It revived in the second half of the 1980s and soared to almost 6 percent in 1991-94. It is projected to average a little over 2 percent during 1997-2004.

The political and economic reform in the erstwhile USSR, Eastern Europe and other parts of the world have given an added thrust to the globalization of the world economy.

25.3   GLOBALIZATION OF BUSINESS

Meaning and Dimensions

Globalization in its true sense is a way of corporate life necessitated, facilitated and nourished by the transnationalization of the World economy and developed by corporate strategies. Globalization is an attitude of mind – it is a mind-set which views the entire world as a single market so that the corporate strategy is based on the dynamics of the global business environment. International marketing or international investment does ot amount to globalization unless it is the result of such a global orientation.

Companies which have adopted a global outlook stop "thinking of themselves as national marketers who venture abroad and start thinking of themselves as global marketers. The top management and staff are involved in the planning of world-wide manufacturing facilities, marketing policies, financial flows and logistical systems. The global operating units report directly to the chief executive or executive committee, not to the head of an international division. Executives are trained in world-wide operations, not just domestic or international. Management is recruited from many countries. Components and supplies are purchased where they can be obtained at the least cost, and investments are made where the anticipated returns are the greatest.

A truly global corporation views the entire world as a single market; it does not differentiate between domestic market and foreign markets. In other words, there is nothing like a home market and foreign market – there is only one market, the global market.

As Kenichi Ohmae observes in his well known book The Borderless World, a global corporation develops a genuine equidistance of perspective. That is, managers with a truly global orientation consciously try to set plans and build organizations as if they view all key customers equidistant from the corporate centre. For example, the managers of Honda, which has operations in several parts of the world, do not think or act as if the company were divided between Japanese and overseas operations. Indeed, the very word 'overseas' has no place in Honda's vocabulary because the corporation sees itself as equidistant from all its key customers. At Casio, the top managers gather information directly from each of their primary markets and then sit down together once a month to lay out revised plans for global product development.

25.4   Stages of Globalization

Normally, a firm passes through different stages of development before it becomes a truly global corporation. Typically, a domestic firm starts its international business by exporting. Later it may establish joint ventures or subsidiaries abroad. From an international firm it may them develop into a multinational firm and, finally, into a global one.

Ohmae identifies five different stages in the development of a firm into a global corporation. The first stage is the arm's length service activity of essentially domestic company which moves into new overseas markets by linking up with local dealers and distributors. In stage two, the company takes over these activiteis on its own. In the next stage, the domestic-based company begins to carry out its own manufacturing, marketing and sales in the key foreign markets. In stage four, the company moves to a full insider position in these markets, supported by a complete business system including R&D and engineering. This stage calls on the managers to replicate in a new environment the hardware systems and operational approaches that have worked so well at home. It forces them to extend the reach of domestic headquarters, which now has to provide support functions such as personnel and finance, to all overseas activities. All through stage four, the headquarters mentality continues to dominate. Different local operations are linked their relation to each other established by their relation to the centre.

In the fifth stage, the company moves towards a genuinely global mode of operation. In this context Ohmae points out that a' company's ability to serve focal customers in markets around the globe in ways that are truly responsive to their needs as well as to the global character of its industry depends on its ability to strike a new organizational balance. What is called for is what Akio Morita of Sony has turned global localization, a new orientation that simultaneously looks in both directions.

Getting to stage give, however, means venturing onto new grounds altogether. Ohmae argues that to make this organizational transition a company must denationalize their operations and create a system of values shared by corporate managers around the globe to replace the glue a nation based orientation once provided.

Ohmae further observes that today's global corporations are nationality-less because consumers have become less nationalistic. True global corporations serve the interests of customers, not governments. They do not exploit local situations and then repatriate all the profits back home, leaving each local area poorer for their having been there. They invest, they train, they pay taxes, they build up infrastructure and they provide good value to customers in all the countries where they do business. IBM Japan, for instance, has provided employment to about 20,000 Japanese and over the past decade has provided three times more tax revenue to the Japanese government than has the Japanese company, Fujitsu.

25.5 ESSENTIAL CONDITIONS FOR GLOBALIZATION

There are, however, some essential conditions to be satisfied on the part of the domestic economy as well as the firm for successful globalization of business. They are :

1. Business Freedom

There should not be unnecessary Government restrictions which come in the way of globalization, like import restrictions, restrictions on sourcing finance or other factors from abroad, foreign investments, etc. That is why the economic liberalization is regarded as a first step towards facilitating globalization.

2. Facilities

The extent to which an enterprise can develop globally from home-country base depends on the facilities available like the infrastructural facilities.

3. Government Support

Although unnecessary government interference is a hindrance to globalization, government support can encourage Globalization. Government support may take the form of policy and procedural reforms development of common facilities such as the infrastructural facilities, R&D support, financial market reforms an so on.

4. Resources

Resources are one of the important factors which often decides the ability of a firm to globalize. Resourceful companies may find it easier to thrust ahead in the global market. Resources include finance, technology, R&D capabilities, managerial expertise, company and brand image, human resource, etc. It should, however be noted that many small firms have been very successful in international business because of one other advantage they possess.

5.   Competitiveness

The competitive advantage of a company is a very important determinant of success in global business. A firm may derive competitive advantage from any one or more of the factors such as low costs and price, product quality, product differentiation, technological superiority, after sales service, marketing strength etc. Sometimes small firms may have an edge over others in certain aspects or times of business.

25.6   GLOBALIZATION OF INDIAN BUSINESS

India's economic integration with the rest of the wold was very limited because of the restrictive economic policies followed until 1991. Indian firms confined themselves, by and large to the home market. Foreign investment by Indian firms was very insignificant.

With the new economic policy ushered in after 1991, there has, however, been a change. Globalization has in fact become a buzzword with Indian firms now and many are expanding their overseas business via different strategies.

This chapter takes a look at the hurdles and prospects in globalization of Indian business and the different globalization strategies.

25.7   OBSTACLES TO GLOBALIZATION

The Indian business suffers from a number of disadvantages in respect of globalization of business. The important problems are the following.

Government Policy and Procedures

Government policy and procedures in India are among hte most complex, confusing and cumbersome in the world. Even after the much publicized liberalization, they do not present a very conducive situation. One prerequisite for success in globalization is swift and efficient action. Government policy and the bureaucratic culture in India in this respect are not that encouraging.

High Cost

High cost of many vital inputs and other factors like raw materials and intermediates, power, finance, infrastructural facilities like ports, etc., tend to reduce international competitiveness of the Indian business.

Poor Infrastructure

Infrastructure in India is generally inadequate and inefficient and therefore, very costly. This is a serious problem affecting the growth as well as competitiveness.

Obsolescence

The technology employed, mode and style of operations, etc., are, in general, obsolete and these seriously affect the competitiveness.

Resistance to Change

There are several socio-politcal factors which resist change and this comes in the way of modernization, and rationalization and efficiency improvement. Technological modernization is resisted due to fear of unemployment. The extent of excess labour employed by the Indian industry is alarming. Because of this labour productivity is very low and this in some cases more than offsets the advantages of cheap labour.

Poor Quality Image

Due to various reasons, the quality of many Indian products is poor. Even when the quality is good, the poor quality image of India has become a handicap.

Supply Problems

Due to various reasons like low product capacity, shortages of raw materials and infrastructure such as power and port facilities, Indian companies in many instances are not able to accept large orders or to keep up delivery schedules.

Small Size

Because of the small size and the low level of resources, in many cases Indian firms are not able to compete with the giants of other countries. Even the largest of the Indian companies are small compared to the multinational giants.

Lack of Experience

The general lack of experience in managing international business is another important problem.

Limited R&D and Marketing Research

Marketing Research and R&D in other areas are vital inputs for development of international business. However, these are poor in Indian business.

Expenditure on R&D in India is less than one per cent of the GNP while it is two to three per cent in most of the developed countries. In 1994-95, India's per capital R&D expenditure was less than $3 when it was between $100 and $825 for most of the developed nations.

Growing Competition

Competition is growing, not only from the firms in the developed countries but also from those in developing countries. Indeed, the growing competition from the developing country firms is a serious challenge to India's international business.

Trade Barriers

Although the tariff barriers to trade have been progressively reduced thansk to the GATT/WTO, the non-tariff barriers have been increasing, particularly in the developed countries. Further, the trading blocs like the NAFTA/EU, etc., could also adversely affect India's business.

25.8   FACTORS FAVOURING GLOBALIZATION

Although India has several handicaps, there are also a number of favourable factors for globalization of Indian business.

Human Resources

Apart from the low cost of labour, there are several other aspects of human resources in India's favour. India has one of the largest pools of scientific and technical manpower. The number of management graduates is also surging. It is widely recognized that given the right environment, Indian scientists and technical personnel can do excellently. Similarly, although labour productivity in India is generally low, given the right environment it will improve substantially. While several countries are facing labour shortage and may face diminishing labour supply, India presents the opposite picutre. Cheap labour has particular attraction for several industries.

Wide Base

India has a very broad resource and industrial base which can support a variety of businesses.

Growing Entrepreneurship

Many of the established industries are planning to go international in a big way. Added to this is the considerable growth of new and dynamic entrepreneur who could make a significant contribution to the globalization of Indian business.

Growing Domestic Market

The growing domestic market enables the Indian companies to consolidate their position and to gain more strengh to make foray into the foreign market or to expand their foreign business.

Niche Markets

There are many marketing opportunities abroad present in the form of market niches. Such niches are particularly attractive for small companies. Several Indian companies have become very successful through niche marking.

Expanding Markets

The growing population and disposable income, and the resultant expanding internal market, provides enormous business opportunities.

Transnationalization of World Economy

Transnationalization of the world economy, i.e., the integration of the national economies into a single world economy as evinced by the growing interdependence and globalization of markets is an external factor encouraging globalization of India business.

NRIs

The large number of non-resident Indians who are resourceful in terms of capital, skill, experience, exposures, ideas, etc. is an asset which can contribute to the globalization of Indian business. The contribution of the overseas Chinese to the recent impressive industrial development of China may be noted here.

Economic Liberalization

The economic liberalization in India is an encouraging factor of globalization. The delicensing of industries, removal of restrictions on growth, opening up of industries earlier reserved for the public sector, important liberalizations, liberalization of policy towards foreign capital and technology, etc., could encourage globalization of Indian business. Further, liberalization in other countries increases the foreign business opportunities for Indian business.

Competition

The growing competition, both from within the country and abroad, provokes many Indian companies to look to foreign markets seriously to improve their competitive position and to increase business. Sometimes, companies enter foreign market as a counter – competitive strategy, i.e., to fight the foreign company in its own home market to weaken its competitive strength.

25.9   GLOBALIZATION STRATEGIES

Indian industry can move towards globalization by different strategies such as developing exports; foreign investments including joint ventures and acquisitions; strategic alliance, licensing and franchising, etc.

25.9.1 Exporting

Export is one of the important paths to globalization. With the economic liberalization an environment for globalization of Indian exports, is slowly emerging. In a truly globalized environment, the exports will also be very much global: the sourcing of finance, materials and managerial inputs will be global, based on purely business considerations.

In fact, in the early 1950s India's economic position was much better than that of most of the countries. Among the developing countries, India had a relatively boardbased industrial structure and significant export market share for several commodities. However, advantage could not be taken of this position due to the absence of an effective export development strategy.

India has potential for significantly increasing the exports of many products if appropriate measures are taken. As a matter of fact, in case of number of products several other developing countries which started their exports much later are way ahead of India while India's progress has been slow. Fourteen thrust product groups were identified quite some time back for export development. However, the progress has been hampered by such problems as inadequacy of production capacities; deficiencies of product development encompassing design, quality, finish and packaging, technological factors, etc. Similarly, although 34 items were identified for extreme focus no commendable progress could be made so far.

The point is that although there are a number of products with large export potential, India failed to exploit the potential satisfactorily. Because of the advance made by other developing countries in the export of such products – although the situation has now become more difficult for India – there still exists a lot of scope for substantially increasing the exports of many of these products.

With the right policy and procedural reforms coupled with institutional support, with technological upgradation and modernization and enlargement of production facilities, with thrust on quality and value added products; with improvements in infrastructural facilities and with right marketing strategy, great strides could be made in the export of a number of products.

According to the projections of Business Today, if the Central Government adopts specific strategies and makes policy changes, 16 important export sectors (viz., textiles, leather, gems and jewellery, granite, tea, processed foods, marine products, tobacco, two-wheelers, steel, aluminium, drugs, spices, software, construction and tourism) can generate $ 55 billion to $ 68 billion of exports by the years 2000 – a three to four fold jump from the 1992 level.

Broadly there are three strategies to increase the export earnings, viz.,

i)   increase the average unit value realization
ii)   increase the quantity of exports
iii)   export new products

One of the key considerations in exports should be to achieve maximum unit value realization. Value-added exports is a much needed graduation for India to enhance the foreign exchange earnings. For example, while 20 million kg. of tobacco exports can earn India Rs.100 crore foreign exchange, if converted to cigatettes, the same quantity of tobacco would earn Rs.400 crore foreign exchange. A very disquieting fact is that India's agricultural exports still are mostly commodity exports, i.e., they are exported mostly in bulk form and the progress achieved in value-added exports is not significant.

Value added exports assume greater significance particularly in view of the stagnation or fall in the exportable surplus of several commodities like pepper, cardamom, tea, coffee, etc.

The major part of India's manufactured exports end up in the low-price segments of the foreign markets. Quality upgradation and marketing efforts are needed to reach the upper segments and to achieve enhanced value realization. Technology imports or foreign collaborations are required towards this end in many cases.

In many cases, what comes in the way of increasing exports is the supply constraints. This is true of a number of manufactured products as well as agricultural commodities. Given the constraints for area expansion, increase in agricultural production should come mostly from increase in productivity which is very low in India. In respect of many industrial products, the production capacity is very low and highly fragmented so that there are a large number of cases of Indian firms not being able to accept offers from abroad for purchase of large quantities of the products which are far beyond the capacity of these firms to supply.

One of the important ways to increase exports is to expand the export basket by adding new products and achieving substantial sales abroad. The share of nontraditional items in India's exports has increased very significantly. However, a lot of potential still remains untapped.

For identifying new products for exports there are two important courses: (i) Explore the export opportunities for product currently produced in India, (ii) Identify products with good demand abroad which can be competively produced and supplied by India.

An important export opportunity for India and other developing countries is provided by the vacation of certain industries or market segments by the developed country firms due to various reasons like environmental consideration, lack of competitiveness, declining industry attractiveness, etc. For example, the developed countries are phasing out production of a wide range of chemicals due to increased expenditure on overheads and high labour costs.

Given the capabilities and limitations of the Indian companies and the international environment, appropriate strategies should be formulated to market different products abroad.

Market niching is the right strategy for many Indian companies. Several Indian companies have indeed successfully used this strategy in the foreign markets.

In some cases, a company can adopt the strategy of straight extension, i.e., extenidng the same product as marketed in the home country to the foreign markets. It is particularly relevant in respect of other developing countries with similar market characteristics as India. A large number of the cases, however, demand quality upgradation, product modification or product development.

25.9.2 Foreign Investment

It is simply not possible to maintain substantial market standing in an important area unless one has a physical presence as a producer. Otherwise one will soon lose the 'feel' of the market.

Besides the advantage of getting a feel of the market, offshore investments are encouraged by such factors as cost advantage, trade barriers, etc. The demand for local content is also satisfied by production in the respective countries.

Foreign investment by Indian companies has so far been very limited. The attractiveness of the domestic market, lack of global orientation, government regulations, etc., have been responsible for this.

At the beginning of 1995, a total of 300 wholly owned subsidiaries (58 in operation and 242 under implementation) were there by Indian companies. The operational ventures were dispersed in 40 countries.

With the economic liberalization and growing global orientation, many Indian companies are setting up manufacturing / assembling / trading bases abroad, either wholly or in partnership with foreign firms. These would help these companies to increase their intenational business. Indian companies have also been making huge investments abroad on acquisitions.

The leader in establishing manufacturing bases abroad is the Aditya Birla group. Aditya Birla, whom the Forbes called India's only international businessman, made this strategic move as early as 1970s. The group's drive to set up business overseas is that "we want a predominance in the industries that we enter. The objective is to be a low-cost, high-quality and global standard player".

A number of large and small Indian companies are investing abroad as part of their globalization strategy. Seveal of these overseas investments aim not only at expansion of production base and business abroad but also at consolidation of the domestic business. The Ballapore Industries of the Thapars are setting up a giant paper mill in Indonesia at an estimated cost of Rs.1800 crore. A plantation put up on 2,50,00 hectares of land will feed the mill. Any surplus pulp may be exported to India to feed Thapar paper mills here. The significance of this should be viewed against the possible wood and pulp shortage in future in India. The Ceat expects that when the tariff barriers between the SAARC countries come down, part of the South Indian market could be served by its tyre plant in Sri Lanka.

Indian companies are also establishing production facilities abroad to get an easy entry into the regional trade blocs. For example, a base in Mexico opens the doors to the

NAFTA region for the Arvind Mills. Similarly Cheminor Drugs, one of the Dr. Reddy's Labs Group of companies, has set up a subsidiary in New Jersey.

25.9.3 Mergers and Acquistions

Mergers and Acquisitions (M & As) are a very important market entry as well as growth strategy. M & As have certain advantages. They may be used to acquire new technology; M & As would have the effect of eliminating reducing competition. One great advantage of M & As in some cases is that they provide instant access to markets and distribution network. As one of the most difficult areas in international marketing comprises distribution, this is some times the most important objective of M & As. For example, Vijay Mallya's UB group acquired a small British company, Wiltshire Brewery. The attraction of Wiltshire for UB was that the former offered a ready made chain of 300 pubs throughout Britain which could be used for the marketing of UB's brands of beer like Kingfisher, Kalyani etc. The UB group has gone for such acquisitions in USA and S.Africa.

A number of other Indian companies have also resorted to acquisition of companies abroad to gain a foothold in the foreign market and to increase the overseas business. There was a spate of such take-overs of East German firms making India one among the top ten investors in the former Communist region of Germany. With the growing global orientation of the Indian companies, there has been a flurry of buyouts abroad, both big and small.

Apart from the big players, a host of lesser known companies have bought out cash strapped plants in Europe, USA, etc.

25.9.4 Joint Ventures

Joint venturing is a very important foreign market entry and growth strategy employed by Indian firms. It is an important route taken by pharmaceutical firms like Ranbaxy, Core, Lupin, Reddy's, etc.

In several cases joint ventures, as in the case of foreign subsidiaries, help Indian firms stabilize and consolidate their domestic business, besides the expansion of the foreign business. Esser Gujarat's joint ventures in countries like Indonesia and Bangladesh to manufacture cold rolled (CR) stell have resulted from a strategy to create an assured market for its hot rolled (HR) coil mother plant at Hazira (HR coils are inputs for manufacturing CR steel products).

Essel Packaging has taken the joint venture route to expand its business abroad. The joint ventures abroad convert the laminate into tubes to be marketed in foreign markets. The centralization of the laminates production in India enables the company to reap enormous economies of scale. The high cost of transportation of tubes over laminates makes the conversion at laminates into tubes in the foreign markets more profitable. Further, the establishment of tube production facilities in foreign markets helps to pre-empt competition.

The liberalization of policy towards foreign investment by Indian firms along with the new economic environment seems to have given joint ventures a boost. At the beginning of 1995, although there were 177 joint ventures, (with a total equity of Rs.179 crore) in operation, there were 347 (total investment Rs.1400 crore) under implementation. Not only the number of joint ventures is increasing but the number of countries and industries on the Indian joint venture map is also expanding. Further liberalization, like enhancement of the investment limit of automatic clearance, is needed for a fast expansion of the Indian investment abroad.

25.9.5 Strategic Alliance

Strategic alliance provides enormous scope for the Indian business to enter/expand the international business. This is particularly important for technology acquistiion and overseas marketing. This is also an important international marketing strategy employed by several Indian firms.

25.9.6 Licensing and Franchising

Licensing and franchising, which involve minimal commitment of resource and effort on the part of the international marketer, are easy ways of entering the international market.

Many Indian firms can use licensing or franchising for the overseas market; particularly the developing countries. For example, Ranbaxy has licensing arrangement in countries like Indonesia and Jordan.

25.9.7 CONCLUSION

The intent of globalization is efficiency improvement and market optimization taking advantage of the opportunities of the global environment. Therefore, in many cases, Indian companies have to globalize to survive and grow in the emerging competitive environment.

The limitations of national markets, the diversity and unevenness of resource endowments of different nations, complexity of technological developments, differences in the levels of development and demand parterns, differences in production efficiencies and costs, technological revolution in communication and other fields, etc., mandate globalization.

The Confederation of Indian Industry (CII) was reported to be formulating a plan to help develop about a hundred Indian corporates to become multinationals by the year 2000. When we consider the fact that there are at present about 40,000 multinationals in the world with more than 2.5 lakh foreign affiliates, 100 multinationals for a country of the size of India is palpably insignificant. This however, should be regarded as a significant achievement when one courts the fact that there is hardly any MNC in India now. Even a tiny country like South Korea, which started the five year plans about a decade later than India, has such well known names as Hyundai, Samsung and Daewoo.

The restrictive economic policies of the past severely effected the competitiveness and growth of the Indian Industry in general. The new economic policy, albeit suffering from certain defects, is a welcome change.

If the Indian firms have the facility to obtain the latest technology in the world, to raise finance from the cheapest source and procure the materials from the best in the world, they are on equal footing with the foreign firms in many respects. And if the Indian firms can muster some edge ever the foreign firms in respect of labour cost, productivity, product quality features, etc., that could be a competitive advantage.

In many cases, size is an important factor which influences the competitive power. Economic liberalization by pruning down the list of industries reserved for the public sector, delicensing and amending the MRTP Act has provided an environment which enables companies to grow fast, both internally and externally. The growth plans of many Indian companies indicate a great leap forward. The turnover of Reliance is projected to more than double from about Rs.10,000 crore to Rs.20,000 crore in a short span. The Modern Group's turnover has more than doubled from Rs.525 crore in 1994-95 in two years time, a fifth of it being exports. The Kirloskar group which had a turnover of Rs.1300 crore, in 1995 is targeting about Rs.7000 crore by the year 2000. The Rs.6000 crore ITC group is positioning itself to become a prominent Indian MNC by the turn of the century. Out of the turnover of Rs.4280 crore of its flagship company in 1993-94, Rs.882 crore was from exports. The Arvind Mills, whose projected turnover is 1996-97 was about Rs.1100 crore, is planning to more than triple it to $ 1 billion by the turn of the century. The increase in the size could keep the companies on a strong footing to make further dent in both the domestic and foreign markets. In short, the Indian industry is where they can make jumps compared to the past situation of limping forward.

Several Indian companies are already leading players. The Ispat group of the Mittals which has units in countries like the US, Canada, Indonesia, Trinidad and Tobago is the largest sponge iron producer in the world. The Aditya Birla group is the world's largest player in viscose fibre and carbon black and also the largest refiner of palm oil. Essel Packaging, which is already the world's second largest integrated producer of laminated tubes is aiming to climb upto the number one position. Arvind

Mills, one of the world's largest producer of denim cloth, is making further thrusts. When its ongoing projects are fully implemented, Reliance Industries would be the second largest producer in the world to be fully integrated from naphtha to fabris. India is also a major player in two-wheelers and bicycles. India is the largest producer of several agricultural commodities.

Liberalization in India and in other countries pose a real challenge to the Indian business to prove its mettle. The 1990s should turn out to be a decade of the 'take off' the Indian business.

25.10 LIBERALIZATION

Basically globalization is a concept by which the globe becomes one unified entity cutting across the political, economic and regional barriers. As such globalization demands:

a.   The product or a service rendered by the firm should be minimum possible cost. The product should also withstand competition with other firms in the national as well international markets.

b.   World trade is subjected to less restriction.

c.   There is economic liberalization. The process of globalization in financial sectors i.e the money and capital market operates globally.

d.   The developed countries should invest in developing countries through Multi National Companies (MNC).

A corporation can be said to be global in true service when,

a.   It provides a product or a service of a brand which is recognized and accepted by the world market, and is export oriented.

b.   The entire system of the organisation quality of the product is approved and is upto the level as mentioned in ISO : 9000.

c.   It has a overseas marketing and distribution system.

d.   It operates a branch of the firm in the operational area with the assistance and finance of the local people but retaining its laid down share.

The personnel and financial functions should be with the parental company and the headquarters in the prime country.

25.11 ESSENTIAL REQUIREMENTS FOR A FIRM TO BECOME A GLOBAL UNIT

1. Establish a R&D so as to develop product and technology and discover new technologies in the field.

2. Product development should be a routine affair. Every effort should be made to develop new products.

3. It should have a strategic response to market feedback, so as to know the change in demands, fashion, technology, etc.

4. Quick and effective attendance to consumer complaints and their removal in the minimum possible time.

5. Commitment to satisfy the customer by providing the right quality of the product or services in right quantity at right time and right price.

6. Organization should be flexible enough to meet the changes and still satisfy the customer demands.

7. Quick decision making system with enough flexibility.

25.12 REVIEW QUESTIONS

1. Write short notes on Globalization?
2. What are the essential conditions for Globalilzation?
3. List out the obstacles in globalization and explain.
4. Define Liberalization.
5. Explain the term globalization strategies.

INTERNATIONAL MANAGEMENT

26.1   INTRODUCTORY OBSERVATIONS

In the present-day-management literature, one finds a large number of principles of management and a good number of management theories concerning areas like leadership, motivation, organizational theory, and organizational behavior and so on. However, there is a need, and, of course, an urgent need to develop what we many call a unified global management theory' i.e. a theory-

- Which contains fundamental managerial concepts, principles and techniques - applicable to most of management situations; and

- which provides useful guidelines and hints to managers, all over the word, involved in practicing management, in various types of group endeavors, for better managing.

Developing a global management theory is not an easy task or an arm-chair exercise. Yet, with efforts of practitioners, scholars and researchers; it may be possible to develop such a theory; as in the present-day-times, one can notice tendencies towards developing a unified global management theory.

26.2   TENDENCIES TOWARDS DEVELOPING A UNIFIED GLOBAL MANAGEMENT THEORY

Tendencies towards developing a unified global management theory may be classified into the following three categories:

(a)   Historical tendencies.
(b)   Conceptual tendencies
(c)   Modern tendencies

Let us describe the major factors, comprised in each of the above stated three categories.

(a)   Historical Tendencies

Some of the tendencies which favor the development of a global management theory and which have a historical origin or background are described below:

(i)   System's Approach to Managing:

System's approach to managing, though thought to be new, is not really new. Scholars comment that it is something like old wine is a new bottle. The core of the concept of system's approach is the recognition of the inter-relationships existing among various parts of an enterprise; and the relationship of the enterprise with the environment (i.e. the supra system). In fact, practitioners of management in the past also appreciated this sort of relationship and provided for it while managing their enterprises but, of course, without using the word system. Again, modern practitioners of management, the world over, manage by the system's approach; as no manager can overlook the significance of interrelationship among various parts of their organization. Certainly then, the system's approach to a managing is one of the building blocks, in developing an integrated global management theory.

(ii)   Contingency or Situational Approach to Managing:

According to contingency or situational approach to managing, there is no universally accepted best way of managing all situations; the best system of managing depends on the realties of managerial situations. Intelligent managers in the past, always decided things, in view of the realities of the situation. Managers of to-day also, everywhere, appreciate and implement the contingency approach to managing; as this approach is nothing but common sense approach. Therefore, a universal belief by managers, everywhere, in the situational approach underpins the efforts involved in developing a unified global management theory.

(b)   Conceptual Tendencies:

Some of the conceptual tendencies favoring the development of unified global management theory are described below:

(i)   Popularity and use of principles of management:

There are a large number of principles of management concerning various managerial concepts and functional areas of management. Many management principles command universal recognition and implementation. Principles of management are popular and useful in that, it is easier to teach, do research and practice management; when one proceeds according to principles.

By testing the validity of existing principles, and developing new principles on the basis of empirical studies; scholars and researchers can provide a useful foundation on which to build a solid and unified global management theory. In fact, a theory of management could be built only around principles of management.

(ii)   Operational School of Management - most popular way of structuring management knowledge:

Management textbooks based on operational school (i.e., analyzing managerial jobs in terms of functions of planning, organizing, staffing, directing, controlling and co-ordinating) are used around the word. Practicing managers, everywhere, concern themselves with functions of planning, directing, controlling etc; while performing their managerial jobs in real life situations. Though may schools of management have grown in the present-day-times and many more are likely to emerge in future; there is no doubt that operational school will continue to retain its dominance over other school of management thought.

As such, the operational school is likely to provide the cementing force to efforts engaged in developing a unified global management theory.

(iii)   Confluence of leadership and motivation concepts
(Confluence means the fact of two or more things becoming one).

Motivation is not only the heart of management; it is also the core of the process of leadership an exercise through which the manager (acting as a leader) tries to influence the behavior of subordinates, for an enthusiastic attainment of groups objectives. In fact, a leader is a flop till he / she is able to motivate subordinates; so that the subordinates see in the leader the means of attaining their personal objectives.

There is no controversy over the role of a manager moulded into a leader. Further, leader's main weapon is the motivational technique. Hence, the confluence of leadership and motivation, which is just conceptual (and not newly innovated); provides a useful building block in developing a unified global management theory.

(c) . **Modern Tendencies**

Some of the modern tendencies favoring the developing of a unified global management theory are described below:

(i)   MNCs Management Practices

Multi-National Corporations (MNCs) management practices, provide the modern building blocks for developing a unified global management theory. While making decisions in areas of planning, organizing, leading and controlling; managements of MNCs must deal with new and different situations characteristic of many cultural perspectives, nations, governments, labor unions and other factors in the global area. Hence, management concepts, principles and techniques followed by MNCs may provide useful pillars to support the building of a unified global theory of management.

(ii)   Case study approach to management education

Case study approach to imparting management education is rather new. It seeks to bridge the gulf between theory and practice of management. In case study approach, management knowledge and experience are imparted to students, trainees and others by analyzing international management cases, of diverse natures. Distilling basics of management from analyses of leading management cases is certainly going to make useful building material available for developing a unified global management theory.

(iii)   Emphasis on behavioral approach to managing

Behavioral approach to managing is a positive contribution of the neo-classical approach to management. Now-a-days, behavioral approach, emphasizing on inter-personal and inter-group behavioral patterns, is being increasingly used in all functions of management i.e. planning, organizing, staffing, directing and controlling.

Managers, in all leading organizations, all over the world, realize as to how difficult it is to understand and modify human behavior, for organizational purposes. New fields of managing which are emerging in view of the recognition of the behavioral aspects of managing are - Organizational Development (OD) and Organizational Behavior (OB).

Fundamentals of OD and OB are likely to make meaningful contributions towards developing a unified global management theory.

(iv)   Professionalisation of Management

Management is getting professionalized, more and more, day-by-day everywhere, in the world. There is no doubt that professional managers follow a more comprehensive and broad-minded approach to managing enterprises. Innovations by, and experience of, professional managers is likely to make positive contributions towards developing a unified global management theory.

(v)   Technological Revolution

Technology in the world is getting so much advanced now-a-days, that experts speak of a 'technological revolution' - the commercial world is passing through. Experts, researchers, and practitioners recognize the impact of technology on organizational structure, organizational behavior and may other aspects, having a bearing on managerial effectiveness.

Efforts of managers, in coping with new technological implications, may provide useful hints for developing managerial concepts and techniques; which might be utilized in developing a unified global management theory.

(vi)   Environment of Global Competition

In an environment of global competition, many co-operations feel problems of their survival, not the speak of growth. This problem applies to corporate enterprises (especially tiny enterprises) all over the world. Managements of many countries can contribute, under the circumstances, to management theory and practice, by suggesting hints for more effective planning, flexible approach to organizing, better management of human resources etc. - as means for ensuring survival and prosperity amidst globally increasing intense competitive conditions. Such suggestions of leading managements, all over the world, can provide building material for developing a unified global management theory.

(vii)   Glossary of Management Concepts and Terms

(Glossary means a list of technical or special words, in a particular context, explaining their meanings).

One of the greatest obstacles in developing a unified global management theory has been the problem of semantics. Management people, authors, researchers etc. tend to use the same terms in different ways or use different terms for the same concept. Fortunately, the Fellows of the International Academy of Management (comprising management scholars and leaders, from over thirty countries) have undertaken the development of a glossary of management terms and concepts, in a number of languages. Such glossary may be a great aid in developing in unified global management theory.

26.3   REVIEW QUESTIONS

1.   What do you understand by the phrase a 'unified global theory of management'? Identify and explain some of the major tendencies, favoring the development of a unified global theory of management.

MODEL QUESTION PAPERS

H 383

B.E. / B.Tech. DEGREE EXAMINATION, APRIL / MAY 2004.

Sixth Semester

Electrical and Electronics Engineering

MG 331 - PRINCIPLES OF MANAGEMENT

Time: Three Hours   Maximum: 100 marks

Answer ALL Questions.

PART A - (10 x 2 = 20 marks)

1.   Define ethics
2.   Explain the social responsibility of business.
3.   Define planning
4.   What are the different types of planning?
5.   Explain the terms decision and decision - making.
6.   What is span of control?
7.   What are the advantages of decentralization?
8.   Name the various types of communication.
9.   What are the different motivational theories?
10.   Explain franchising.

PART B - (5 x 16 = 80 marks)

11.   (i)   Describe theory X and theory Y.   (8)

      (ii)   Explain the various sources of recruitment. What are their advantages
             and disadvantages?   (8)

12.   (a)   Explain Henry Fayol's principles of management.   (16)

                              Or

      (b)   Describe the various elements of planning.

13.   (a)   (i)   Describe the various types of decision.   (8)
              (ii)   Explain the steps in rational decision - making.

                                    Or

       (b)   How are individual ethics formed? Also explain the arguments for and
              against social responsibility and organizational approaches to social
              responsibility.   (16)

14.   (a)   (i)   Distinguish between formal and informal organization.   (8)
              (ii)   Describe departmentation by process. What are its advantages and
                     disadvantages?

                                    Or

       (b)   (i)   Explain the functions of Human Resources Management   (8)
              (ii)   Explain the various methods of performance appraisal.   (8)

15.   (a)   (i)   What are the barrier to effective communication? Explain
                     them.   (10)
              (ii)   Explain the qualities required for effective leadership.   (6)

                                    Or

       (b)   (i)   Why do companies decide to go international? Also explain the
                     merits and limitations of multinational companies.   (6)
              (ii)   Explain how companies go international and also explain how
                     they affect organization complexity and managerial involvement
                     abroad.   (10)

$$\boxed{\text{N 1123}}$$

B.E. / B.Tech. DEGREE EXAMINATION, NOVEMBER / DECEMBER 2004

Sixth Semester

Electrical and Electronics Engineering

MG 331 - PRINCIPLES OF MANAGEMENT

Time: Three Hours   Maximum: 100 marks

Answer ALL Questions.

PART A - (10 x 2 = 20 marks)

1. State any one definition of management.
2. What are the functions of managers?
3. Sate the steps in planning.
4. What are the benefits of management by objectives?
5. Define span of management.
6. What is meant by functional authority?
7. Define theory - X.
8. State the Maslow's hierarchy of needs.
9. What is the managing concept in France?
10. State the factors influencing managing in Australia.

PART B - (5 x 16 = 80 marks)

11. (i)   Explain the nature and purpose of international business and multinational corporations.   (8)

    (ii) Describe the trend towards a unified global theory of management.   (8)

12. (a)   Describe the various approaches to management.   (16)

                              Or

    (b)   Explain the nature and importance of ethics in managing and ways to institutionalize and raise ethical standards.   (16)

13. (a)   Discuss about the nature and types of premises and forecasts in detail.   (16)

                              Or

(b)   Explain the importance and limitations of rational decision making.   (16)

14. (a)   Describe the basic patterns of traditional departmentation and explain the advantages and disadvantages of each.   (16)

Or

(b)   Discuss the major principles to be kept in mind in developing organization structure.

15. (a)   What are the characteristics of written, oral and nonverbal communication? Explain them in detail.

Or

(b)   Explain the managerial techniques that are especially useful for operations, planning and control as well as other areas of enterprise operation.   (16)

$$\boxed{\text{R 230}}$$

B.E. / B.Tech. DEGREE EXAMINATION, APRIL / MAY 2005.

Sixth Semester

Electrical and Electronics Engineering

MG 331 - PRINCIPLES OF MANAGEMENT

Time: Three Hours   Maximum: 100 marks

Answer ALL Questions.

PART A - (10 x 2 = 20 marks)

1.   Explain the importance of planning.
2.   Explain ethical dilemma.
3.   Explain organizing.
4.   Explain controlling.
5.   Explain global outsourcing.
6.   What is social responsibility?
7.   What do you mean by the term "bounded rationality" in decision making?
8.   What are the various types of decision making models?
9.   Explain chain of command.
10.   Explain departmentalization.

PART B - (5 x 16 = 80 marks)

11.   Explain the following approaches for ethical decision.

    (i)   Utilitarian approach
    (ii)   Individualism approach
    (iii)   Moral - rights approach
    (iv)   Justice approach.

12.   (a)   (i)   Differentiate between strategic and tactical planning.   (8)

(ii)   Explain the characteristics of objectives. What are the requirements of good objectives? Also mention its benefits   (8)

Or

(b) (i)   Explain environmental appraisal. What are the factors which need to be studied for environmental appraisal?   (8)

(ii)   Explain the different types of policies. Also explain the guidelines to be followed for effective policy-making.   (8)

13. (a)   Explain the various methods of departmentalism. Also discuss the factors to be taken into consideration while framing various departments.   (16)

Or

(b) (i)   Discuss the factors determining span of control.   (8)

(ii)   What are the advantages and disadvantages of matrix type of organization?   (4)

(iii)   Explain the essential requirements of a good appraisal system. (4)

14. (a)   Explain the following motivational theories :

(i)   Herb erg's motivation - Hygiene theory

(ii)   Maslow's need theory.   (16)

Or

(b)   Explain the contributions of Taylor and Gilberth to management.   (16)

15. (a) (i)   Explain the factors affecting managerial ethics.   (8)

(ii)   Explain the various steps involved in the selection of an employee.   (8)

Or

(b)   Explain the economic, legal - political and socio-cultural factors to be considered in the international business environment.   (16)

B 514

B.E. / B.Tech. DEGREE EXAMINATION, NOVEMBER / DECEMBER 2005

Sixth Semester

Electrical and Electronics Engineering

MG 331 - PRINCIPLES OF MANAGEMENT

Time: Three Hours   Maximum: 100 marks

Answer ALL Questions.

PART A - (10 x 2 = 20 marks)

1. Define Management.
2. Define ethics.
3. Why is it important to study the various management theories that have been developed?
4. What do you mean by planning?
5. Differentiate between managerial "effectiveness" and "efficiency".
6. Define Staffing.
7. Explain Leading.
8. Define Motivation.
9. Define Leadership.
10. What is "noise" is a communication system?

PART B - (5 x 16 = 80 Marks)

11. (i) Explain in detail the procedure of decision - making.   (8)
    (ii) Explain the steps that make up the formal planning process.   (8)

12. (a) (i) Explain the levels of ethical questions in business. Also explain ethical language.   (8)
        (ii) Explain the basic tenets of common morality.   (8)

                                        Or

    (b) (i) Write short notes on management theory and practice.   (8)
        (ii) Describe the models of corporate social responsiveness.   (8)

13. (a) (i)   What is division of work? What are its advantages and disadvantages? What does an organization chart show? Also explain the importance of organizational structure.   (8)

          (ii) What is a functional structure? How is it different from a product/market structure? What are the advantages and disadvantages of each?   (8)

                                          Or

     (b) (i)   Explain line and staff authority. Also explain the guidelines for effective delegation.   (8)

          (ii) Explain the steps of hiring sequence. Is this sequence the same under all conditions? Why or why not?   (8)

14. (a) (i)   Explain the expectancy model of motivation.   (8)
          (ii) Describe the common barriers to effective interpersonal communication. How may these barriers be overcome?   (8)

                                          Or

     (b) (i)   Distinguish between authoritarian, democratic and Laissez - Faire leadership styles and their managerial implications.   (8)

          (ii) Compare and contrast decision support systems, expert systems and conventional management information systems.   (8)

15. (a) (i)   Why do companies decide to go international? Explain.   (8)

          (ii) What economic variable should managers be aware of before they invest in other countries? Why?   (8)

                                          Or

     (b) (i)   Describe the four stages of corporate internationalization identified by Christopher Korth and explain how they effect organization complexity and managerial involvement abroad. (10)

          (ii) Write short notes on the future of global management.   (6)

H 1438

B.E. / B.Tech. DEGREE EXAMINATION, MAY / JUNE 2006

Sixth Semester

Electrical and Electronics Engineering

MG 331 - PRINCIPLES OF MANAGEMENT

Time: Three Hours   Maximum: 100 marks

Answer ALL Questions.

PART A - (10 x 2 = 20 marks)

1. Define Management.
2. What is meant by ethics?
3. What is the purpose of planning?
4. State any two decision making strategies?
5. Give two examples for line organization.
6. Define decentralization.
7. Define productivity.
8. State the types of information.
9. What is meant by preventive control?
10. Define performance appraisal.

PART B - (5 x 16 = 80 marks)

11. (i)   Describe about unified management theory in detail.   (8)
    (ii) What is meant by global management theory? Explain in detail. (8)

12. (a)   "Management is a Science" – Discuss on this Statement.   (16)

                              Or

    (b)   Explain the social responsibility of an individual.   (16)

13. (a)   Explain the objectives of planning in any organization and also explain
          the planning strategies.   (16)

                              Or

    (b)   What is meant by planning premises? Explain in detail.   (16)

14.   (a)   Discuss about the nature and purpose of organizing.   (16)

                                    Or

       (b)   Explain the techniques involved for selection process.   (16)

15.   (a)   Explain any two motivational theories with examples.   (16)

                                    Or

       (b)   What are the types of leadership styles? Briefly explain them. (16)

K 1152

B.E. / B.Tech. DEGREE EXAMINATION, NOV. / DEC. 2004

Seventh Semester

Computer Science Engineering

MG 331 - PRINCIPLES OF MANAGEMENT

(Common to Electronics and Communication Engineering)

Time: Three Hours   Maximum: 100 marks

Answer ALL Questions.

PART A - (10 x 2 = 20 marks)

1.   What is meant by Productivity?
2.   What is Social Audit?
3.   How would you evaluate the importance of a decision?
4.   State briefly Tows Matrix.
5.   State the factors that influence Job design?
6.   What are the sources of organizational conflict?
7.   What is meant by Brain Storming?
8.   List out few leadership traits.
9.   What are the dangers in budgeting?
10.   What is value engineering?

PART - B (5 x 16 = 80 marks)

11.   (i)   What are the important aspects of the system approach to Manager Selection?   (8)

      (ii)   What are the main characteristics of organization development?   (8)

12.   (a)   (i)   Define Management. What are the functions managers perform to attain the set goals?   (9)

             (ii)   List and discuss the benefits and limitations of some codes of ethics.   (7)

                                    Or

(b)   (i)   What are different types of plans ? Explain.   (8)

        (ii)   Explain briefly the benefits and weakness of MBO.   (8)

13.   (a)   (i)   Explain modern approaches to decision making under uncertainty.   (10)

        (ii)   Explain how formal organization is different from informal organization. Illustrate.   (6)

Or

(b)   (i)   Explain the concept of functional authority. How do you delegate it?   (10)

        (ii)   How does a leader influence organization culture?   (6)

14.   (a)   (i)   What are some possible implications of theories X and Y, staffing, leading and controlling?   (7)

        (ii)   Explain any three theories of Motivation   (9)

Or

(b)   (i)   Explain different styles of leadership based on authority.   (8)

        (ii)   What are communication barriers and suggest measures how communication be made effective?   (8)

15.   (a)   (i)   Define controlling as a managerial function and explain the basic control process.   (10)

        (ii)   State briefly the nature and applications of information technology.   (6)

Or

(b)   (i)   Explain how operations research helps to enhance productivity.   (8)

        (ii)   What do you understand by principle of Preventive Control? Explain its advantages.   (8)

S 290

B.E. / B.Tech. DEGREE EXAMINATION, APRIL / MAY 2005

Seventh Semester

Computer Science and Engineering

MG 331 - PRINCIPLES OF MANAGEMENT

(Common to Electronics and Communication Engineering)

Time: Three Hours   Maximum: 100 marks

Answer ALL Questions.

PART A - (10 x 2 = 20 marks)

1.   Define social audit.
2.   List the important functions of managers.
3.   Mention the three approaches generally adopted by managers in selecting an alternative.
4.   Enumerate the advantages of functional organization grouping.
5.   Broadly classify the tests that are commonly used in the selection of people for job.
6.   State the objectives of sensitivity training.
7.   Distinguish between motivation and satisfaction.
8.   What are the four basic ingredients of leadership skill?
9.   State the principle of preventive control.
10.   Write some of the requirements that must be fulfilled to ensure the JIT method to work.

PART - B (5 x 16 = 80 marks)

11.   (i)   Discuss about the general steps involved in the operations research procedure.   (9)
      (ii)   Explain the assumptions and advantages of principle of preventive control.   (7)

12.   (a)   (i)   Give an account of various steps involved in planning.   (8)
             (ii)   Explain briefly the benefits and weaknesses of Management By Objectives.   (8)

Or

     (b)   (i)   Enumerate the Fayol's Principles of Management.   (6)

            (ii)   State and explain the eight recommendations that should be considered by managers for successful implementation of strategies.   (10)

13.   (a)   (i)   Write short notes on any two important modern approaches to decision making under uncertainty.   (6)

            (ii)   Discuss about the factors determining an effective span of management.   (10)

                                Or

     (b)   (i)   Briefly explain the factors determining the degree of decentralization of authority.   (10)

            (ii)   Give a brief account of at least six mistakes in organizing.   (6)

14.   (a)   (i)   Give a brief account of the skills and personal characteristics needed by managers.   (6)

            (ii)   Discuss about the various steps in the formulation of career strategy.   (10)

                                Or

     (b)   Discuss in detail about the various approaches followed in organizations for manager development.   (16)

15.   (a)   (i)   Enumerate the assumptions of Mc Gregory's theory X and theory Y.   (8)

            (ii)   Write short notes on Maslow's hierarchy of needs.   (5)

           (iii) Briefly explain about the three types of basic motivating needs proposed by Mc Cleeland.   (3)

                                Or

     (b)   (i)   Give a brief account of various leadership styles based on use of authority.   (4)

            (ii)   Discuss about the barriers and breakdowns in communication.   (12)

A 415

B.E. / B.Tech. DEGREE EXAMINATION, NOV. / DEC. 2005

Seventh Semester

Computer Science Engineering

MG 331 - PRINCIPLES OF MANAGEMENT

(Common to Electronics and Communication Engineering)

Time: Three Hours

Maximum: 100 marks

Answer ALL Questions.

PART A - (10 x 2 = 20 marks)

1. What are the objectives of planning?
2. What do you understand by management science theory?
3. Name the different types of organizational structure.
4. What do you understand by effective organizing?
5. What is the purpose of Human Resource Management?
6. Mention any two functions of manager.
7. Define motivation.
8. Mention any two leadership qualities.
9. Define productivity.
10. Define operations management

PART B - (5 x 16 = 80 marks)

11. (i) Describe the different objectives of planning (8)
    (ii) Discuss the factors for strategies policies and planning premises (8)

12. (a) Define decision making and explain the process of decision making that affects the efficiency of the business decisions (16)

    Or

    (b) (i) Explain the line organization with a neat sketch (8)
        (ii) Explain the concept of decentralization (8)

13.   (a)   (i)   Explain the different types of selection procedure in an organization   (8)

            (ii)   Explain the importance of performance appraisal of Human Resource Management   (8)

Or

     (b)   (i)   Discuss the role of manager   (8)

            (ii)   Discuss how manager can be helpful in organizational development   (10)

14.   (a)   (i)   Discuss the different theories of motivation   (8)

            (ii)   Explain how motivation helps an organization to improve productivity   (8)

Or

     (b)   (i)   Explain the importance of strong leadership in the creation of cohesive work in an industrial organization   (8)

            (ii)   Discuss the importance of communication in a modern industrial organization   (8)

15.   (a)   Explain in detail the systems and process of controlling control techniques   (16)

Or

     (b)   Explain the preventive control mechanism towards achieving a unified global management theory   (16)

J 1313

B.E. / B.Tech. DEGREE EXAMINATION, MAY / JUNE 2006

Seventh Semester

Computer Science and Engineering

(Common to Electronics and Communication Engineering)

MG 331 - PRINCIPLES OF MANAGEMENT

Time: Three Hours   Maximum: 100 Marks

Answer All Questions

PART - A (10 x 2 = 20 Marks)

1. What do you understand by mission?
2. List out Mc Kinsey's 7-S framework approach.
3. What is meant by informal organization?
4. List any four limitations of decentralization?
5. State and brief the stages in recruitment process
6. Write four steps in formulating a career strategy
7. What are four 'Brain Storming' ideas?
8. What are the barriers of communication?
9. Explain what is meant by 'Globalization'?
10. What are the essential features of Japanese style of business management? State any four.

PART B - (5 x 16 = 80 Marks)

11. (i) Define staffing. Describe the system approach to staffing   (8)

    (ii) What are the main characteristics of organization development? How does OD differ from manager development?   (8)

12. (a) (i) what are the functions managers perform to attain the set goals? Explain.   (9)

(ii) Explain the major social responsibilities of a business towards different claimants. (7)

Or

(b) (i) What are the different types of plan? Explain (8)

(ii) How can strategies be implemented effectively? (8)

13. (a) (i) What determines the span of management and hence the levels of organization? (8)

(ii) Explain briefly the importance and limitations of rational decision making (8)

Or

(b) (i) Why has there been a conflict between line and staff for so long and so many companies? How can this conflict be removed? (9)

(ii) Define organization culture. How does a leader influence organization culture (7)

14. (a) (i) Explain Theory X and Theory Y assumptions. (9)

(ii) Explain briefly any three theories of motivation (7)

Or

(b) (i) Define leadership. Explain Fielder's Contingency approach to leadership (8)

(ii) Briefly describe the communication process model. 'Lack of upward communication can be disastrous'-Give reasons. (8)

15. (a) (i) Define controlling as a Managerial function. Explain the basic control process. (8)

(ii) What are the challenges faced by IT Managers? Explain the ways by which IT can help managers at different levels. (8)

Or

(b) (i) Explain briefly the difference between Direct control and preventive control (8)

(ii) Point out some of the operational differences between a domestic firm and a multinational corporation and discuss their importance (8)

GLOSSARY

Accountability: It is the obligation to carry out responsibility and exercise authority in terms of performance standards established.

Action Research: The method through which organizational development and change agents learn what improvements are needed and how the organization can best be aided in making improvement.

Affiliate: A company owned or controlled by another corporation through ownership of 10 per cent or more of outstanding voting stock.

Auditing: The process of verifying the validity of an organization's financial statements and records by outsiders or by members of the organization.

Balance sheet: A statement showing a company's assets, liabilities and net worth at a given time.

BCG matrix: A corporate portfolio management approach that examines the rate of market growth and market share of each of a corporation's business units to help top management develop a balance between those business units that absorb cash and those that provide it.

Behavior Modification: An approach to motivation based on the law of effect that behavior which leads to rewarding consequences tends to be repeated, and behavior with negative consequences tends not to be repeated.

Benchmarking: Comparing a company's practices and processes with the world's best standards for the purpose of closing the gap with them.

Board Of Directors (BOD): An apex body for decision making; the members of the board exercise their authority and responsibility collectively.

Boston Consulting Group (BCG): A two-by-two product portfolio analysis using market growth rate with relative market share. (It defines its segments as dogs, cats, stars and question marks. These different businesses are categorized in terms of cash flow).

Break-even analysis: A mathematical procedure for studying the relationships between cost, sales volume and profit.

Budgets: Formal quantitative statement of the resources allocated to specific programmes or projects for a given period.

Bureaucratic control: A method of control that employs strict rules and regulations to help ensure desired behavior by organizational units often used by multinational enterprises to control subsidiaries.

Business unit strategy: The level of strategy that concerns a portion of a company which is large and distinct enough to be considered a separate business.

Capacity planning: The determination of the amount of products of services that an operations system should be capable of producing.

Case method: It is a method of training through which case studies provide learning experiences that help the learner to develop habits and skills of analysis, reasoning, imagination and judgment.

Centralization: It is concentration of authority at certain central points within an organization.

Chain of command: The hierarchy of authority, encompassing all organization members, which extends from the top to the bottom of the organization.

Challenge of change: The strategy implementation process involves a change, either minor or major, if it affects a large number of people cutting into deeper issues like beliefs, values, etc., it is a major change.

Change agent: The individual leading or guiding the process of a change in an organizational situation.

Channel: The medium of communication between a sender and a receiver.

Chaos management style: When both the Board of Directors and top management have little or no involvement in the decision - making process of the company, their style is described as the chaos management style.

Charismatic leaders: Those leaders, who, through their personal vision and energy, inspire followers and have a major impact on their organization; also called transformational leaders.

Client system: The individual group or organization which is the target of a planned change.

Closed system: A system that does not interact with its environment.

Coercive power: The negative side of reward power, based on the influencer's ability to punish and seek conformance from subordinates.

Collaborative bargaining: The process of negotiating and administering agreements between labor and management concerning wages, working conditions and other aspects of the work environment.

Command group: A group composed of a manager and his or her subordinates, who interact with each other towards a common objective.

Commission groups: Groups whose members are usually appointed by government officials, charged with administrative, regulatory, or legislative tasks.

Committee: A formal organizational group, usually relatively long-lived, created to carry out specific organizational tasks.

Communication network: A set of channels within an organization or group through which communication travels.

Competition: The situation in which two or more parties strive towards mutually incompatible goals and cannot interfere with each other.

Competitive advantage (or edge): The position achieved by a business enterprise over its competitors by intensifying functional differentiation of its products, exploiting competitors' weaknesses, taking aggressive initiatives through search for improvements / innovations and by superior competitive performance.

Computer-Aided Design (CAD): The process of designing products interactively with computers.

Computer-Based Information System (CBIS): A formal system for providing various levels of management with information through the use of computers.

Conceptual skill: The mental ability to guide and coordinate an organization's activities by understanding the organization as a whole, as well as an understanding of the interdependence of its parts.

Contingency approach: The view that the management techniques that best contribute to the attainment of organizational goals might vary in different types of situations or circumstances.

Continuous improvement: Constant, ceaseless attempts to fulfill the customer's expectations.

Continuous - process production: A production technology that yields long flows of homogeneous materials, such as oil refining.

Continuous reinforcement: A reinforcement schedule in behavior modification, in which individuals are immediately rewarded/punished for their good/bad behavior.

Controllable variable: A part of a problem situation that can be manipulated to achieve a solution.

Controlling: The process of monitoring actual organizational activities to see that they conform to planned activities, and correcting flaws or deviations.

Cooperation: The process of working together to attain mutual objectives.

Coordination: The integration of the activities of the separate part of an organization to accomplish organizational goals.

Corporate social responsibility: The concept that corporations have an obligation to act for the good of society.

Corporate values: Beliefs held by managers of an organization concerning what is desirable or good. The broad objectives pursued by a business enterprise and the priority attached to these objectives give some idea about its corporate values.

Critical Path Method (CPM): A network analysis technique used to schedule and control work on projects for which the time required to complete the task is specified / limited.

Cultural control: A method of control that emphasizes implicit and informal leading based on a broad company culture, associated with many large Japanese companies.

Data: Raw, unanalyzed facts, figures and events.

Decentralization: The delegation of power and authority from higher to lower levels of an organization, often accomplished by the creation of small, self-contained organizational units.

Decision making: The process of identifying and selecting a course of action to solve specific problems.

Decision Support System (DSS): An easily accessible microcomputer - based information system that aids individual managers in planning and decision making.

Decoding: The interpretation and translation of a message into meaningful information.

Delegation: It is the entrustment of responsibility and authority to a subordinate and the creation of accountability for the successful accomplishment of the task.

Delphi method: A survey of expert opinion that includes each expert's review of the other's ideas; the experts identify is not disclosed to the others in order to ensure that the decision is not through consensus.

Departmentalization: The grouping into departments of work activities those are similar and logically connected.

Diversification: This results when a firm adds new products or enters into new markets which may be related or unrelated to the existing business.

Divestment strategy: Divestment implies stripping or getting rid of loss-making operations or units.

Division of work: The breakdown of a complex task into components so that individuals are responsible for a limited set of activities, instead of the task as a whole.

Dysfunctional conflict: Any conflict that results in decreased efficiency and greater factionalism within an organization.

Effectiveness: The ability to determine appropriate objectives doing the right things.

Efficiency: The ability to minimize the use of resources in achieving organizational objectives; in common parlance, smart work.

Electronic Data Processing (EDP): Storage and analysis of data using computers.

Electronic mail (E-mail): Data and text circulated through interlinked computers.

Empowerment: Giving people the power to solve problems and ensure quality.

Encoding: The translation of information into a series of symbols for communication.

Entrepreneur: The originator a new business venture; a person who starts a business activity and ventures to take risk.

Environmental factors: These are both global and national factors which influence business the important factors being economic, technological, socio-cultural, political, legal, and international.

Equity theory: A theory of job motivation emphasizing the role played by an individual's belief in the equity or fairness of rewards and punishment in determining his or her performance and satisfaction.

Expectancy approach: A method of motivation specifying that effort to achieve high performance is a function of the perceived likelihood that high performance can be achieved and will be rewarded if achieved, and that the reward will be worth the effort expanded.

Expert power: Power based on the belief or understanding that the influencer has specific knowledge or relevant expertise which the influencer does not have.

Expert System (ES): An advanced computer program that emulates the problem-solving abilities of human experts through the use of artificial intelligence.

Export Processing Zone (EPZ): A physically fenced-in industrial estate developed by host country governments to facilitate manufacture by foreign as well as domestic investors, primarily for exports.

External audit: The check of a firm's financial statements and records for validity, accuracy and completeness by accounting personnel from outside the organization.

External environment: The environment outside the organization (government, political, social, economic, cultural factors, etc.)

Fail-safe: Technical or procedural solutions incorporated with the product's design to minimize error.

Fear of failure: The fear of not reaching organizational/personal goals and of potential public embarrassment if such failures are recognized.

Fear of success: Fear of the burden and stress that may accompany success and the envy and dislike it generates in others.

Financial budget: Budgets that detail how the organization intends to spend money during the financial year and where that money will come from.

First-line managers: Managers who are responsible for the work of operating employees only, and who do not supervise other managers. They are the first or the lowest level of managers in an organizational hierarchy.

Fishbone diagram: A method designed by quality garu Koaru Ishikawa to trace the causes and effects of problems.

Forecasting: The attempt, using specific techniques, to predict outcomes and project future trends.

Foreign Direct Investment (FDI): The primary measure of cross-border investment of TNCs. FDI involves giving managerial controlling power to the foreign investor.

Formal authority: Power rooted in the general understanding that specific individuals or groups have the right to extent influence within certain limits by virtue of their position within an organization.

Franchise: A business arrangement in which a person gets the right to manufacture market or distribute the products or services of a company and use the company's name to do business.

Functional conflict: Any conflict that has positive, constructive and non-divisive results.

Functional layout: The organizing of physical production arrangements to foster a specific purpose such as storage or sales.

Functional-level strategy: The level of strategy that establishes a framework for the management of organizational functions, such as marketing or production, so that they conform to the business unit-level strategy.

Functional organization: A form of departmentalization in which employees are divided according to the functions they perform: production, marketing finance, etc.

Game theory: A method of analyzing and predicting the rational behavior of people in competitive and conflict situations.

General Manager: The individual responsible for all activities such as production, marketing and finance, for an organization.

Geocentric: The attitude that accepts both similarities and differences among countries and takes a balanced view towards the management of operations in every nation.

Global village: In a liberalized economy, the boundaries between cultures and nations are blurred and people think of the world as a "global village".

Goal: The basic purpose for which an organization has been brought into existence.

Grapevine: The various paths through which informal communication is passed through an organization, including the single-strand gossip, probability and cluster chains.

Group cohesiveness: The degree of solidarity and positive feeling held by individuals towards their group.

Group Decision Support System (GDSS): The use of a computerized information system in a group meeting to make more efficient use of information for group decisions.

Hawthorne effect: The possibility that workers who receive special attention will perform better simply because they receive that attention; one interpretation of Elton Mayo and his colleague's studies.

Holding Company: A company having control over one or more firms through ownership of the latter's stocks.

Human Resource Audit: The analysis and appraisal of an organization's current human recourses.

Human Resources Information System (HRIS): A system, frequently computerized, for collecting, storing, maintaining, retrieving, and validating data concerning an organization's personnel.

Human resources planning: Planning for the future personnel needs of an organization, taking into account both internal activities and factors in the external environment.

Human Skill: The ability to work with, communicate with, an motivate individuals to work in groups.

Inspection: A system of comparing products and services with specified requirements to ensure conformity.

Induction and orientation: Activities intended to ease an individual's entrance into an organization through introducing the individual to the organization and providing information on it.

Influence: Any action or example of behavior that causes a change in the attitude or behavior of another person or group.

Informal communication: The grapevine or any communication within an organization that is not officially sanctioned.

Informal groups: Unofficial groups created by members of an organization without the express encouragement of managers.

Informal organization: The undocumented and officially unrecognized relationship between members of an organization, which inevitably emerge out of the personal and group needs of employees.

Information ownership: The possession by certain individuals of unique information and knowledge concerning their work.

Inputs: Resources from the environment that enter any system, such as an organization

Installation: The part of a management science effort in which a mathematical model is developed and used with actual data.

Integration: The degree to which employees of various departments work together in a unified way.

Internal audit: The monitoring within an organization of the validity, accuracy and completeness of its financial statement and records.

Internalization: The third dimension of a management science effort in which the concepts and methodology of management science become part of the thinking of managers, allowing them to recognize appropriate times to use these techniques.

Job enlargement: The combining of various operation at a similar level into one job to provide more variety for workers, and thus increase motivation and satisfaction.

Job enrichment: The combining of several activities from a vertical cross section of the organization into one job to provide the worker with more authority and responsibility.

Job shop production: The production of small batches of custom-made products.

Job Specialization: The division of work into standardized, simplified tasks.

Just-in Time (JIT): A production system that eliminates inactive production inventory through delivery to the production line of parts and suppliers exactly when they are needed.

Kaizen: A Japanese term implying continuous improvement, involving every employee in every company function at all levels on an organization.

Large batch / mass production: The production of large quantities of similar items, often on a assembly line.

Lateral communication: Communication between departments of an organization that generally follows the work flow, thus providing a direct channel for co-ordination and problem solving.

Leader-member relations: The quality of interaction between a leader and his or her subordinate; according to Fred Fielder, it is the most important influence on the manager's power.

Leadership: The process of directing and inspiring workers to perform the task-related activities of the group.

Leadership functions: The group maintenance and task related activities that must be performed by the leader, or someone else, for a group to perform effectively.

Leadership styles: The various patterns of behavior favored by leaders during the process of directing and influencing workers.

Leading: The process of directing and influencing task-related activities of organization members.

Linear Programming (LP) Model: A mathematical model used to determine the optimum allocation of limited resources to attain a goal.

Local Area Network (LAN): An intra-organizational, user-oriented computer network that allows users to communicate with each other and to share facilities for data storage.

Management: The process of planning, organizing, staffing, directing and controlling the work of organization members and of using all available organization resources tor each stated organizational goals.

Management Audit: A systematic, comprehensive examination of the quality of management in an organization in order to bring about improvement.

Management By Crisis: A management style which focuses on problems as they arise.

Management By Objectives (MBO): A formal set of procedures that establishes and reviews progress towards common goals for managers and subordinates.

Management Game or Business Game: An educational or training activity in which trainee is required to take decisions as if in real-life management problem and is then presented with the results of each decision.

Management Information System (MIS): A formal, usually computerized, structure for providing management with complete and up-to-date information.

Management Performance: The measure of how efficient and effective a manager is, or how well he or she determines and achieves appropriate objectives.

Management Science (MS): Mathematic techniques for modeling, analysis and solution of management problems.

Managers: Individuals, who plan, organize, lead and control other individuals in the process of pursuing organization goals.

Market Niche Strategy: A marketing strategy which aims to focus on small gaps or niches in the market, and then introduces suitable products at competitive prices to capture those small markets.

Matrix organization: An organizational structure which is a combination of the functional and product types of organizations.

Mentors: Individuals who pass on the benefits of their knowledge to other individuals who are usually younger and less experienced.

Message: The encoded information sent by a sender to a receiver.

Middle Managers: Managers in the mid-range of the organizational hierarchy, who are responsible for other managers and sometimes for some operating employees.

Mission: The unique reason for an organization's existence that makes it different from all others.

Mission statement: Formal description of what a quality improvement project intends to accomplish.

Motivation: Is the technique adopted by managers to create willingness on the part of subordinates to give their best to the organization.

Network analysis: A Technique used for scheduling complex projects that contain interrelationships between activities or events.

Networking: The linking of groups of computers, either intra organizationally or inter organizationally, so that they can communicate with each other and share common data bases and resources.

Niche strategy: In marketing management, niche means focusing around a product or a market; it is a strategy involving a very low degree of risk and represents they typical behavior of small companies.

Noise: Anything that confuses, disturbs, diminishes or interferes with smooth communication.

Objectives: The targeted goals of an organization towards which resources and efforts are channeled.

One-way Communication: Any communication from the sender without feedback from the receiver.

Open System: A system that interacts with its environment.

Operational Plans: Plans that detail the implementation of strategic plans.

Operations: The production activities of an organization.

Operations Management: The planning, organizing, directing and controlling of an organization's production/ operations system.

Operations System: The organizational system or subsystem whose function is to transform inputs into desired outputs.

Organizational conflicts: Disagreement between individuals or groups within the organizational stemming from the needs to share scarce resources or engaged in interdependent work activities, or from differing statuses, goals, or cultures.

Organizational Culture: The set of important understandings, such as norms, values, attitudes and beliefs, shared by organizational members.

Organizational design: The determination of the organizational structure that is most appropriate for the strategy, people, technology, and task of the organization.

Organizational Development (OD): At the heart of organizational development is the concern for the vitalizing, energizing, actualizing, activating and renewing of organizations through technical and human resources.

Organizational goals: The purpose, mission and objectives that are the reason for an organization's existence and that form the basis of its strategy.

Organizational Life Cycle: The pattern of developmental changes that typically occurs in an organization.

Organization of Method (O&M): The body of knowledge concerned with the examination of the method of an organization covering any or all aspects or organization from classical procedures to management structure. O&M is often an application of methods of study and sometimes work measurement techniques to office procedures.

Organizing: The process of arranging an organization's structure and coordinating its managerial practices and use of resources to achieve its goals.

Outputs: Transformed inputs that are returned to the external environment as products or services.

Out of Control: Situation during which the critical parameters of a process exceed pre-defined limits.

Overload: The condition of being unable to meet all the various performance expectations held by oneself and others.

Pareto analysis: A technique used to identify the most important cause of a problem using the Pareto principle.

Partial reinforcement: In behavior modification, a schedule of reinforcement in which rewards are given intermittently.

PDCA cycle: A four-step process of Plan-Do-Check-Act, devised by Japanese firms on Ed Deming's principles.

Performance appraisal; The process of evaluating an individual's performance by comparing it to existing standards or objectives.

Planning: The process of establishing objectives and suitable courses of action before taking action.

Pokka-Yoke: Shigeo Shingo's principle of eliminating errors by eliminating the possibility of making mistakes.

Policy: A standing plan which is a guideline to decision making, where a manager has certain discretion or it is solutions to recurring problems.

Polycentric: The attitude that all countries are different and difficult to understand; therefore, foreign offices must be relied upon to know what works best in their own countries.

Positive reinforcement: In behavior modification, any consequence that results in the repetition of a given behavior.

Post-action control: A control method that uses the results of a completed action to guide changes in future activities.

Power: The ability to exert influence; that is, the ability to change the attitudes or behavior of individuals or groups.

Pre-action controls: A control method that budgets for all necessary material, financial, and human resources before an action is begun.

Production: The transformation of organizational resources into finished goods and services.

Productivity: A measure of the performance of a worker or an operations system relative to resources utilization: or output divided by input.

Program Evaluation and Review Technique (PERT): A network analysis technique, using estimates of time required to complete tasks, which is used to schedule and control projects for which task completion times cannot be predicted fairly precisely.

Programme: A single use that covers a relatively large set of organizational activities and specifies major steps, their order and timing, and the unit responsible for each step.

Programmed decisions: Solutions to routine problems determined by rule, procedure, or habit.

Purpose: The primary role of an organization in society or the aim of producing a good or service.

Qualitative forecasting: A judgment-based forecasting technique used when hard data are scarce or difficult to use.

Quality assurance: Activity that confirms whether or not a product or service meets the specifications promised by the supplier or expected by the customer.

Quality Circle: Periodic meeting of labor and management personnel to solve quality control and productivity problems.

Quality Control: The process of ensuring that goods and services meet predetermined standards.

Quantitative Overloading: The situation that occurs when an individual is given more tasks than he or she can accomplish at a given time.

Ratio analysis: The process of stating key figures from an organization's financial statement as fractions or percentages of one another, to assist in the assessment of its financial performance or condition.

Realistic Job Preview (RJP): A description provided by an organization's financial statement as fractions or percentage of one another, to assist in the assessment of its financial performance or condition.

Reality shock syndrome: An individual's reaction to the different between high job expectations and the frustrating day-to-day realities of the workplace.

Recruitment: The development of a pool of candidates in accordance with a human resources plan for applying a job.

Refreezing: Transforming a new behavior pattern into a norm through reinforcement and supporting mechanisms.

Responsibility centre: Any organizational unit that is headed by a manager responsible for the unit's activities; major types include revenue, expense, profit and investment centre.

Reward system: A system of performance motivation through wage increases, bonuses, promotions, and so on.

Risk: 1. Probability of loss or failure in a business venture or related to a particular decision or course of action.

2. Hazard (e.g. fire, accident, etc) covered by a contract of insurance.

Risk management: Function associated with reducing the risk or loss to a firm, particularly loss due to fire, accidents, etc.

Role conflict: A situation in which an individual is confronted by two or more incompatible demands.

Role perception: The individual's understanding of the behavior needed to accomplish a task or perform a job.

Satisfiers: Positive motivating factors in the work environment, including achievement, responsibility, recognition, and advancement.

Scalar principle: The concept that a clear line of authority through an organization must exist if delegation is to work successfully.

Scenario construction: The building of a logical, hypothetical description of sequences of events so as to examine the dynamics of alternative sets of conditions.

Scientific management: A management approach, formulated by Frederick Taylor and other between 1890 and 1930, that sought to scientifically determine the best method for performing any task and for selecting, training and motivating workers.

Sensitivity training: An early personal growth technique at one time fairly widespread in organizational development efforts, that emphasizes increased sensitivity in interpersonal relationships.

Seven 'S': Strategy, structure, system, staff, style, skills and super-ordinate goals of an organization.

Simulation models: Models (usually computerized) of situations that are too complex for standard mathematical equations to describe effectively.

Situational leadership theory: An approach to leadership developed by Paul Hersey and Kenneth H. Blanchard that described how the leaders should adjust their leadership style in response to their subordinate, expressing desire for achievement, experience, ability and willingness to accept responsibility.

Span of management: The number of subordinates who can be effectively managed by a supervisor or manager.

Staff: The individuals or groups who provide line managers with advice and services.

Staffing: The process of recruiting, placing, training, and developing personnel.

Stakeholders: Those groups or individuals who are directly or indirectly affected by an organization's pursuit of its goal.

Standing committees: Permanent committees that exist to respond to a continuing organizational need.

Statistical Process Control (SPC): Use of statistical methods to analyze a production process to prevent undesirable variations.

Statistical Quality Control: Use of statistical techniques to ensure that the produc conforms to specifications.

Steering controls: Controls designed to detect any deviation from a predetermined standard, and to allow corrections to be made prior to the completion of a specific sequence of actions. Also known as feed forward controls.

Stockholders: Owners of corporate stocks also called shareholders.

Strategic Business Unit (SBU): A term developed by General Electric Co. USA to identify distinctive business or product divisions, each responsible for growth and profitability, and each of which may be planned independent of the other business.

Strategic control: The process of checking strategy implementation progress against the strategic plan at periodic or critical intervals to determine if the corporation is moving towards its strategic objectives.

Strategic decisions: These decisions encompass the definition of the business, products and markets to be served, functions to be performed and major policies needed for an organization to execute these decisions to achieve objectives.

Strategic management: It is a stream of decisions and actions which leads to the development of an effective strategy or strategies to help achieve corporate objectives.

Strategic planning: The active formulation by top management of an organization's objectives, and definition of the strategies for achieving them.

Strategic plans: Comprehensive plans designed to define and achieve the long-term objectives of the organization.

Strategy: The broad programme for defining and achieving an organization's response to the environment over time.

Stress: The tension and pressure that result when an individual views a situation. It is the wear and tear caused by life.

Structure: The arrangement and interrelationship of the components of an organization - or it is the "Manner in which a building or organization or other complete whole is constructed." (Oxford dictionary)

Subsystems: Those parts comprising the whole system.

Super ordinate goals: Higher-level goals that encompass lower-level goals; also, the significant meaning or guiding concept that an organization imbibes in its members.

Synergy: A situation in which the whole is greater than its parts. In organizational terms, the fact that department that interact cooperatively can be more productive than if they operate in isolation, for example 2+2=5.

Taguchi methods: Techniques developed by Genichi Taguchi to cut variables and, therefore, costs, to a minimum in design and production.

Task force: A temporary group formed to address a specific problem.

Task structure: A word situation variable that, according to Fred Fiedler, helps determines a manager's power. In structured tasks, the manager's power is diminished.

Team building: A method of improving organizational effectiveness at the team level by diagnosing barriers to team performance, and improving inter-team relationships and tasks accomplishment.

Telecommuting: The use of computers to enable individuals to work at home, sending only the work (via telephone or data network) to the work place.

Theory X: The assumption that the average employee dislikes work, is lazy, has little ambition and must be directed, coerced, or threatened with punishment to perform adequately.

Theory Y: The assumption that the average person can enjoy work, be committed to objectives and seek responsibility.

Theory Z: According to William Ouches, the management believes that the key to productivity and quality is the development and participation of all employees.

The Peter Principle: In a hierarchy, every employee tends to rise to his level of incompetence.

Total Quality Management (TQM): It is an approach to improving the effectiveness, of flexibility, of a business as a whole. It is essentially a way of organizing and involving the whole organization, every department, every activity, every single person at every level.

Transactional analysis: An approach to improving interpersonal effectiveness, sometimes used in organizational development efforts, which concentrates on the styles and content of communication.

Uncontrollable variable: A part of a problem situation that cannot be manipulated in the short run, and thus constrains the set of feasible solutions.

Unfreezing: Making the need for change so obvious that the individual, group, or organization can readily see and accept that change must occur.

Unit Production: The production of individual goods or services that are tailored to a customer's specifications.

Valence: The value or motivating strength of a reward to the individual.

Vertical communication: Any communication that moves up or down the chain of command.

Vertical Information system: Means through which data are transmitted up and down the managerial hierarchy.

Video conferencing: Meeting held via telecommunications, usually by satellite television transmission, rather than by face-to-face contact.

Waiting-Line Model (queuing): A management science technique for determining the most appropriate number of servicing units in situations with waiting lines.

Wholly owned subsidiary: A company completely controlled by a parent or holding company. The parent or holding company owns the entire voting stock of the subsidiary company.

Zero-Base Budgeting (ZBB): A budgeting approach in which all of the organization's activities, the existing ones and the proposed new ones, are considered on an equal footing in resource allocation decisions, rather than using the previous years' budget as a starting point.

Zero-defect: A defect - free product or service used as a target by companies in quality practices.

REFERENCES

1. David R.Hampton, Management, McGraw-Hill International Editions, 1987.

2. Heinz Weihrich, Harold Koontz, Management, McGraw-Hill International editions, 1994.

3. S.N.Chary, Production and Operations Management, Tata McGraw-Hill Publishing Co., Ltd., 1996.

4. K.K.Ahuja, Management & Organization, CBS Publishers & Distributors, 1993.

5. Joseph, L. Massie, Essentials of Management, Prentice-Hall of India Pvt. Ltd., 1996.

6. P.C.Tulsian, Vishal Pandey, Business Organization and Management, Pearson Education.

7. Konni, Donnel, C.O., Weighrich, H. Management, McGraw-Hill International Book, Co., 1997.

8. R.Paneerselvam, Production and Operations Management, Prentice Hall India Pvt. Ltd., 1999.

9. P.C. Tripathi, P.N.Reddy, Principles of Management, Tata Mc Graw Hill Publishing Co., Ltd., 1991.

10. V.S.P.Rao, P.S.Narayana, Principles of Management, Konark Publishers Pvt., Ltd., Delhi, 1989.

11. R.D.Agarwal, Organization and Management, Tata Mc Graw Hill Publishing Co., Ltd., 1993.

12. R.D.Agarwal, Principles and Practice of Management.

13. R.Srinivasan, S.A.Chunawalla, Management Principles and Practice, Himalaya Publishing House, 1997.

14. Satya Saran Chaterjee, An Introduction to Management, Its Principles and techniques, The World Press Pvt., Ltd., Calcutta, 1993.

15. Ivancevich, Donnelly, Gibson, Management, Principles and Functions, All India Publishers, 1991.

16.   Gene Burton, Manab Thakur, Management Today, Principles and Practice, Tata Mc Graw Hill Publishing Co., Ltd., 1995.

17.   P.N.Reddy, S.S.Gulshan, Principles of Business Organization and Management.

18.   V.S.P.Rao, P.S.Narayana, Management Concepts & Thoughts, Konark Publishers Pvt., Ltd., Delhi, 1989.

19.   R.S.Gupta, Principles of Management, S. Chand & Company, 2005.

20.   G.B.Mamoria, S.V.Gankar, Management, Text & Case, Himalaya Publishing House.

21.   Martand Telsang, Industrial Engineering and Production Management, S. Chand & Company, 1998

22.   O.P. Khanna, Industrial Engineering and Management, Dhanpat Rai & Sons, 1989.

23.   K.Anbuvelan, Principles of Management, Laxmi Publications, New Delhi, 2007.

24.   K.Anbuvelan, Management concepts for Civil Engineers, Laxmi Publications, New Delhi, 2005.

25.   Shyamal Banerjee, Principles and Practice of Management, Oxford & IBH, 1981.

26.   L.M. Prasad, Principles and Practice of Management, S. Chand & Sons, 2006.

27.   Francis Cherunilam, International Business, Wheeler Publishing, 1998.

SUBJECT INDEX